BE A BETTER BYSTANDER

BE A BETTER BYSTANDER

Transforming Passive Observers into Active Responders

George Schreer

BLOOMSBURY ACADEMIC
NEW YORK · LONDON · OXFORD · NEW DELHI · SYDNEY

BLOOMSBURY ACADEMIC
Bloomsbury Publishing Inc, 1359 Broadway, New York, NY 10018, USA
Bloomsbury Publishing Plc, 50 Bedford Square, London, WC1B 3DP, UK
Bloomsbury Publishing Ireland, 29 Earlsfort Terrace, Dublin 2, D02 AY28, Ireland

BLOOMSBURY, BLOOMSBURY ACADEMIC and the Diana logo are trademarks of Bloomsbury Publishing Plc

First published in the United States of America 2026

Copyright © Bloomsbury Publishing Inc 2026

Cover design by Jason Enterline
Cover images © istock/bubaone

All rights reserved. No part of this publication may be: i) reproduced or transmitted in any form, electronic or mechanical, including photocopying, recording or by means of any information storage or retrieval system without prior permission in writing from the publishers; or ii) used or reproduced in any way for the training, development or operation of artificial intelligence (AI) technologies, including generative AI technologies. The rights holders expressly reserve this publication from the text and data mining exception as per Article 4(3) of the Digital Single Market Directive (EU) 2019/790.

Bloomsbury Publishing Inc does not have any control over, or responsibility for, any third-party websites referred to or in this book. All internet addresses given in this book were correct at the time of going to press. The author and publisher regret any inconvenience caused if addresses have changed or sites have ceased to exist, but can accept no responsibility for any such changes.

A catalog record for this book is available from the Library of Congress.

ISBN: HB: 979-8-8818-0590-6
PB: 979-8-8818-0591-3
ePDF: 979-8-8818-6783-6
eBook: 979-8-8818-0592-0

Typeset by Deanta Global Publishing Services, Chennai, India
Printed and bound in the United States of America

For product safety related questions contact productsafety@bloomsbury.com.

To find out more about our authors and books visit www.bloomsbury.com and sign up for our newsletters.

Contents

List of Figures   vi
List of Photos   vii
Preface   viii

Part I   The Unresponsive Bystander

1. Background on Bystander Behavior   3
2. Identifying Obstacles That Impede Bystander Helping   13

Part II   Transforming Passive Bystanders Into Active Responders

3. Evidence-Based Strategies to Boost Bystander Behavior   41
4. Confronting Alcohol- and Health-Related Emergencies   63
5. Confronting Bullying and Cyberbullying in Schools   97
6. Confronting Sexual Misconduct   125
7. Confronting Bias   153
8. Promoting Allyship   181

Index   211
About the Author   213

Figures

1.1	Situational Model of Bystander Intervention	9
2.1	Situational Model of Bystander Intervention	16
3.1	Theory of Planned Behaviour	56
4.1	Theory of Planned Behaviour	71
5.1	Theory of Planned Behavior	109
7.1	Theory of Planned Behavior	168

Photos

2.1	© iStock/Feodora Chiosea. Stock illustration ID:1269878901.	15
2.2	© iStock/Estradaanton.	17
2.3	© iStock/BibleArtLibrary.	18
2.4	© iStock/Tetiana Lazunova.	19
2.5	© iStock/xavierarnau.	20
2.6	© iStock/Page Light Studios.	21
2.7	© iStock/Hafiez Razali.	22
2.8	© iStock/925324030.	25
2.9	© iStock/ImageegamI.	28
2.10	© iStock/Rawpixel.	29
2.11	© iStock/Diy13.	30
3.1	© iStock/JayLazarin.	47
3.2	© iStock/goc.	57
4.1	© iStock/goc.	70
4.2	© iStock/AndreyPopov.	79
4.3	© iStock/sabelskaya.	81
4.4	© iStock/elenabs.	82
4.5	© iStock/ST.art.	83
4.6	© iStock/fmajor.	85
4.7	© iStock/ollo.	86
4.8	© iStock/almagami.	87
5.1	© iStock/SolStock.	99
5.2	© iStock/monkeybusinessimages.	100
5.3	© iStock/Egoitz Bengoetxea Iguaran.	101
8.1	© iStock/Vladimir Vladimirov.	201

Preface

Picture this scenario, you are at a beach relaxing with your favorite book and beverage, when a woman sitting on a nearby blanket listening to a "boombox" (portable media player popular in the 1970s and 1980s) asks you if you could "watch her things?" while she goes to use the restroom. Like most people dealing with this mild imposition, you might sheepishly say something like, "Um . . . OK, no problem." Soon after, she leaves, and sure enough, a few minutes later a "thief" walks up to the unattended blanket and steals the woman's radio. Would you honor your obligation and yell for the thief to stop (and when he inevitably ignores you), get up from your comfy beach blanket and chase the culprit down? Based on the results of a classic field study testing this exact scenario, the answer was a resounding yes! In fact, over 90 percent of bystanders tried to stop the thief when they felt responsible for the victim's belongings compared to a default condition in which just 20 percent who did not feel directly responsible for the victim's things (in this case, the victim had simply made small talk before walking away) (Moriarty, 1975). Studies such as this remind us, that under the right conditions, people can become selfless and active responders.

Unfortunately, in many situations where help is needed, the right conditions are usually not readily available. Instead, many obstacles are present that prevent good people from intervening. Typically, in cases involving sexual harassment, bullying, discrimination, and even health-related emergencies, the default is often to either passively stand by and watch or look the other way while quickly passing by (Sword & Zimbardo, 2015). Indeed, one large review found that even though peers were present in approximately 80 percent of bullying episodes, bystanders intervened less than 20 percent of the time (Polanin, Espelage, & Pigott, 2012). Likewise, in cases of acute alcohol poisoning or sexual assault, although bystanders were typically present during these incidents, they typically elected not to intervene (Schipani-McLaughlin, Salazar, & Vivolo-Kantor, 2019). And even when it comes to health-related emergencies, most bystanders fail to provide cardiopulmonary resuscitation (CPR) for acute cardiac events (Sasson, Meischke, Abella, et al., 2013).

When reflecting on these findings, a typical reaction is *"How could people just stand by and watch this horrible event happen?"* followed by the typical knee-jerk response, "these people are obviously heartless and selfish." After all, only a cold-hearted, remorseless person would fail to heed the screams of a person being assaulted or ignore the hurt in the eyes of someone being bullied or harassed. While many are quick to point the finger at people's deep-rooted personality flaws, others put the blame on the de-evolution of modern society using such terms as "moral decay," "apathy," or "alienation" (see Gilovich, Keltner, Chen, & Nisbett, 2019; Myers & Twenge, 2019).

Rather than attribute bystander inaction to callousness, moral decay or indifference, many social science and public health researchers believe the focus should instead focus on the bystander's immediate social environment (i.e., dynamics present in the situation). According to one well-established theory of bystander intervention (Latané & Darley, 1970), there are numerous obstacles a bystander must navigate through in order for help to be given. Complicating matters further, at each step there are numerous impediments that preclude the bystander from helping.

Chapter 1 addresses this helping model and sets the stage for the complexities facing bystanders in emergency situations. It will soon become apparent that, by definition, emergencies "emerge" suddenly without warning, they require immediate attention, and most ordinary people have little experience dealing with them. Chapter 2 will identify some of the common barriers that inhibit helping during an emergency situation. Chapter 3 will look at the many evidence-based strategies people can use to overcome these obstacles and become active responders. In the remaining chapters, we will look at how validated helping models can be used to promote helping in specific real-world emergency situations including: alcohol-related and health-related emergencies (Chapter 4), bullying/cyberbullying (Chapter 5), sexual assault (Chapter 6), and discrimination (Chapter 7). In the final chapter (Chapter 8), we will discuss the importance of allyship, with particular emphasis on how to become an anti-racist ally. Each of these chapters will address what strategies bystanders can use to become active responders as well as strategies public health educators can use to design more effective intervention/training programs.

Although we will identify numerous obstacles inhibiting people from helping, bystanders can make a huge difference. With the right knowledge and practical toolkit to intervene, passive bystanders can easily be transformed into active responders. So, let's get started.

Part I

The Unresponsive Bystander

Background on Bystander Behavior

1

- Key Terms in This Chapter 3
- Tragic Murder of Kitty Genovese 4
- Why People Don't Help in Emergencies 6
- Situational Model of Bystander Intervention (SMB) 8
- Importance of Bystanders 10
- Summary 10

Key Terms in This Chapter

altruistic helping: people are motivated to help others without any need for personal gain

bystander[1]: an individual who is present at an incident where somebody needs help and is left with a choice to take action or remain uninvolved

bystander effect: people are less likely to help in groups than when they are alone

egoistic helping: people are motivated to help others by personal gains such as praise, honor, and status

Kitty Genovese: a woman viciously attacked and murdered while walking home after a late-night shift as bar server to her residence in Queens, New York (1964)

Situational Model of Bystander Intervention (SMB): proposes that bystanders typically go through a series of five decision-making steps before help will be given

social responsibility norm: a sense of duty and obligation, in which people are expected to respond to others by giving help to those in need of assistance

Tragic Murder of Kitty Genovese

We can understand the reticence of people to become involved in an area of violence, but when they are in their homes, near phones, why should they be afraid to call the police?
—A shocked NYC police officer after learning that no one allegedly called the police during the Kitty Genovese attack (Gansberg, 1964)

In the notorious case that made terms such as "bystander apathy" and "diffusion of responsibility" part of the American lexicon, bar server **Kitty Genovese** was viciously attacked and murdered while walking home after a late-night shift to her residence in Queens, New York. The brutal attack took place over thirty minutes, beginning on a dark sidewalk and ending inside an apartment vestibule. Despite Kitty screaming, *"Oh, my God! He stabbed me! Help me!"* it was alleged that nobody went to her aid or called

---

1 In this book, the term **bystander** is used as a neutral term to refer to an individual who is present at an incident where somebody needs help and is left with a choice to take action or remain uninvolved. A *passive bystander* is a person who is present at an incident but does not intervene (synonyms include passerby, onlooker, witness, and spectator), while an *active bystander* is a person who takes action when observing an incident (synonyms include active responder and upstander) (Darley & Latané, 1968; Fischer, Krueger, Greitemeyer, et al., 2011).

the police until she was already dead.[2] According to newspaper accounts like the one mentioned above, several neighbors in surrounding buildings reported hearing screams, but decided it was probably just a drunken brawl or a lovers' quarrel. Chillingly, the convicted killer, Winston Moseley, seemed to intuitively understand this peculiarity of human behavior. When asked during his trial why he continued the attack after seeing a man turn on his lights, he said, "I had a feeling this man would close his window and go back to sleep, and sure enough he did" (McFadden, 2016).

While Kitty Genovese may have become the "poster child" for bystander apathy, many modern examples of bystander passivity during sexual assault incidents have been reported. In one disturbing case, investigators allege that as many as twenty high school students watched the gang rape of a teenage girl in the courtyard outside a California high school homecoming dance, and allegedly no one reported it to authorities even though the attack went on for almost two hours (see *Police: As many as 20 present . . .*). In another case of extreme callousness, a group of young men from Chicago live-streamed on Facebook the sexual assault of a fifteen-year-old girl to an audience of over forty viewers; once again, nobody called the police (see *Gang rape of Chicago teen . . .*). Of course, these brazen acts of insensitivity are not limited to the United States. In one chilling incident from India, police reported that while a young girl was sexually assaulted by a mob on a busy street, an off-duty TV journalist felt compelled to film the event but did not intervene (see *Indian anger . . .*).

Besides sexual assaults, there have been numerous reports of bystanders standing idly by in other emergency situations. Chilling video footage captured a horrifying scene of an immigrant woman being knocked to the ground and repeatedly kicked in the head, while three men simply watched from a nearby building. One advocate for immigrants lamented, *"When I look at the video, the inaction is what's heartbreaking. If you are being attacked, the community will not be standing for you."* (see *Editorial: The bystander effect . . .*). In another tragic case from India, a man hit by a car lay injured and bleeding for twelve hours while large numbers of people passed by without offering any form of help (Kazmi, 2017).

---

2 Recently, several facts of the Kitty Genovese case have been disputed. In one archival study, researchers found that there is no clear evidence that 38 people (as originally reported) witnessed the murder or that all of the bystanders remained inactive. Importantly, however, this does not nullify the hundreds of studies supporting the "bystander effect." As the authors state, *"We are not claiming that challenges to the story of the witnesses invalidate the tradition of work on bystander intervention"* (Manning, Levine, & Collins, 2007, p. 556).

Why People Don't Help in Emergencies

Although tragic incidents such as these inspire both laypeople and social scientists to examine why ordinary people may not help in emergency situations, let's briefly discuss what factors motivate individuals to provide help when a sudden, unexpected crisis arises.

Our motivation to help is dictated by powerful social norms of how we ought to behave (Berkowitz, 1972). Just as social norms remind us to not chew food with our mouths open, they also remind us to provide help to those who need it. So, if a person with a leg brace drops a book, we typically adhere to the norm and pick it up for them. If there is a well-publicized blood shortage, many more people will visit their local blood bank than usual.[3] This **social responsibility norm** involves a sense of duty and obligation, in which people are expected to respond to others by giving help to those in need of assistance (see *Understanding altruism . . .*). The teachings of many religions are based on the social responsibility norm that we should, as good human beings, reach out and help other people in need.

Besides social norms, our willingness to help others is also influenced by self-serving and selfless motivations. **Egoistic helping** occurs when people are motivated by personal gains such as praise, honor, and status. This type of helping would also include the evolutionary need to preserve one's genes. Evolution predicts that we should have a stronger desire to help victims that are genetically similar to us, thus maximizing the chances that our genes will survive. To illustrate evolution's impact, think about who you would rescue first from a burning building: a family member or a friend. Typically, the higher the risk, the more people are willing to help their kin over their comrade (Baumeister & Bushman, 2011).

In contrast to egoistic helping, **altruistic helping** occurs when people are motivated to help others without any need for personal gain. To illustrate this form of helping, imagine you are part of a study where you watch somebody get a small electric shock every time they make a mistake. Would you be willing to trade places with that person? Participants made to feel empathic concern (i.e., identify with the person in pain) for the person being shocked were more willing to take their place, even when told they could leave the experiment or when their personal sacrifice would go unnoticed (Fultz, Batson, Fortenbach, et al., 1986). These results may sound surprising;

---

[3] In the days after the Sept. 11 terrorist attacks in New York City (US), there was a tremendous outpouring of support to donate blood, but unfortunately most of the blood had to be discarded because the amount expended the need and could not be stored. There were calls to come back later when the need would be greater, but sadly most people ignored those pleas (see *Blood donation surge . . .*).

however, empathy is a powerful motivator toward helping. Many studies have found that both the severity of the emergency and the level of victim distress trigger an empathic emotional reaction from bystanders that motivates them to intervene (Batson, Batson, Griffitt, et al., 1989).

Motives to help are not always static, however. They can change over time. For example, imagine if you were contacted by the local Red Cross asking you to donate blood during a severe shortage. If you agree to roll up your sleeves, what is your motivation? Perhaps it is for altruistic reasons, such as providing service to those in desperate need or perhaps it is for more egoistic reasons such as the respect and admiration that you will surely receive from others. To illustrate how motives can change over time, researchers found that experienced blood donors were more motivated by altruistic reasons, while novice donors were more motivated by selfish reasons (Paulhus, Shaffer, & Downing, 1976).

Whether true altruistic helping exists is debatable. After all, any time a person helps someone in need they are typically going to feel good about themselves, which, to some degree, is self-serving. Even if a person makes a large anonymous donation to a worthy cause, chances are they will still take pride in their own generosity. So, is that truly altruistic? In any event, rather than debating whether true altruism exists, one renowned researcher posed that a better question might be *"Isn't it great that natural selection selected human beings to be able to get pleasure from helping others?"* (Baumeister & Bushman, 2011, p. 273).

Indeed, there are lots of studies to back up the notion that humans are hardwired to help. For example, in one dramatic study, German toddlers who saw an adult researcher drop a marker out of their reach typically crawled over to the marker, picked it up, and handed it back to the researcher. Interestingly, if the researcher simply threw the marker on the ground the infants did not retrieve it, indicating they could infer the adult's mental state (Warneken & Tomasello, 2006). Likewise, a majority of American toddlers watching an adult "accidentally" drop a piece of fruit, retrieved the fruit, even shortly before their snack time, when they were likely to be hungry (Barragan, Brooks, & Meltzoff, 2020). Furthermore, Israeli infants shown a video of a square figure being "bullied" by a round figure were more willing to play with the square figure later (Uzefovsky, Paz, & Davidov, 2019). Studies like these show that even very young children are able to exhibit some degree of empathy for helping those in need.

Besides being hardwired to help, there is also some compelling evidence that our brains are hardwired for empathy. Several neuropsychological studies using fMRI scans show that the threat of shock to a friend (but not a stranger) is nearly identical to the brain activity displayed under threat to the self (Beckes, Coan, & Hasselmo, 2013). Thus, if a friend is under threat, it feels the same as if we ourselves are under that same threat.

Now that we have discussed the underlining motives behind why people help those in need, it's time to look at the flip side: *Why people might avoid helping in emergency situations?* One explanation is that while social norms dictate that we ought to help those who need it, we are also faced with competing social norms such as *"it is impolite to stare," "mind your own business,"* and *"don't be a snitch."* Opposing norms like these may reduce the likelihood that help will be given in an emergency situation.

Accounts of Genovese's murder prompted researchers to try to understand how seemingly ordinary, compassionate people could watch or hear such a brutal attack, and yet not intervene. Because the murder took place in a large metropolitan city (NYC), both social theorists and laypeople chalked up the apparent callousness of the bystanders to the profound apathy, alienation, and urban decay perceived to be rampant in large urban cities during that time. The consensus was big cities are cold, "urban jungles," where residents have little time or interest in helping their fellow citizens.

Not everyone, however, blamed the tragedy on vague concepts such as "alienation" and "urbanization" or misleading and oversimplified concepts such as apathy. The most vocal opponents of the bystander apathy explanation were a pair of social psychologists, John Darley and Bibb Latané. Rather than attribute bystander inaction to apathy and indifference, they contend to better understanding the failure of bystanders one needs to consider the situation itself. In other words, the situational factors in the bystander's immediate social environment are of utmost importance in determining an individual's reaction to an emergency, and whether a person helps or not may *"lie in the various decisions the bystander must make before he intervenes"* (Latané & Darley, 1970, p. 28). Based on this premise, they developed a 5-step model of bystander intervention we will use throughout this book.

Situational Model of Bystander Intervention (SMB)

According to the **Situational Model of Bystander Intervention (SMB)**, bystanders must deal with a sequence of cognitive decision-making steps before any help will be given. As shown in **Figure 1.1**, there are five steps one must pass to become an active bystander: *Step 1:* Notice the event, *Step 2:* Interpret the event as an emergency, *Step 3:* Take responsibility to help,

Situational Model of Bystander Intervention

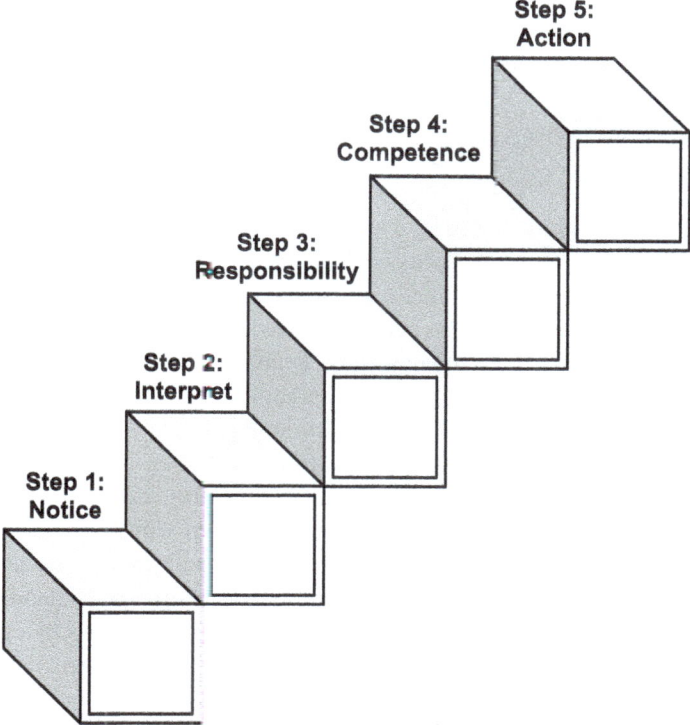

Figure 1.1 Situational Model of Bystander Intervention

Step 4: Possess the competency to help, and *Step 5:* Take action to help. Note how this model implies a bystander is bombarded with a rash of split-second decisions that influence whether they will help or not. Indeed, as they prophetically state, *"The bystander to an emergency is in an unenviable position. It is perhaps surprising that anyone should intervene at all"* (Latané & Darley, 1970, p. 31).

Complicating matters further, crowds of people can inhibit helping at each of these crucial steps. This phenomenon has been defined as the **bystander effect**—the tendency for people to help less when in groups than when they are alone (Latané & Darley, 1970). There is a large body of research supporting the bystander effect. One large review of the literature found that people in groups who witnessed staged emergencies (e.g., falls, thefts) in areas like classrooms and hallways were 50 percent *less* likely to help compared to when alone, and equally important, much *slower* to react to the emergency (Latané & Nida, 1981). Indeed, a recent meta-analysis from over fifty bystander intervention studies also confirmed the robustness of the bystander effect.[4]

Importance of Bystanders

An important question to ask is, if bystanders face so many obstacles and are often reluctant to help, why focus on them at all? There are several important reasons worth considering. First, a bystander, is by definition, a witness to a live event where help may be necessary. Second, when bystanders witness a potential real-world emergency (e.g., health-related emergency, assault, bullying) they can offer immediate, "on the spot" help when it is most needed. Third, if bystanders can be transformed from passive to active participants, the sense of accountability shifts away from the victim and is now firmly placed on the actions of strangers, friends, and the community at large. Fourth, if more bystanders make the option to help when needed, ideally, new helping norms can be created, which should help to increase people's sense of responsibility to stand up for others. Thus, because bystanders are often the first line of defense in emergency situations, it follows that getting bystanders to become active participants will greatly benefit society (Banyard, Moynihan, & Crossman, 2009).

Summary

Tragic incidents like the Kitty Genovese murder show us that even decent, respectable bystanders may not always help when it seems obvious to others that they should. Rather than attribute bystander inaction to callousness or apathy, many researchers today believe the focus should be on the bystander's immediate social environment. According to the **Situational Model of**

---

4 Although, the bystander effect is quite robust in laboratory settings, current research suggests that it might be less prevalent in certain types of real-world public disturbances. For example, a recent international study examining over 200 video clips containing public disputes (i.e., arguments and assaults) captured by surveillance cameras from three different locations (the Netherlands, United Kingdom, and South Africa), found that bystanders intervened in a whopping 90 percent of the aggressive conflicts! (Philpot, Liebst, Levine, et al., 2019). While the adage that "there is strength in numbers" may hold true for a very specific form of publicly violent dispute (primarily drunken bar fights), the findings say very little about the extent to which the likelihood of victim helping varies across wider social contexts such as bystander passivity present during sexual assaults, bullying, and discrimination.

Bystander Intervention (SMB), bystanders must resolve a series of five steps before help can be given. Complicating matters further, at each step there are numerous impediments that preclude the bystander from helping. In the next chapter we will identify many of these common obstacles.

References

Banyard, V. L., Moynihan, M. M., & Crossman, M. T. (2009). Reducing sexual violence on campus: The role of student leaders as empowered bystanders. *Journal of College Student Development, 50*, 446–457.

Barragan, R. C., Brooks, R., & Meltzoff, A. N. (2020). Altruistic food sharing behavior by human infants after a hunger manipulation. *Scientific Reports, 10*, 1785.

Batson, C. D., Batson, J. G., Griffitt, C. A., et al. (1989). Negative-state relief and the empathy: Altruism hypothesis. *Journal of Personality and Social Psychology, 56*, 922–933.

Baumeister, R. F., & Bushman, B. J. (2011). *Social psychology and human nature* (2nd ed.). Wadsworth.

Beckes, L., Coan, J. A., & Hasselmo, K. (2013). Familiarity promotes the blurring of self and other in the neural representation of threat. *Social Cognitive and Affective Neuroscience, 8*, 670–677.

Berkowitz, L. (1972). Social norms, feelings, and other factors affecting helping and altruism. In L. Berkowitz (Ed.), *Advances in experimental social psychology* (pp. 63–108). Academic Press.

Blood donation surge after 9/11 waned fast. (2003, May 6). Retrieved from https://consumer.healthday.com/circulatory-system-information-7/blood-disorder-news-68/blood-donation-surge-after-9-11-waned-fast-513060.html

Darley, J. M., & Latané, B. (1968). Bystander intervention in emergencies: Diffusion of responsibility. *Journal of Personality and Social Psychology, 8*, 377–383.

Editorial: The bystander effect and why we don't always step up to help. (2021, April 1). Bangor Daily News (ME).

Fischer, P., Krueger, J. I., Greitemeyer, T., et al. (2011). The bystander-effect: A meta-analytic review on bystander intervention in dangerous and non-dangerous emergencies. *Psychological Bulletin, 137*, 517–537.

Fultz, J., Batson, C. D., Fortenbach, V. A., et al. (1986). Social evaluation and the empathy-altruism hypothesis. *Journal of Personality and Social Psychology, 50*, 761–769.

Gang rape of Chicago teen was watched live by 40 people on Facebook, no one called cops. (2017, March 1). Retrieved from https://www.nbcnews.com/news/us-news/gang-sex-assault-chicago-teen-was-watched-live-40-people-n736616

Gansberg, M. (1964, March 27). *37 who saw murder didn't call the police.* New York Times.

Indian anger over media footage of girl being sexually assaulted. (2012, July 12). Retrieved from https://www.theguardian.com/world/2012/jul/15/india-media-sexual-assault-girl

Kazmi, Z. (2017, August 19). *Delhi accident victim: Why don't people step forward to help? It's the 'bystander effect.'* Hindustan Times (India).

Latané, B., & Darley, J. M. (1970). *The unresponsive bystander: Why doesn't he help?* Appleton-Century-Crofts.

Latané, B., & Nida, S. (1981). Ten years of research on group size and helping. *Psychological Bulletin, 89,* 308–324.

Manning, R., Levine, M., & Collins, A. (2007). The Kitty Genovese murder and the social psychology of helping: The parable of the 38 witnesses. *American Psychologist, 62,* 555–562.

McFadden, R. D. (2016, April 5). *Winston Moseley, 81, killer of Kitty Genovese, dies in prison.* New York Times.

Paulhus, D. L., Shaffer, D. R., & Downing, L. L. (1976). Effects of making blood donor motives salient upon donor retention: A field experiment. *Personality and Social Psychology Bulletin, 3,* 99–102.

Philpot, R., Liebst, L. S., Levine, M., et al. (2019). Would I be helped? Cross-national CCTV footage shows that intervention is the norm in public conflicts. *American Psychologist, 75,* 66–75.

Police: As many as 20 present at gang rape outside school dance. (2009, October 28). Retrieved from http://www.cnn.com/2009/CRIME/10/27/california.gang.rape.investigation/index.html

Understanding altruism: Self and other concerns. (n.d.) Retrieved from https://opentextbc.ca/socialpsychology/chapter/understanding-altruism-self-and-other-concerns/

Uzefovsky, F., Paz, Y., & Davidov, M. (2019). Young infants are pro-victims, but it depends on the context. *British Journal of Psychology, 111,* 322–334.

Warneken, F., & Tomasello, M. (2006). Altruistic helping in human infants and young chimpanzees. *Science, 311,* 1301–1303.

Identifying Obstacles That Impede Bystander Helping

2

Key Terms in This Chapter 13

Identifying Obstacles to Help Using the Situational Model of Bystander Intervention 14

Obstacles at Step 1: Noticing a Problem Exists 14

Obstacles at Step 2: Interpreting Event as an Emergency 22

Obstacles at Step 3: Taking Responsibility to Help 24

Obstacles at Step 4: Possessing the Competence to Help 27

Obstacles at Step 5: Taking Action to Help 30

Summary 34

Key Terms in This Chapter

belief in the just world theory: proposes that people have an inherent need to believe that the world is just (i.e., people get what they deserve)

bystander effect: people are less likely to help in groups than when they are alone

compassion fatigue: the gradual desensitization to helping those in need

cost-reward model: proposes that helping is more likely to occur when the costs for helping are low and when the costs for not helping are high

diffusion of responsibility: reduction in responsibility based on the assumption others who are present will help

Good Samaritan laws: laws protecting well-meaning people from being sued or prosecuted for unintentional injury or wrongful death

pluralistic ignorance: incorrectly assuming that others are thinking and feeling the same as us

self-efficacy: confidence that an individual has in their ability to accomplish a specific task

situational ambiguity: an incident that is not clearly defined (e.g., an "unconscious" man lying on a park bench), thus making several interpretations plausible

Situational Model of Bystander Intervention (SMB): proposes that bystanders typically go through a series of five decision-making steps before help will be given

social exchange theory: proposes that we have a desire to maximize benefits and minimize costs

Identifying Obstacles to Help Using the Situational Model of Bystander Intervention

According to the **Situational Model of Bystander Intervention (SMB)** (Latané & Darley, 1970), bystanders must deal with a sequence of five cognitive decision-making steps before any help will be given. Complicating matters further, at each step, there are numerous impediments that preclude the bystander from helping. In this chapter, we will identify the common barriers bystanders encounter at each of the steps.

Obstacles at Step 1: Noticing a Problem Exists

Question: *If a blind man is waiting at a busy intersection, what are the odds you would notice he needs help?*

Identifying Obstacles That Impede Bystander Helping 15

Photo 2.1 © iStock/Feodora Chiosea. Stock illustration ID:1269878901.

Picture the typical city dweller in this scenario: contending with the incessant traffic noise, scrolling through their Instagram feed, rushing to get to work on time. It's no wonder many bystanders may innocently miss an incident entirely. In today's world, because inattention has partially become an adaptive learned response, we will start with identifying the obstacles that prevent us from noticing a problem exists in the first place.

Social Norms Inhibiting Attention

Social norms reminding us to *"mind your own business"* or that it is *"impolite to stare"* may inadvertently conflict with prosocial norms reminding us to help those in trouble. To illustrate, imagine you witness a violent interaction between a man and a woman at a bar (see Photo 2.2). At one point the woman screams, *"Get away from me, I don't know why I married you."* Would you intervene? What if instead, the woman screamed out, *"Get away from me, I don't even know you."* Would you intervene here? As you might predict, American subjects tested under these conditions intervened much *less* frequently when the staged fight was between a married couple than between two strangers. When asked why they did not feel comfortable intervening in the domestic dispute, the most common response was *"I felt it was none of my business"* (Shotland & Straw, 1976). Likewise, a Spanish team of researchers found that subjects reading hypothetical scenarios of domestic abuse were less willing to intervene if they interpreted the incident as a "private matter" (Gracia, Garcia, & Lila, 2009). Studies like these show that we tend to strictly adhere to the privacy norms of others, especially when the others appear to know each other (e.g., a "lover's quarrel").

Situational Model of Bystander Intervention

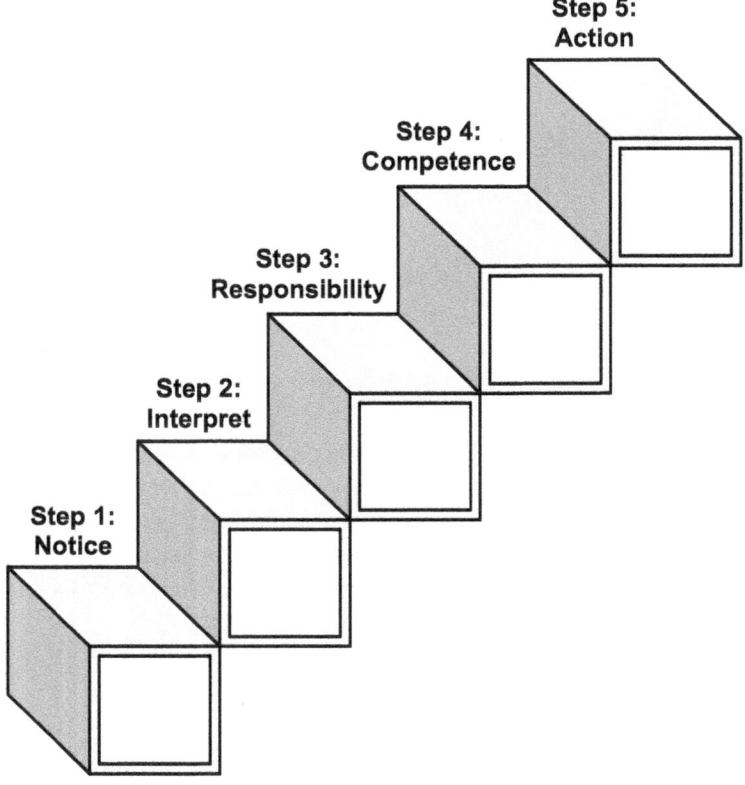

Figure 2.1 Situational Model of Bystander Intervention

Time Pressures

Imagine you are a seminary student from a large university and you are asked to give a brief sermon about the Parable of the Good Samaritan (you know the folktale where both laypeople and clergymen completely ignore a gravely injured man who would surely have died if it were not for the help of one "good" Samaritan) (see Photo 2.3). To create additional pressure, you are also told that your speech will be recorded, and due to space concerns, you will need to walk to a building on the other side of campus. While walking between the buildings, you encounter a shabbily dressed man slumped in the alleyway coughing and moaning. *Would you offer help? Of course you would, right?* After all, you are a seminary student preoccupied with religious thoughts of

Photo 2.2 © iStock/Estradaanton.

piety and kindness. Well, *what if you were also told that due to a scheduling error you were running late and needed to get to this other building ASAP?* Apparently, adding this time constraint can have a huge effect on helping. In the actual study, when compared to seminary students from an American university who were not in a hurry to reach their destination, those who were in a rush were 6X *less* likely to offer help (Darley & Batson, 1973). This study shows that even good-intentioned, virtuous people may succumb to the time pressures that often dictate our busy lives.

As the "Good Samaritan" study implies, when pressed for time, people are less likely to provide help to others, but whether or not you get help may partly depend on cultural sex roles. In some cultures, the social norm "women and children first" implies, in times of potential sudden death, women, and children should be given higher priority than men. In the case of the *Titanic* which hit an iceberg and sunk in 1912 and the *Lusitania* which was hit by a German U-boat torpedo and sunk in 1915, the Captains of both ships issued the "women and children first" order. Notably, however, archival evidence appears to show that it was only followed in the *Titanic* disaster (Frey, Savage, & Torgler, 2010). According to the researchers, because the *Lusitania* sank so quickly relative to the *Titanic*, the social norm of women and children first did not have time to activate, so instead it was replaced with the more selfish mantra of "every man for themselves." This archival

Photo 2.3 © iStock/BibleArtLibrary.

study suggests that when people have little time to react, more selfish survival instincts kick in faster than the prosocial norms of helping.

Preoccupation

Besides social norms and time pressures inhibiting us from helping, our attention is often preoccupied with other matters such as our obsession with our cell phones. Now, of course cell phones serve a lot of valuable functions (e.g., support our need to stay connected, provide important news updates, etc.), but they can also be highly distracting (see Photo 2.4).[1] In one study, college students from an American university, using a driving simulator, showed reduced ability to recognize objects placed directly in their visual field, even while using a hands-free cell phone (Strayer, Drews, & Johnston, 2003). Likewise, another study found that cell phone users walking through an American college campus typically remained completely oblivious to a unicycling clown riding past them (Hyman, Boss, Wise, et al., 2010). Applying this "perceptual blindness" research to helping behavior, people

---

[1] While distracting, cell phones can be a powerful way to galvanize people for a specific cause. In one instance, when Haiti was hit with a massive hurricane, Americans contacted via text messaging raised more than $30 million for Haitian relief efforts (see *Mobile giving to help Haiti . . .*).

Photo 2.4 © iStock/Tetiana Lazunova.

using their cell phones in a large American city were 8X *less* likely to help a person with a leg brace who dropped a stack of magazines, presumably because their phones preoccupied their attention, thus making them less likely to notice their immediate surroundings (Puryear & Reysen, 2013).

Ironically, although cell phones can fulfill our basic need to belong, they may simultaneously decrease the motivation for further connection. In support of this premise, researchers found that American subjects asked to use their cell phones for just three minutes to contact friends were much *less* willing to volunteer their time to help a charity (Pocheptsova, 2012). Thus, although cell phones provide a valuable need for social connection, they may simultaneously reduce the motivation to provide needed help to others.[2]

Sensory Overload

The sensory overload from smartphones, earbuds, and other various gadgets may also prevent us from noticing someone in distress or hearing someone's

---

2 As a cultural strategist friend of mine eloquently opined, *"Phones are such a bizarre layer between viewer and events. People film a concert, watch on their small phone screen even with the band in front of them, or take photos of a spectacular sunset on the beach, confining their eyes to the small screen rather than the expansive view. They become distanced from the thing they're watching, less fully immersed in the scenes as a result, and may be less impacted or affected by unpredictable raw emotions."* (B. Legato, personal communication, June 21, 2024).

Photo 2.5 © iStock/xavierarnau.

cries for help. This can be especially troublesome in big, urban centers. City dwellers are often overloaded with additional sensory input (people, noise, vehicles) (see Photos 2.5 and 2.6) and may be especially prone to adapt to the sensory overload by intentionally "tuning out" low-priority stimuli (e.g., a homeless person asking for loose change). In his research on city life, eminent social psychologist Stanley Milgram eloquently describes sensory overload as *"the inability of a system to process inputs [such as sights, sounds, foot traffic] from the environment because there are too many inputs for the system to cope with, or because successive inputs come so fast that Input A cannot be processed when Input B is presented"* (Milgram, 1970, p. 153). According to Milgram, to adapt to sensory overload, less time must be given to each input and/or low-priority inputs must be disregarded. To test this assumption, bystanders from either New York City or the less clamorous neighboring suburbs were approached by a child claiming to be lost and in need of help. Consistent with the sensory overload explanation, help was given considerably *less* often in the urban NYC areas relative to the suburban NYC areas (Solomon, Solomon, & Maiorca, 1982). Likewise, a Dutch study showed there was much *less* help in areas with high environmental input level (measured by sound level, traffic count, pedestrian count, and building count) compared to low environmental input (Korte, Ypma, & Toppen, 1975).

Photo 2.6 © iStock/Page Light Studios.

Compassion Fatigue

Another problem facing urban residents when deciding whether to offer help or not is **compassion fatigue**—the gradual desensitization to helping those in need. Originally applied to health care professionals dealing with sick and vulnerable populations, city dwellers may also experience a form of moral exhaustion that makes them less likely to help others (see *Traumatic stress & the news audience* . . .). As Milgram articulates, *"There are practical limitations to the Samaritan impulse in a major city. If a citizen attended to every needy person, if he were sensitive to and acted on every altruistic impulse that was evoked in the city, he could scarcely keep his own affairs in order"* (Milgram, 1970, p. 156). In addition to practical limitations, city people may be more suspicious of others asking for help due to the high number of scam artists and hustlers, making them less trusting of an apparent "victim" in need of help (Myers & Twenge, 2019). Of course, this type of fatigue should not exonerate somebody from ignoring a person in need, but it does show that in high-density places like big cities, inattention is often the default response.

Remarkably, although compassion fatigue may be a common problem in big cities, it can also be demonstrated in a laboratory setting. In one study, Swedish college students exposed to large amounts of information stressing the need to help the less fortunate (i.e., moral exhaustion), showed

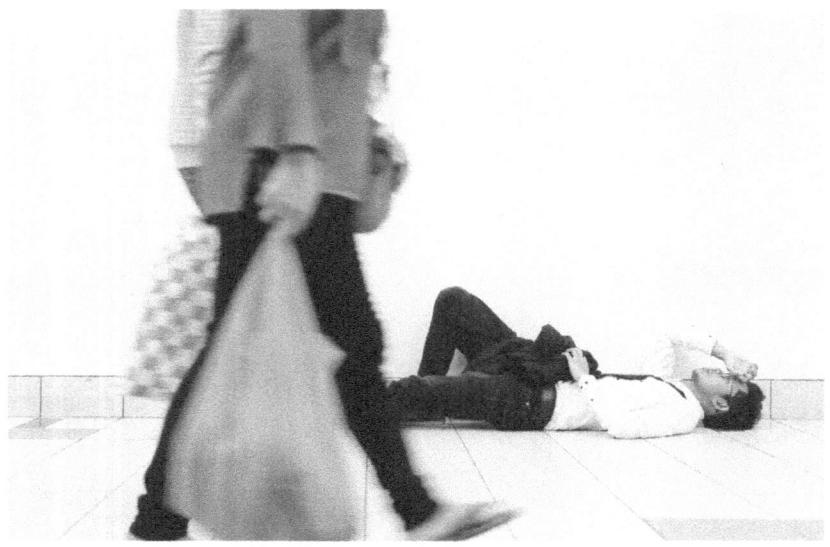

Photo 2.7 © iStock/Hafiez Razali.

less willingness to engage in altruistic acts such as charity giving, again demonstrating how compassion fatigue and helping others are often inversely related (Kajonius, 2014).[3]

Obstacles at Step 2: Interpreting Event as an Emergency

Question: *If you see a man on the sidewalk of a busy street walking awkwardly and clutching his sides, would you make the assumption he needs help?*

For many, the answer to the question above seems relatively obvious: "of course I would." On the other hand, however, the situation is not entirely clear. Is the man truly in need of help or is he just drunk or perhaps mentally unstable? As Photo 2.7 implies, each passerby may have a different interpretation of the event, but what they all have in common is the default justification to remain unresponsive. In this section, we look at obstacles that prevent us from identifying a potential problem as a real emergency.

---

3 New research suggests that rather than assuming that compassion is a limited resource leading to compassion fatigue, compassion should be seen as an energizing experience that motivates people to care about others in need (Gainsburg, 2023).

Situational Ambiguity

Imagine you are working alone on a survey as part of a study and suddenly a stream of non-lethal white smoke starts filling the room. *How would you respond to this odd occurrence?* The rational thing to do would be to investigate where the smoke is coming from and then go alert the researcher. In one classic study, this is what most male students from an American university did when they were filling out the survey alone. However, when in the presence of real bystanders or staged "bystanders" who were told to ignore the smoke, most subjects remained unresponsive and did not report the smoke (Latané & Darley, 1968). When asked why they did not go for help, the typical response was *"I wasn't sure if it was a really a true emergency."* This implies there was **situational ambiguity**—an incident that is not clearly defined thus making several interpretations plausible. When others around us don't seem concerned we are typically less likely to see the situation as a serious problem.

Pluralistic Ignorance

So why might we interpret situations differently when in a group than when alone? One explanation is that in groups, we tend to look at what everyone else is doing before we decide to act. So, if nobody else seems concerned, we may come to the wrong conclusion that taking action is not necessary. Incorrectly assuming that others are thinking and feeling the same as us is defined as **pluralistic ignorance**. Metaphorically, it's like each bystander giving a collective group shrug which signals to others that there is nothing to worry about.

Many studies have illustrated the concept of pluralistic ignorance. In one study, pairs of college students from and American university were drawing sketches of animals when they overheard a loud crash from a workman outside in the hallway who had apparently "fallen" off a ladder. Notably, subjects were much *less* likely to come to his aid if they were seated back-to-back compared to face-to-face (Darley, Teger, & Lewis, 1973). This is presumably because they could not see the expression of concern on their partner's face but only notice his or her unresponsiveness, they were more likely to incorrectly assume that the incident did not require immediate attention.

As the previous study implies, the degree of pluralistic ignorance may depend on your relationship with the other bystanders. For instance, imagine you witness an incident with a friend or with a complete stranger. *In which situation would you expect pluralistic ignorance to be greater?* One prediction is that it would be higher among strangers because while strangers are, by definition, unfamiliar with each other's nonverbal reactions, friends can be quite adept at reading each other's nonverbal cues. In support of this hypothesis, male undergraduates from an American university who overheard a woman "fall" and badly twist her ankle, were much *less* likely to help when paired with a stranger than when paired with a close friend. Moreover, the researchers noticed that while strangers typically glanced furtively at one another, friends were much better at conveying their concerns both nonverbally and verbally, thus greatly increasing the chance they would interpret the situation correctly (Latané & Rodin, 1969).

Group Visualization

In the above-mentioned studies, real groups of people were present during a potential emergency. Remarkably, researchers have also found that people simply asked to visualize being in a crowded movie theater (vs. empty theater) were less likely to help in a subsequent, unrelated task (Garcia, Weaver, Moskowitz, & Darley, 2002). Apparently, merely imagining being in a group may lower one's sense of personal accountability.

Interestingly, when interpreting events, our brains may also respond differently when in groups than when alone. In a recent study using neuroimaging, researchers found that when Scottish participants in a virtual reality experiment witnessed an emergency with increasing numbers of bystanders, a decrease in activity was observed in brain regions (e.g., medial prefrontal cortex) linked to helping and prosocial behavior (Hortensius & de Gelder, 2018). This study provides some compelling evidence that our brains may actually respond differently to emergencies when in the presence of others than when alone.

Obstacles at Step 3: Taking Responsibility to Help

> **Question:** *If you see a guy pummeling another guy outside a crowded bar, is it your responsibility to notify the bouncer?*

As Photo 2.8 implies, bystanders often assume someone else will step up and take responsibility. In one real-world example, a man from India was hit by a car but did not receive any help from the numerous bystanders present. This tragic event prompted India's director of Mental Health and Behavioral Sciences to state, *"When you see someone being bashed up and don't intervene but no one stops it. Everyone thinks, 'mera kya lena dena hai'?"* (translation: *"what have I got to do with this?"*) (Kazmi, 2017). As

Photo 2.8 © iStock/925324030.

we will see in this section, there are several obstacles that preclude us from feeling any responsibility to help.

Diffusion of Responsibility

Imagine you are a first-year college student taking part in a study allegedly dealing with campus life. You are seated in front of a microphone and told other first-year students in adjacent rooms will share their thoughts about adjusting to college via a closed intercom system. You are told that when each person is talking your microphone will be turned off in order to avoid talking over each other. Things progress normally for a while when suddenly you hear one of the other "subjects" appear to have a full-blown seizure. To reduce any ambiguity you may be experiencing, he breathlessly says: *"I could really-er-use some help so if somebody would-er-give me a little h-help-uh-er-er-er-er-er c-could somebody-er-er-help-er-uh-uh-uh (choking sounds) . . . I'm gonna die-er-er-I'm . . . gonna die-er-help-er-er-seizure-er"* (more choking sounds, then silence) (Darley & Latané, 1968, p. 379). *What would you do?* Students from an American university tested in this scenario were 3X *less* likely to report the seizure to the experimenter when they believed others were present during the group interaction compared to when they thought they were alone. Furthermore, the more "bystanders" they believed were listening, the longer their delay to respond.

In another showing diffusion of responsibility in groups, female participants working on a group exercise involving being stranded on a deserted island who overheard a male "partner" make a sexist comment about another group member *("She's pretty hot. I think we need more women on the island to keep the men satisfied")* typically failed to confront him, especially when other women were present (Swim & Hyers, 1999). Similar to the real-world Kitty Genovese murder, observers in these studies were under the impression that because others were witnessing the same event as them it was no longer their responsibility to help.

Apparently, this tendency to spread responsibility can begin at a relatively young age. As one study found, 5-year-old American children were much less likely to help an experimenter who dropped her cup on the ground when in the presence of two other unresponsive child bystanders than when alone (Plotner, Over, Carpenter, & Tomasello, 2015). Based on post-interviews, children in the group bystander condition were 4X *less* likely to say it was "their job to help" compared to children tested alone. The authors believe these findings have practical applications in that *"interventions to promote helpfulness in bystander-type situations should address the issue of diffusion of responsibility early in development"* (Plotner et al., 2015, p. 505).

Victim Deservingness

According to a phenomenon referred to as the **belief in the just world theory** (Lerner, 1980), people have an inherent need to believe that the world is just. Applying this concept to helping behavior, this theory predicts that if the victim needs help through no fault of their own, people will feel a sense of responsibility to help, however, if the victim is perceived to be the cause of their plight, intervention will be less likely because the victim is blamed for their predicament. On one level, this makes sense intuitively. For example, *who is more likely to receive help after falling: a person on crutches or a person who appears to be drunk?* Most people would probably feel a greater obligation to help the person on crutches because they are not seen as the cause of the problem, while the inebriated person is seen as at least partially responsible for the problem. In support of the just world theory, bystanders were much less likely to intervene in cases of sexual assault if they believed the victim was intoxicated or dressed provocatively (Burn, 2009; Workman & Freeburn, 1999). Similarly, British college students were much less likely to give donations to victims of a "man-made" catastrophe (e.g., civil war) than to victims of a natural disaster (e.g., hurricane) (Zagefka, Noor,

Brown, et al., 2011).[4] Together, these studies clearly show that people often feel less responsibility to help if the victim is perceived to have brought this problem upon themselves.

Victim Dissimilarity

Imagine you receive a call from a man you quickly realize has dialed the wrong number. Before you hang up, he pleads with you that his car has broken down and that he is calling from a pay phone and has run out of change *(Note: this study was conducted prior to cell phones when a dime was needed to use a "pay" phone)*. He asks you if you would call his girlfriend (or boyfriend) to let them know that he is running late for their one-year anniversary. *Would you help the poor guy out?* Apparently, the answer depends on whether the caller appeared to be gay or straight. Both male and female (presumably heterosexual) adults living in the United States were far *less* likely to help male callers who they perceived to be homosexual than callers they perceived to be heterosexual (Shaw, Borough, & Fink, 1994). This suggests that the less similar a person is to you, the less likely they will get help.[5]

Obstacles at Step 4: Possessing the Competence to Help

Question: *If someone sitting next to you on a subway train was having convulsions and difficulty breathing, would you try to intervene?*

Similar to the other scenarios mentioned earlier, your first response may be a resounding "Of course I would do something to help!" *But, what if—like many people faced with this problem—you have no idea how to administer life-saving techniques?* As Photo 2.9 shows, there are some basic steps bystanders can take to help, but often they lack the confidence to perform them. In this section, we will look at how our lack of competence creates a major obstacle for providing help, even when we feel some sense of responsibility to do something.

Self-efficacy is the confidence that an individual has in their ability to accomplish a specific task (Bandura, 1995). For our purposes, bystander

---

4 Of course there are other reasons for why people may be less likely to help a country during a civil war such as a lack of a clear solution or feeling their actions will make little difference.
5 Apparently, this tendency for in-group favoritism is a relatively universal phenomenon. In a large, cross-cultural study across forty-two countries, people tended to cooperate more when their partner came from the same country compared to when they came from a different country (Romano, Sutter, Liu, et al., 2021).

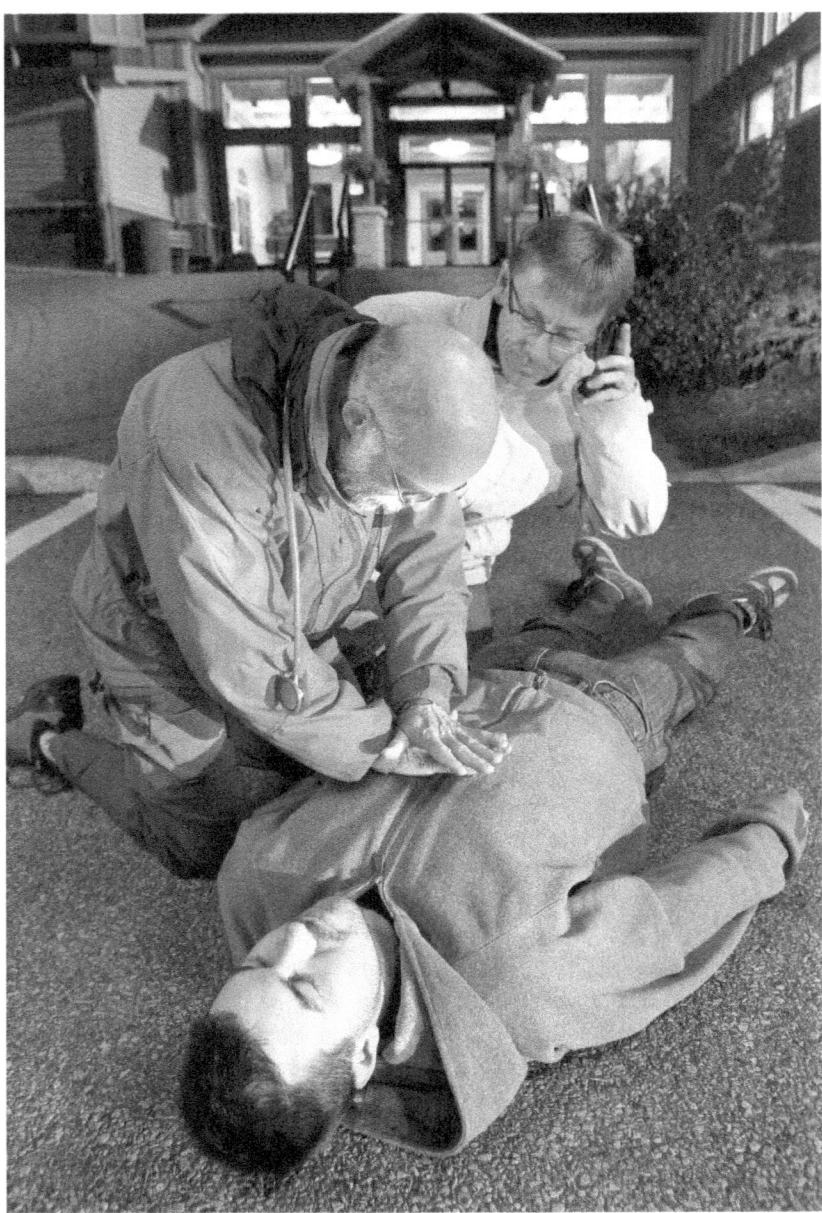
Photo 2.9 © iStock/Imageegaml.

efficacy refers to the confidence one has in their ability to successfully help in an emergency situation. As we will see, bystander incompetence is strongly associated with bystanders remaining frozen and inactive.

Lack of Competence

Based on the **SMB**, bystanders should be more likely to intervene if they feel they have the competence and ability (i.e., self-efficacy) to intervene. If they lack competence, however, the theory predicts they will be more willing to defer helping to other bystanders or health care professionals. Revisiting one of the scenarios mentioned earlier, imagine you are participating in a study and you overhear a workman fall off a ladder in the hallway you had just walked past a few minutes earlier (see Photo 2.10) *Would you jump out of your chair and run outside to help him?* Again, it may depend on your level of competence. If you do not have the training to administer first aid you might be less willing to get involved than if you have training in that area. To illustrate, in one study low competent subjects (college students attending an American university with little first aid training) when paired with another bystander were less likely to help the injured victim than when they were alone (i.e., they showed the typical bystander effect). High competent subjects (registered nurses), however, did not show the bystander effect; they were just as likely to help when in pairs as when alone (Cramer, McMaster, Bartell, & Dragna, 1988). Interestingly, when debriefed both high and low

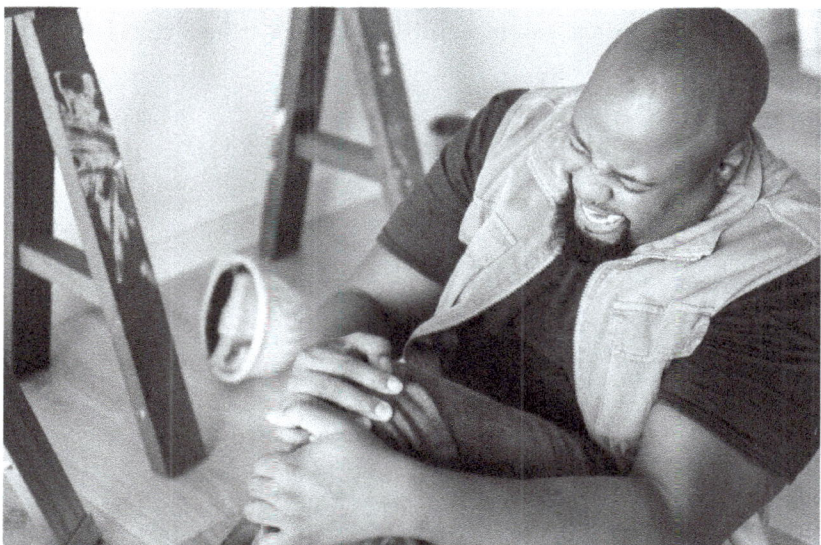

Photo 2.10 © iStock/Rawpixel.

competent subjects thought they should do something, but that belief only translated into action for the high competent subjects. Presumably nurses are well-versed in dispensing first aid and thus have confidence in their ability to help, whereas most students lack first aid training and thus may prefer to defer helping in this scenario.

Fear of Screwing Up

In a life-threatening scenario, another reason people may avoid helping is the fear they might make the situation worse. They might think, *"What happens if while trying to administer CPR to a person who is not breathing, I accidentally break one of the victim's ribs or damage their trachea? Could I be sued or prosecuted for negligence?"* Fortunately, most states have **Good Samaritan laws** protecting well-meaning people from being sued or prosecuted for unintentional injury or wrongful death (see *Good Samaritan laws* . . .). Therefore, as long as you were trying to help in good faith, most states have laws that protect you from unintentional negative outcomes.

Obstacles at Step 5: Taking Action to Help

> **Question:** *If you encounter a stranger with a stab wound, and you have some basic first aid skills, would you still offer help?*

As Photo 2.11 illustrates, some emergencies have inherent risks for helping. In life-threatening situations, especially, there are often high costs for getting

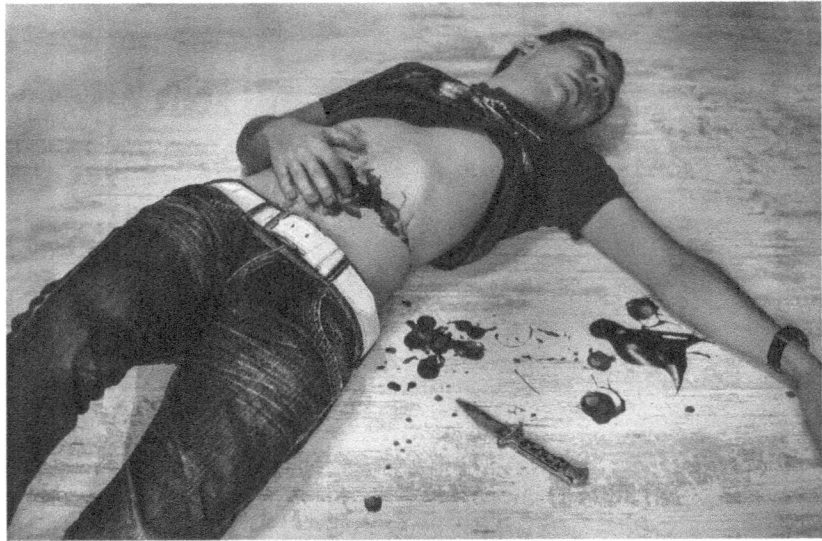

Photo 2.11 © iStock/Diy13.

involved such as unsanitary conditions (blood, bodily fluids, diseases), danger (threat to personal safety), and time commitment (police reports, testifying in court). As we will see in this section, even though a person may feel some sense of responsibility to help and also possess the basic skills to provide assistance, there are numerous perceived risks that may prevent them from taking action.

Risks Exceed Benefits

People are less likely to offer help if the situation involves a high cost-to-benefit ratio. According to **social exchange theory** (Thibaut & Kelley, 1959), we have a desire to maximize benefits and minimize costs. Let's use donating blood as an example. If you focus on the costs to give blood (pain of needle prick) or the benefits in not donating (no pain), chances are you will not sign up for the next community blood drive. However, if you focus on the benefits to donate (helping people who desperately need a blood transfusion) or the costs to *not* help (people could die) you will probably be more likely to roll up your sleeve (Myers & Twenge, 2019).

For some people, the sight of blood is fear-inducing and repulsive. Based on this common phobia, one might predict that emergencies where the victim is bleeding should increase the costs to intervene. As predicted, bystanders who witnessed a "victim" with a cane collapse in a subway car in NYC were less likely to help the victim when he was bleeding from the mouth, presumably because the costs to intervene were greater (Piliavin & Piliavin, 1972). Thus, the **cost-reward model** of helping predicts that the higher the costs are to help relative to the rewards, the less likely people will intervene.

Danger/Fear of Physical Harm

Another cost to intervene is the potential threat to personal safety. In one study discussed earlier, patrons at a bar in the United States who overheard a fight between a man and a woman were much less likely to intervene if they thought it was a lover's quarrel *("Get away from me, I don't know why I married you")* than if they thought the argument was between two strangers (*"Get away from me, I don't even know you"*) (Shotland & Straw, 1976). Many people did not feel comfortable intervening in the married condition because they felt it was none of their business. Another potential reason, however, is that the danger of intervening is often seen as more costly in the marital spat scenario. After all, the husband, in this case, could become belligerent and take his anger out on you or maybe the wife could berate you for snooping into their private matter. Not surprisingly, then, when deciding whether to butt into a conflict, the costs to intervene are substantially higher when it appears to be a domestic dispute than a stranger situation.

To show how costs are calculated before making a decision to help, here is another scenario: imagine you are on your daily subway commute and you observe a menacing looking male "passenger" physically threaten another subway rider. A short time later, you observe a "tourist" who clearly looks lost, approach this belligerent man and ask him whether the train is stopping at a particular station. Consistent with his nasty persona, the man purposely gives the naïve traveler incorrect information. *Would you intervene in this case and let the tourist know the man gave them wrong information?* Compared to a control group who did not see the man act aggressively, most subjects on a NYC subway tested in this threatening condition elected *not* to intervene, undoubtedly because they perceived that the costs of personal injury were too high to risk helping (Allen, 1972). Together, these studies show that bystanders may avoid helping in potentially volatile situations due to a fear of physical harm, retaliation from the perpetrator, or even provoking the aggressor to further violence against the victim.

People who see the world as a dangerous and frightening place (Gerbner, Gross, Morgan, & Signorielli, 1980) might also be prone to avoid offering help because they assume any involvement may ultimately threaten their personal safety. In support of this premise, Chinese researchers found that the more people feared crime within their community, the less they were willing to offer help in a pickpocketing scenario (Zhong, 2010). Thus, the fear of living in a dangerous world (perceived or real) may prevent helping in situations deemed high-risk.

Risk of Damaging Interpersonal Relationships

Another risk that poses an obstacle to bystander intervention is the fear of damaging interpersonal relationships with friends, colleagues, or supervisors. For example, imagine this scenario taken from a bystander training video: *"José recalled his mentor's advice about networking, so when he was at the company's holiday party and saw two colleagues talking to the regional Vice President, he walked right over to say hello. The VP responded, 'Thanks, I'll take another white wine please.'"* (Scully & Rowe, 2009, p. 4). In this scenario, rather than correct the VP, the assumption is that many people will remain silent in order to avoid any potential awkwardness and maintain a good relationship with their boss.

Embarrassment/Social Inhibition

Besides the fear of getting hurt or damaging relationships, another risk to helping is the fear of negative evaluation (looking foolish) from others. Socially anxious people tend to avoid responding in social situations in order to eschew the social disapproval they expect to get from others (Zoccola, Green, Karoutsos, et al., 2011). In theory, then, people with a high fear of negative evaluation should be less likely to help in social situations because they become preoccupied with how they might be judged, instead of focusing their attention on the problem at hand. Thus, one can predict that some people may avoid giving someone the Heimlich maneuver or CPR out of concern that if they perform poorly they may be judged harshly. In support of this notion, when reluctant witnesses (students from an American university) to a staged theft were asked why they failed to intervene, the most common responses were to avoid both looking foolish and the possible humiliation of having been fooled or deceived (Denner, 1968). Similarly, students from an American university who scored high on the fear of negative evaluation scale were less likely to help a person who "accidentally" knocked over a stack of paper and books compared to those with a low fear of negative evaluation (Karakashian, Walter, Christopher, & Lucas, 2006). In another study, researchers found that students from an American college who were high in masculinity (e.g., *"I publicly restrict emotions and feelings in order to maintain a macho demeanor"*) were less likely to help in a simulated choking incident (similar to the seizure study described earlier). The researchers concluded that perhaps *"highly masculine subjects fear potential embarrassment and loss of poise, so they may be reluctant to intervene in emergencies"* (Tice & Baumeister, 1985, p. 420).

Not surprisingly, these social inhibitions against helping found in adults also apply to children. In one study done in the United States, older children (aged 10–11) who heard sounds of another child's severe distress from an adjoining room were *less* likely to help than younger children (aged 5–6). Consistent with the findings using adult subjects, the older children reported an increased concern about being negatively evaluated by peers which, coincidentally, might also explain why they were less likely to communicate with others when deciding how to handle the incident (Staub, 1970).[6]

---

6 Although concern about being judged by peers can inhibit helping, complete strangers can also induce feelings of embarrassment. In one recent study, participants asked to imagine doing embarrassing things in public (e.g., falling on the ground, mistaking one person for another) were more concerned about leaving a bad impression and feeling embarrassment when the bystanders were strangers than when they were friends. Apparently, when people are among strangers, they are more likely to worry about being negatively judged because the bystanders would only have this one situation with which to judge them (Tang, Li, Zheng, et al., 2023).

Another potential obstacle related to embarrassment is the awkwardness over the concern that the recipient might not welcome support, but instead feel offended or see the help as a threat to their self-esteem (Nadler & Fisher, 1986). In a series of studies, students from an American university were asked to reach out via email to a peer on campus they had lost touch with who was currently dealing with an issue and in need of social support. After sending the email, the participants were asked to report their degree of awkwardness and negativity. The recipients, in turn, were asked to rate how awkward they felt as well as the warmth conveyed by the email. In general, the recipients rated the unsolicited help much more positively than the helpers expected (Dungan, Munguia Gomez, & Epley, 2022). One explanation for this gap is that helpers may undervalue the impact of their support because they focus more on how competent their support appears, whereas recipients may focus more on the warmth of the gesture. As the researchers concluded, *"Agonizing over what to say or do may mistakenly keep people from expressing a sentiment whose value to a recipient also comes from the warmth it conveys"* (Dungan et al., 2022, p. 1310). Thus, because helping others can feel risky or awkward, bystanders may overestimate the costs of helping a recipient in need. Collectively, these studies show that for some people, the cultural ideal to look "poised and collected under stress" may ironically prevent them from providing help to those who need it most.

Summary

According to the **SMB**, rather than attribute bystander unresponsiveness to apathy and indifference, we must understand that bystanders are faced with a series of decision-making steps they must pass through in order to become an active responder. At each step there are numerous barriers preventing us from becoming helpful bystanders (see Figure 2.1). In this chapter, we identified some of the common barriers that inhibit helping at each step of an emergency situation. In the next chapter we will look at some evidence-based strategies people can use to overcome these obstacles and become more active responders.

References

Allen, H. (1972). Bystander intervention and helping on the subway. In L. Bickman & T. Henchy (Eds.), *Beyond the laboratory: Field research in social psychology.* McGraw-Hill.

Bandura, A. (1995). *Self-efficacy in changing societies.* Cambridge University Press.

Burn, S. M. (2009). A situational model of sexual assault prevention through bystander education. *Sex Roles, 60,* 779–792.

Cramer, R., McMaster, M., Bartell, P., & Dragna, M. (1988). Subject competence and minimization of the bystander effect. *Journal of Applied Social Psychology, 18,* 1133–1148.

Darley, J. M., & Batson, C. D. (1973). From Jerusalem to Jericho: A study of situational and dispositional variables in helping behavior. *Journal of Personality and Social Psychology, 27,* 100–108.

Darley, J. M., & Latané, B. (1968). Bystander intervention in emergencies: Diffusion of responsibility. *Journal of Personality and Social Psychology, 8,* 377–383.

Darley, J., Teger, A., & Lewis, L. (1973). Do groups always inhibit individuals' responses to potential emergencies? *Journal of Personality and Social Psychology, 26,* 395–399.

Denner, B. (1968). Did a crime occur? Should I inform anyone? A study of deception. *Journal of Personality, 36,* 454–465.

Dungan, J. A., Munguia Gomez, D. M., & Epley, N. (2022). Too reluctant to reach out: Receiving social support is more positive than expressers expect. *Psychological Science, 33,* 1300–1312.

Frey, B. S., Savage, D. A., & Torgler, B. (2010). Interaction of natural survival instincts and internalized social norms exploring the Titanic and Lusitania disasters. *Proceedings of the National Academy of Sciences USA, 107,* 4862–4865.

Gainsburg, I., & Cunningham, J. L. (2023). Compassion fatigue as a self-fulfilling prophecy: Believing compassion is limited increases fatigue and decreases compassion. *Psychological Science, 34,* 1206–1219.

Garcia, S. M., Weaver, K., Moskowitz, G. B., & Darley, J. M. (2002). Crowded minds: The implicit bystander effect. *Journal of Personality and Social Psychology, 83,* 843–853.

Gerbner, G., Gross, L., Morgan, M., & Signorielli, N. (1980). The 'main-streaming' of America: Violence profile number 11. *Journal of Communication, 30,* 10–29.

Good Samaritan laws: What exactly do they protect? (2019, January). Retrieved from https://www.lhsfna.org/index.cfm/lifelines/january-2019/good-samaritan-laws-what-exactly-do-they-protect/

Gracia, E., Garcia, F., & Lila, M. (2009). Public responses to intimate partner violence against women: The influence of perceived severity and personal responsibility. *Spanish Journal of Psychology, 12,* 648–656.

Hortensius, R., & de Gelder, B. (2018). From empathy to apathy: The bystander effect revisited. *Current Directions in Psychological Science, 27,* 249–256.

Hyman, I. E., Boss, S. M., Wise, B. M., et al. (2010). Did you see the unicycling clown? Inattentional blindness while walking and talking on a cell phone. *Applied Cognitive Psychology, 24,* 597–607.

Kajonius, P. (2014). The effect of information overload on charity donations. *International Journal of Psychology and Behavioral Sciences, 4,* 41–50.

Karakashian, L. M., Walter, M. I., Christopher, A. N., & Lucas, T. (2006). Fear of negative evaluation affects helping behavior: The bystander effect revisited. *North American Journal of Psychology, 8,* 13–32.

Kazmi, Z. (2017, August 18). Delhi accident victim: Why don't people step forward to help? It's the 'bystander effect.' *Hindustan Times*. Retrieved from https://www.hindustantimes.com/delhi-news/delhi-accident-victim-why-don-t-people-step-forward-to-help-it-s-the-bystander-effect/story-24sFtMP0VMT4w0NesCvwJJ.html

Korte, C., Ypma, I., & Toppen, A. (1975). Helpfulness in Dutch society as a function of urbanization and environmental input level. *Journal of Personality and Social Psychology, 32,* 996–1003.

Latané, B., & Darley, J. M. (1968). Group inhibition of bystander intervention in emergencies. *Journal of Personality and Social Psychology, 10,* 215–221.

Latané, B., & Darley, J. M. (1970). *The unresponsive bystander: Why doesn't he help?* Appleton-Century-Crofts.

Latané, B., & Rodin, J. A. (1969). A lady in distress: Inhibiting effects of friends and strangers on bystander intervention. *Journal of Experimental Social Psychology, 5,* 189–202.

Lerner, M. J. (1980). *The belief in a just world: A fundamental delusion.* Plenum.

Milgram, S. (1970). The experience of living in the cities. *Science, 3,* 1461–1468.

Mobile giving to help Haiti exceeds $30 million. (2010, January 21). Retrieved from http://www.nbcnews.com/id/34850532/ns/technology_and_science-wireless/t/mobile-giving-help-haiti-exceeds-million/#.XUh3vehKjIU

Myers, D. G., & Twenge, J. M. (2019). *Social psychology* (13th ed.). McGraw Hill.

Nadler, A., & Fisher, J. D. (1986). The role of threat to self-esteem and perceived control in recipient reaction to help: Theory development and empirical validation. In L. Berkowitz (Ed.), *Advances in experimental social psychology* (Vol. 19, pp. 81–122). Academic Press.

Piliavin, J. A., & Piliavin, I. M. (1972). Effect of blood on reactions to a victim. *Journal of Personality and Social Psychology, 23,* 353–361.

Plotner, M., Over, H., Carpenter, M., & Tomasello, M. (2015). Young children show the bystander effect in helping situations. *Psychological Science, 26,* 499–506.

Pocheptsova, A. (2012). Cellphish effects of cellphone use. *Rotman Magazine* (pp. 111–113).

Puryear, C., & Reysen, S. (2013). A preliminary examination of cell phone use and helping behavior. *Psychological Reports, 113,* 1001–1003.

Romano, A., Sutter, M., Liu, J. H., et al. (2021). National parochialism is ubiquitous across 42 nations around the world. *Nature Communications, 12,* 4456.

Scully, M., & Rowe, M. (2009). Bystander training within organizations. *Journal of the International Ombudsman Association, 2,* 1–9.

Shaw, J. I., Borough, H. W., & Fink, M. I. (1994). Perceived sexual orientation and helping behavior by males and females: The wrong number technique. *Journal of Psychology and Human Sexuality, 6,* 73–81.

Shotland, R. L., & Straw, M. K. (1976). Bystander response to an assault: When a man attacks a woman. *Journal of Personality and Social Psychology, 34,* 990–999.

Solomon, H., Solomon, L. Z., & Maiorca, J. (1982). The effects of bystander's anonymity, situational ambiguity, and victim's status on helping. *Journal of Social Psychology, 117,* 285–294.

Staub, E. (1970). A child in distress: The influence of age and number of witnesses on children's attempts to help. *Journal of Personality and Social Psychology, 14,* 130–140.

Strayer, D. L., Drews, F. A., & Johnston, W. A. (2003). Cell phone-induced failure of visual attention during simulated driving. *Journal of Experimental Psychology: Applied, 9,* 23–32.

Swim, J. K., & Hyers, L. L (1999). Excuse me—what did you just say?!: Women's public and private responses to sexist remarks. *Journal of Experimental Social Psychology, 35,* 68–88.

Tang, H., Li, L., Zheng, L., et al. (2023). Social distance of bystanders affects people's embarrassment via changing fear of negative evaluation and feelings of attachment security. *BMC Psychology, 11,* 1–8.

Thibaut, J. W., & Kelley, H. H. (1959). *The social psychology of groups.* Wiley.

Tice, D. M., & Baumeister, R. F. (1985). Masculinity inhibits helping in emergencies: Personality does predict the bystander effect. *Journal of Personality and Social Psychology, 49,* 420–428.

Traumatic stress & the news audience. Retrieved from https://web.archive.org/web/20080715015000/http://www.dartcenter.org/training/selfstudy/3_photojournalism/04.php

Workman, J. E., & Freeburn, E. W. (1999). An examination of date rape, victim dress, and perceiver variables within the context of attribution theory. *Sex Roles, 41,* 261–278.

Zagefka, H., Noor, M., Brown, R., et al. (2011). Donating to disaster victims: Responses to natural and humanly caused disasters. *European Journal of Social Psychology, 41,* 353–363.

Zhong, L. Y. (2010). Bystander intervention and fear of crime: Evidence from two Chinese communities. *International Journal of Offender Therapy and Comparative Criminology, 54,* 250–263.

Zoccola, P. M., Green, M. C., Karoutsos, E., et al. (2011). The embarrassed bystander: Embarrassability and the inhibition of helping. *Personality and Individual Differences, 51,* 925–929.

Part II

Transforming Passive Bystanders into Active Responders

Evidence-Based Strategies to Boost Bystander Behavior

3

Key Terms in This Chapter 42

Increasing Intentions to Help Using the Situational Model of Bystander Intervention (SMB) 42

Counteracting Obstacles for Step 1: Notice a Problem Exists 44

Counteracting Obstacles for Step 2: Interpret Event as an Emergency 46

Counteracting Obstacles for Step 3: Take Responsibility to Help 48

Counteracting Obstacles for Step 4: Gain Competence to Help 51

Counteracting Obstacles for Step 5: Take Action to Help 53

Increasing Intentions to Help Using the Theory of Planned Behavior (TPB) 55

Applying TPB 55

Summary 59

Key Terms in This Chapter

cost-reward model: proposes that helping is more likely to occur when the costs for helping are low and when the costs for not helping are high

descriptive norms: what others *typically* do

Good Samaritan laws: laws protecting well-meaning people from being sued or prosecuted for unintentional injury or wrongful death

injunctive norms: what others *ought* to do

kin-selection theory: predicts that people are more likely to help others who share their genes over those who do not

mindfulness: a receptive attention to present-moment experiences

pluralistic ignorance: incorrectly assuming that others are thinking and feeling the same as us

recategorization: create an inclusive category of "we" by redefining boundaries of "us" vs. "them"

situational model of bystander intervention (SMB): proposes that bystanders typically go through a series of five decision-making steps before help will be given

social identity theory: proposes that we tend to define ourselves by the groups we share

theory of planned behavior (TPB): proposes that the intent to do a behavior depends on three antecedent factors: one's *personal attitude* toward the behavior, the perceived *subjective norms* that relevant others hold about the behavior, and the degree of *perceived behavioral control* (i.e., self-efficacy) one has to do the behavior

zero-tolerance policies: severe disciplinary actions in response to specific types of misbehavior, regardless of the context of the improper behavior

Increasing Intentions to Help Using the Situational Model of Bystander Intervention (SMB)

What hurts the victim most is not the cruelty of the oppressor but the silence of the bystander.
—Elie Wiesel from an interview with Carol Rittner and Sandra Meyers in *Courage To Care: Rescuers of Jews during the Holocaust*. (1986). NYU Press.

As we discussed in Chapter 2, bystanders are often ill-prepared to intervene in high-risk situations due to the numerous obstacles that may be inhibiting their behavior. As the quote above implies, that lack of help (i.e., silence) can be deafening. Fortunately, however, this does not mean that bystanders are doomed to forever remain unresponsive and aloof. In this chapter, we will examine many practical strategies bystanders can use to transform themselves from passive onlookers into active responders.

As we discussed previously, the **Situational Model of Bystander Intervention (SMB)** (Latané & Darley, 1970) proposes that to transform passive spectators into active responders, bystanders must be able to take notice of a potential "problem" (step 1), quickly identify it as an emergency (step 2), experience a sense of responsibility (step 3), possess the skills to intervene (step 4), and perceive the benefits of helping as outweighing the risks of not helping (step 5).

Based on SMB, it would be logical to assume that making people aware of these steps might facilitate their decision to help. In one study, students from an American university who learned about the barriers of intervention such as pluralistic ignorance (step 2), diffusion of responsibility (step 3), and fear of being ridiculed (step 5) were much more likely to help an unresponsive "victim" they encountered later that day who fell off a bicycle, even when in the presence of a nonresponsive "subject." As the researchers remarked, *"Sensitizing persons to social forces in the environment gives them greater freedom to control their own behavior"* (Beaman, Barnes, Klentz, & McQuirk, 1978, p. 410).

Researchers have also looked at what factors bystanders themselves personally think might inhibit their likelihood to help as well as what factors they believe would facilitate helping. In one study, students from an American university asked what barriers they thought might prevent them from helping a victim of sexual assault reported a lack of responsibility (step 3) and inadequate skills to intervene (step 4) as the most common obstacles. In terms of what factors they thought should facilitate helping, the most common responses were whether it was a clear emergency (step 2) and if they felt a strong sense of responsibility to do something (step 3) (Bennett, Banyard, & Garnhart, 2014). Furthermore, students from an American university who completed a questionnaire assessing the five steps of the **SMB** were *less* likely to help as the number of perceived barriers increased (Burn, 2009). As these studies demonstrate, the factors people explicitly perceive as facilitating or hindering helping easily map onto the **SMB**.

Because bystanders can play a valuable role in emergency-type situations, public health researchers have recently begun to design training programs to promote bystander intervention in high-risk incidents such as bullying, sexual assault, and prejudice (Bennett et al., 2014; Berkowitz, 2009; Burn, 2017). Common in all these trainings is that: bystanders learn about the obstacles preventing them from intervening, and subsequently learn effective strategies to overcome these barriers. As one intervention researcher contends, *"Programs intended to promote bystander intervention in situations at-risk for sexual assault may be more effective if they address the barriers identified by a situational model of bystander intervention"* (Burn, 2009, p. 791).

To illustrate, imagine a workplace scenario where during a company meeting you witness your male boss turn to one of the few women present and say to her, *"You should bake the cookies for their next meeting because women are good at that sort of thing."* As a bystander to this event, you can probably envision an inner dialog sounding something like this: *"What did he just say?"* (step 1), *"Was that a sexist remark?"* (step 2), *"Is anyone going to say something?"* (step 3), *"Is there something I should say to make him aware that was inappropriate?"* (step 4), and *"If I say something will it jeopardize my job?"* (step 5) (Ashburn-Nardo, Morris, & Goodwin, 2008). Note how this inner dialog helps you become acutely aware of the obstacles inhibiting your ability to help. In this chapter, we will discuss some of the practical strategies that bystanders can use to overcome common barriers at each step in order to become more active responders (see "What can I do?" boxes).

Counteracting Obstacles for Step 1: Notice a Problem Exists

Promote Vigilance

As we saw in Chapter 2, due to the preoccupation with cell phones, time pressures, and sensory overload, people often fail to notice a problem exists. One way to overcome this problem is to become more vigilant of your surroundings. As the "Good Samaritan" study demonstrated, the seminary students who had time to get to their destination (compared to those feeling rushed) were far more likely to survey their immediate environment, and subsequently respond to a sickly man in need of help (Darley & Batson, 1973). Taking time to be vigilant is essential. While people preoccupied with their cell phones are less likely to notice a person in need of help, those who were not dividing attention with their phones were far more likely to notice the situation (Puryear & Reysen, 2013).

Another way to increase vigilance is through mindfulness training. **Mindfulness**—a receptive attention to present-moment experiences—may help to increase bystander intervention. In one study, White female graduate students from an American university received mindfulness training including focusing attention on the flow of breadth (i.e., full breadth sensations in the nostrils, chest, and abdomen) followed by acknowledging and then letting go of thoughts and bringing attention back to the breath. This group was 3× more likely to help a Black person in staged scenarios (e.g., pick up a stack of dropped papers or offer them their seat when they were on crutches) relative to a group that received sham mindfulness training (Berry, Wall, Tubbs, et al., 2021). One potential explanation for the success of mindfulness is that it helps people to regulate their emotions going into these arousing social interactions. Lower affective arousal may make bystanders less likely to focus on their own physiology and more on the situation at hand (Condon, 2019).

Promote Awareness to Detect Problem

Besides becoming more vigilant of your immediate surroundings, another strategy to become a better bystander is to become more knowledgeable about the particular incident. In other words, *how can you notice a potential "emergency" if you lack the knowledge or awareness to determine if a problem exists?* Let's use workplace prejudice as an example. Although many companies adopt **zero-tolerance policies** on prejudice and discrimination, these policies can only work if prejudice is detected. Unfortunately, due to the subtle nature of contemporary biases, prejudice may not appear obvious to some people, especially those from non-stigmatized groups. Thus, bystanders may fail to notice more hidden forms of prejudice such as avoidance behaviors (e.g., shorter interactions, more speech hesitations, etc.) or the use of "positive" stereotypes to describe a specific group (e.g., *"Black people are natural athletes"*). To illustrate, Black participants (but not White, importantly) from an American university watching a White actor interviewing for a position on a diversity task force rated the actor as *more* prejudiced when he made a reference to Black people's superior athletic ability (Czopp, 2008). This implies that while some Black people may find a "positive" comment racially insensitive, White bystanders might assume (incorrectly) that the comment is harmless, thus reducing the chance they would confront the speaker in this case.

Promoting awareness of the problem is an effective way to get people to become more vigilant that a problem exists. Indeed, the more bystanders learned about sexual violence the greater their intent to intervene, presumably because they are now better able to identify when others are at risk (Banyard, 2008). As we will see in later chapters, the more bystanders learn about the nuances of bullying, prejudice, or sexual assault, the more prepared they will be to intervene.

> ### "What Can I Do?"
>
> The takeaway message at step 1 is: **"If you do not detect a 'problem', then there is no way you can provide any help in this situation."** To become more vigilant, take notice of people and pay attention to your surroundings. Instead of walking with your head down staring at your phone screen, make a concerted effort to reduce social media use when in public so you can pay more attention to your social environment (recall *"texting study"*). Listening with your eyes as well as your ears will make you a more vigilant observer. Another strategy is to educate yourself so you will be more informed if, in fact, a real problem exists. For example, learning about the subtle nature that prejudice has on targets can help you see hidden biases in interactions that others may miss (recall *"prejudice study"*).

Counteracting Obstacles for Step 2: Interpret Event as an Emergency

Promote Transparency and Clarity

Failure to identify the situation as a potential emergency arises from factors such as ambiguity and uncertainty, so it follows that increasing transparency should help people in correctly identifying a situation as a potential emergency. For example, the American Heart Association (www.Heart.org) has begun to educate the public about the warning signs of heart attacks and strokes. The rationale is that by familiarizing people with the warning signs of a particular health-related emergency, they will be more likely to identify the signs as a real emergency.

Of course, some real-world emergency situations such as witnessing a car crash are more well-defined than, let's say, a couple arguing with each other at a bar. So, interpreting whether somebody is in need of help can, at times, be difficult in some high-risk situations. For example, students from an American university were more likely to recognize the importance of intervening in situations that appear high risk to the victim (e.g., *"I should probably check in with my drunk friend before she goes to a room with someone she just met"*), but less likely to identify bystander opportunities that are less apparent (e.g., *"I should challenge a male friend who uses 'b*tch' or 'slut' to describe all women"*) (McMahon, Postmus, & Koenick, 2011).

Promote Actively Seeking Out Information

As research on conformity consistently shows, when we are unsure how to act, we tend to look to others for guidance (Myers & Twenge, 2019). This works well when people around us know what to do, *but what if the situation is ambiguous and they don't know what to do?* According to the concept of **pluralistic ignorance**—if no one else does anything, then we are more likely to incorrectly assume there is not a problem. Thus, *"pluralistic ignorance occurs when ignorant, inactive bystanders look to other ignorant, inactive bystanders and consequently all fail to identify the situation as intervention appropriate"* (Burn, 2009, p. 781).

To counteract pluralistic ignorance, bystanders should be encouraged to verbally express their doubts and concerns in order to communicate to others that there may be problem. In one study, first-year college students from the UK taking part in an active bystander intervention program dealing with sexual assaults on campus showed an increased awareness of the problem and a greater willingness to help, due in part to *"breaking down the ignorance barrier"* and not relying solely on others for cues on how to behave (Bovill & White, 2019).

Promote Prosocial Modeling

People are reluctant to take action if nobody else does. Street performers intuitively know this, so they might ask a "plant" to throw money into their

Photo 3.1 © iStock/JayLazarin.

violin or guitar case to cue others to do the same. Applying modeling to helping scenarios, the presence of a helpful bystander should increase helping among the other bystanders. Consistent with this prediction, a set of field studies found: shoppers at a large department store in the United States were more likely to drop money into a Salvation Army kettle if they first witnessed someone else doing it, and drivers were much more inclined to stop and help another driver with a flat tire if they had earlier driven past a staged scene in which a person with car trouble was observed receiving assistance (Bryan & Test, 1967). In another study looking at prosocial modeling, single shoppers at a mall in the United States who saw someone offer help to a woman who "dropped" her books were more likely to "pay it forward" and later assist a person who dropped a dollar bill (Burger, Bender, Day, et al., 2015).

> ### "What Can I Do?"
>
> The takeaway message at step 2 is: ***"If you think there may be a 'problem,' then do some basic detective work."*** To counter pluralistic ignorance, you should actively seek out information rather than letting others define the situation for you. Remember, when in groups, we often interpret situations differently than if we were alone in that same situation (recall *"smoke study"*). To illustrate, imagine you notice a woman is lying in a somewhat grotesque position in the front seat of her car. Rather than look around to see if others seem concerned that she might be injured or half-dead, you can take the initiative to check out the situation yourself. It never hurts to ask, "Is everything OK?" Note: while doing this, you are also promoting proper social etiquette to other bystanders present (recall *"Salvation Army study"*).

Counteracting Obstacles for Step 3: Take Responsibility to Help

Promote Norms of Responsibility

The diffusion of responsibility is especially likely to happen when social norms do not support prosocial intervention. So, one strategy to reduce the diffusion of responsibility to others is to make the norm of responsibility more visible. For example, imagine you are at a beach relaxing with your favorite book and beverage, when a woman sitting on a nearby blanket listening to a "boombox" (portable media player popular in the 1970s and 1980s) asks you if you could "watch her things?" while she goes to use the restroom. Like most people dealing with this mild imposition, you might say something like,

"Um . . . OK, no problem." After saying OK, she leaves, and sure enough, a few minutes later a "thief" walks up to the unattended blanket and steals the woman's radio. *Would you honor your obligation and yell for the thief to stop (and when he inevitably ignores you), get up from your comfortable beach blanket and chase the culprit down?* Based on the results of a study using this exact scenario on a beach outside New York City, the answer was a resounding yes! In fact, over 90 percent of bystanders tried to stop the thief when they felt responsible for the victim's belongings compared to just 20 percent who did not feel directly responsible for the victim's things (in this case, the victim had simply made small talk before walking away). Results such as this reassure us that under the right conditions, people can be model citizens. As the author proudly boasted *"at a period in history when cries of 'public apathy' abound, it is heartening to find that this mild manipulation is so effective in producing a responsive bystander"* (Moriarty, 1975, p. 376).

In the previous study, the norm of responsibility was manipulated by explicitly asking people if they could "watch their stuff," but *is the norm of responsibility inherent in some cultures more than others?* In one study, researchers investigated the degree people will perform simple helping behaviors (e.g., helping a blind person navigate a crosswalk or helping a person with a leg brace pick up papers they dropped) across various cities from twenty-three countries. Notably, the researchers found a strong trend for cities from Latin American countries (Costa Rica, Mexico, El Salvador, Brazil) to be more helpful than other international cities (incidentally, Los Angeles and New York were dead last). One possible explanation is that the cultural norms in these cities emphasize social responsibility (*simpátia* in Spanish and *simpático* in Portuguese). Based on these findings, the researchers contend that *"Brazilians and New Yorkers are both more likely to offer help in Ipanema than they are in Manhattan"* (Levine, 2003, p. 232). This implies that helping, in some cases, may be less about the characteristics of the individuals and more about the social norms present in their immediate environment.

Promote Social Solidarity

As we discussed in Chapter 1, evolution can play a big role in deciding whether or not to help. To illustrate, if you came home from work and saw your apartment building on fire, you would first probably check to make sure that your family members are safe. Consistent with this outcome, **kin-selection theory** (Darwin, 1859) predicts that people are more likely to help others who share their genes over those who do not. An interesting question to ask is, *does this sense of increased responsibility generalize to victims* *who are not necessarily genetically similar to us, but are still perceived to be part of our in-group?*

According to **social identity theory** (Turner, 1985), we tend to define ourselves by the groups we share. Applying this theory to helping, a shared group identity should increase feelings of responsibility and lead bystanders to act in ways that support the needs of fellow in-group members. To illustrate, imagine you live in the UK and you are a huge fan of the Manchester United football (soccer in America) club. While strolling in a mostly deserted park, you see a "jogger" take a nasty tumble while running down a steep hill. A few seconds later, you see him wincing in pain as he holds his ankle. *Would you be more willing to help him if he was wearing a Manchester United jersey than if he was wearing your archrival, Liverpool's shirt?* Well, apparently how we categorize the victim has a big impact on whether help is given. Self-identified Manchester United fans tested under these conditions were far more likely to offer the "victim" help if he was presumably part of their in-group (Manchester United) rather than if he was wearing a jersey from the dreaded out-group (Liverpool) or an unbranded shirt (Levine, Prosser, Evans, & Reicher, 2005). Likewise, in another study using an immersive virtual environment (in this case, a bar), researchers hypothesized that group affiliation between the bystander and the victim should provide a powerful incentive for the bystander to try to intervene to stop a violent attack. As predicted, UK fans of the English football club team (Arsenal, in this case) who witnessed a virtual bar patron attack a fellow Arsenal fan (in-group) were far more likely to physically intervene and help the virtual victim than if the victim was not an Arsenal fan (out-group). The researchers propose that the *"key to tackling the so called 'walk–on-by' society lies in using the power of group identification to promote social solidarity–and to persuade and empower bystanders to intervene"* (Slater, Rovira, & Southern, 2013, p. 11).

Promote Re-Categorization from "Them" to "Us"

We not only define ourselves by the groups we share, we also tend to categorize people into "us" vs. "them" (Tajfel, 1970). Generally speaking, we feel more responsible to help the "us" than the "them." So, in order to increase your sense of responsibility, *imagine if you could learn to recategorize out-group members from the remote "them" to the more favorable "us"?* In the football study described above, self-identified English football fans were more likely to help a victim if he presumably was a fan of the same football club they supported (Manchester United) than a football club they openly despised (Liverpool). *But what if the social categories were changed from the relatively narrow (exclusive) category of "Manchester fan" to the broader (inclusive) category of "football fan?"* In a follow-up study, when their shared football fan identity was made salient, bystanders were just as likely to help a victim in a Manchester United shirt as they were to help a victim in a Liverpool shirt (Levine et al., 2005). Thus, as the shared identity between bystander and victim increases, the likelihood of helping is often extended to those previously identified as out-group members (i.e., **re-categorization**) (Dovidio & Gaertner, 1999).

"What Can I Do?"

The takeaway message at step 3 is: ***"If you know there is a 'problem,' change your mindset from 'someone else will probably do something' to 'someone else will probably not do something.'"*** To counteract the natural tendency to diffuse responsibility to other bystanders, one simple solution is to always assume responsibility, especially when you are in a group. Remember, in many cases, you might want to help but your default is to assume someone else will take care of it. When we feel a sense of responsibility to help others, that is when our sense of compassion and humanity shines through (recall *"beach study"*). Furthermore, if you begin to cast a wider net of what people are part of your in-group (recall *"English football study"*), you will be amazed at how many more people begin to fall under your wide umbrella of "in-group" member.

Counteracting Obstacles for Step 4: Gain Competence to Help

Promote Self-Efficacy

As we know, even though bystanders may feel responsible to help they may still remain passive because they feel they lack the ability to intervene. Typically, bystanders high in self-efficacy[1] are much more likely to help. Recall in a previous study, compared to the average college student attending an American university, nursing students were much more likely to administer first aid to an injured "victim." Importantly, although both groups felt they should do something to help the victim, the highly competent nurses were much more likely to spring into action, presumably because nurses are well-versed in dispensing first aid (Cramer, McMaster, Bartell, & Dragna, 1988). Likewise, compared to those with little experience with electricity, college

---

1 Self-efficacy (step 4 of the SMB) overlaps with the concept of perceived behavioral control in the Theory of Planned Behavior (TPB) discussed in the next section.

students from an American university who reported having experience with electrical equipment were more likely to help a man whom they observed suffering a serious "shock" while working with this type of equipment (Clark & Word, 1974). Furthermore, researchers from an American university found that the higher a student's self-reported confidence in their ability to intervene in a hypothetical alcohol-related scenario (e.g., *"if they saw a very drunk person being brought upstairs to a bedroom by a group of people at a party"*), the greater their willingness to intervene (Krieger, Serrano, & Neighbors, 2017). Together, these studies dovetail with a recent meta-analysis that found that the presence of highly competent bystanders greatly reduces the bystander effect (Fischer, Krueger, Greitemeyer, et al., 2011).

Promote "Good Samaritan" Laws

In certain helping situations, people may avoid helping because they fear that they may make the situation worse. For example, *what happens if while trying to administer CPR, you accidentally break one of the victim's ribs or damage their trachea? Can you be sued or charged for negligence?* Fortunately, most states in the United States, **"Good Samaritan" laws** that offer limited protection to well-meaning people from being sued or prosecuted if their actions inadvertently contribute to a person's injury or death.[2] As stated on the Laborer's Health & Safety of North America website, *"In most instances, a bystander can't be held liable for not providing assistance. However, that doesn't mean putting yourself in danger like entering a burning building or moving a person who has fallen and may have injured their neck—in both cases it's best to wait for emergency medical personnel. In more common emergency situations, like assisting someone who is feeling dizzy or confused, Good Samaritan assistance can be as simple as providing a blanket, offering water or calling 911"* (see *Good Samaritan laws* . . .).

Focus on Warmth as Well as Competence

Although increasing competence is important to overcome the obstacles at step 4, bystanders often focus too much on their perceived competence at the expense of how positively the recipient will react to the help. Studies show that during a helping scenario, bystanders typically attend more to the competence of their actions, whereas recipients attend more to the warmth

---

2 It should be noted, however, that although these laws are intended to reduce a bystander's hesitation to intervene, they typically only protect someone who acted in a "reasonable" manner while providing the aid, so any gross negligence or recklessness which harmed the victim might still be actionable.

conveyed by the bystander (Epley, Kumar, Dungan, & Echelbarger, 2023). This difference in perspective may create a psychological barrier toward acting prosocially. Therefore, worrying about saying or doing the right thing may lead to avoidance, while shifting attention to the warmth conveyed by a prosocial action may help to increase prosocial behavior.

> ### "What Can I Do?"
>
> The takeaway message at step 4 is: ***"If you don't feel competent to help, then boost your self-efficacy."*** For example, if you don't know how to save someone who is choking on a piece of food sitting at your table, then learn the "Heimlich maneuver" (recall *"nursing study"*) If you are concerned about repercussions, realize that most states have Good Samaritan laws that protect bystanders who acted in good faith (check your local "Good Samaritan laws").

Counteracting Obstacles for Step 5: Take Action to Help

Promote How Benefits to Help Can Outweigh Risks

According to the **SMB**, before we decide on how to help we conduct a subconscious cost-benefit analysis. If the perceived costs to intervene are relatively high compared to the rewards, help is unlikely, however, if we perceive the costs to be relatively low, we will be more likely to provide aid. Furthermore, based on the **cost-reward model** (Piliavin & Piliavin, 1972), helping should occur when the costs for helping are low and when the costs for *not* helping are high. In support of this model, students from an American university participating in a bystander intervention training on sexual assault were more likely to value the benefits of helping (e.g., *"If I intervene, I can prevent someone from being hurt"*) and the costs to not intervene (e.g., *"If I don't do anything, that person is going to get hurt"*) over the costs to intervene (e.g., *"Intervening might cost me a friendship"*) (Banyard, Moynihan, & Plante, 2007). As mentioned in Chapter 2, if you focus on the costs to give blood (pain of needle prick) or the benefits *to not* donate (no pain) chances are you will not sign up for the next community blood drive. However, if you focus on the benefits *to* donate (helping someone who needs a blood transfusion) or the costs to not help (people could die) you will be more likely to roll up your sleeve and get blood drawn (Myers & Twenge, 2019).

Promote Public Self-Awareness

When people are made self-aware, they become more concerned with how others evaluate them. Therefore, in terms of helping, one could predict that when reputational costs for *not* offering help are high, helping should increase, presumably because the presence of other bystanders increases self-awareness, which in turn, affects reputational concerns (i.e., being negatively judged by others for not helping). In support of this prediction, compared to students assigned to the lone bystander condition, Dutch college students using a "busy" online emotional support forum were much more likely to help a person in distress when their screen names were highlighted (van Bommel, van Prooijen, Elffers, & van Lange, 2012). In theory then, promoting public self-awareness in social settings may be an effective way to promote action. In practice (aka the real world), however, the challenge of course is how to raise self-awareness while maintaining an individual's right to privacy. Obviously, using security cameras and running a city like a police state would most certainly increase self-awareness, but at a large cost to personal freedom.

Promote Reducing Inhibitions to Intervene

Ironically, the cultural ideal to look "cool, calm, and collected" under stress may prevent us from providing help in social situations. For example, students from an American college who with a high fear of negative evaluation were *less* likely to help a person who "accidentally" knocked over a stack of books compared to those with a low fear of negative evaluation (Karakashian, Walter, Christopher, & Lucas, 2006). This implies that an effective strategy to transform disengaged bystanders into active responders is by reducing their inhibition to intervene. In support of this strategy, compared to their sober counterparts, Dutch bar patrons who had consumed a fair amount of alcohol helped a person who dropped items on the floor faster in the presence of others, presumably because they felt less social risk (embarrassment) to intervene (van Bommel, van Prooijen, Elffers, & van Lange, 2016). Although consuming alcohol was effective in this case, we should probably look for more practical and ethical ways to reduce inhibitions, and subsequently, promote the impulse to help. A more feasible way to reduce these social inhibitions may be to help people develop strong prosocial tendencies. In one study, students from an American university who reported strong prosocial tendencies (e.g., *"I tend to help people who are in real crisis or need"*) showed less inhibition to help in real-world incidents of sexual assault (Bennett et al., 2014).

> ### "What Can I Do?"
>
> The takeaway message at step 5 is: ***"If you have the ability to help, but are on the fence, focus on the benefits of helping and minimizing the costs."*** Remember, a quick cost-benefit analysis is probably going to lean toward not helping, so to change the ratio in your (or more importantly, the "victim's") favor, focus on how the immediate helping of a stranger feels a lot better than the long-term guilt of not helping (recall *"giving blood study"*). Also realize, in many cases, helping does not need to be (nor should be) heroic or life-threatening, sometimes simply calling 911 or comforting the person is all that is necessary.

Increasing Intentions to Help Using the Theory of Planned Behavior (TPB)

Applying TPB

Although the **SMB** is an incredibly useful model for transforming passive bystanders into active responders, it does not specifically address a broad range of cognitive factors (e.g., attitudes and beliefs) that may also influence bystander behavior (Banyard, Moynihan, Cares, & Warner, 2014). For example, *"What are the bystander's attitudes/beliefs about helping in that scenario?"* and *"What are the attitudes/beliefs of other people who the bystander respects?"* Emerging evidence from public health research suggests that the **Theory of Planned Behavior (TPB)** can help address these missing factors by focusing more on cognitive processes.

According to the **TPB** (Ajzen, 1991), the intent to do a behavior depends on three antecedent factors: (1) one's attitude toward the behavior, (2) the perceived norms that relevant others hold about the behavior, and (3) the degree of perceived behavioral control (i.e., self-efficacy) one has to do the behavior.[3] In general, as your *personal attitude* (beliefs about the behavior and potential outcomes of doing the behavior) is strengthened, the *subjective norms* (perceptions of what important people in your life would do or expect you to do) are aligned with your personal attitudes, and your *perceived behavioral control* (degree of confidence you can do the behavior) is high, your intention to engage in that particular behavior should be stronger (see Figure 3.1).

---

3 Each antecedent factor can subsequently split into two components; these additional components will be addressed in Chapter 6.

Theory of Planned Behavior

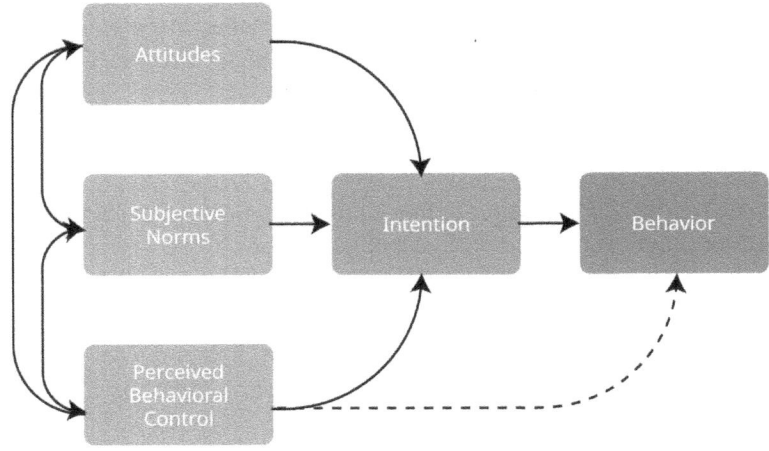

Figure 3.1 Theory of Planned Behaviour

Let's apply the three factors of the **TPB** to recycling. Imagine you are interested in increasing college students intentions to recycle in their dorms. To begin, you would want to strengthen their personal attitudes about recycling, perhaps by having them tour a recycling plant, watch a documentary on the serious environmental problems associated with not recycling, and/or showing them how recycling is personally relevant to them (e.g., can help reduce costs of books). To promote subjective norms, you could hang posters in the dorms showing other students happily engaging in recycling. To increase perceived behavioral control, you could replace standard bins with lids that have cut-out shapes such as circles for bottles and slits for paper. (see Photo 3.2)

Strengthen Bystanders' Attitudes about Helping

For our purposes, we can also apply the **TPB** to helping in real-world emergency situations. To begin, bystanders must have positive attitudes about helping in that particular situation. As we will see in upcoming chapters, this is not always the case. Let's take bullying for an example. When bullying occurs, bystanders may have unsympathetic attitudes toward someone who is bullied *("it's just a harmless 'rite of passage'")* or conclude that any help they give will not make a difference *("I don't expect a positive outcome for*

Photo 3.2 © iStock/goc

a victim who is bullied"). To strengthen their attitudes about confronting bullying, bystanders need to raise their awareness of the impact of bullying on the victim (build empathy) and focus on the positive outcomes of helping. To build empathy, in general terms, bystanders must take on the perspective of the victim (e.g., *"I will become sensitive to other people's feelings, even if they are not my friends"*). In support of this strategy, students who watched a video showing the impact of bullying on the victim as well as emphasizing how bystanders can make a big difference when standing up to bullying showed greater concern for an unknown victim and were more likely to believe their help could make a difference (Doane, Ehlke, & Kelley, 2020). Thus, to become active responders, bystanders must have strong attitudes about moral responsibility, possess empathy, and believe that all people (even strangers) deserve help when faced with an urgent situation.

Based on the **TPB**, it is important to realize that for some behaviors, people may hold the correct attitude but still not engage in the correct behavior. Let's take texting and driving for example. Most people know the dangers of texting and driving, yet these same people might still text and drive if lots of their friends/family members are doing it. Bystanders to emergencies often show the same pattern seen with texting and driving. That is, most bystanders believe that bullying is wrong (i.e., they have the right attitude), but if their attitudes conflict with what their friends would do, then they may fail to get involved.

Emphasize Correct Subjective Norms on Helping

People often take their cues from what other people do. For bystanders to help in a potential emergency, subjective norms (what would other people do?) must be salient and clearly pro-helping. These subjective norms are often defined as **descriptive norms** (what others *typically* do) and **injunctive norms** (what others *ought* to do). Often these norms are aligned, for example, students shouldn't talk on a cell phone during class because it is disrespectful (injunctive) and the vast majority of students do not engage in this behavior (descriptive).

During emergency situations, however, there is an interesting paradox— often people are aware of the injunctive norm (e.g., binge drinking is dangerous), yet wrongly assume that the descriptive norm is most of their peers do not feel the same way. Typically this results in doing what they think others are doing, which, in this case, is not helping. In one example, researchers found that males from an American university tended overestimate the extent to which other males hold sexist attitudes, and this in turn, increased their reluctance to challenge those attitudes for fear of being ostracized (Berkowitz, 2010). One way to counteract this misperception is to show male students that their peers actually hold *less* sexist attitudes than they believe. In one study, male students from an American university who were given accurate information on their peers" attitudes toward sexist language (rather than relying on their biased perceptions) were more willing to challenge a sexist-related incident (Kilmartin, Smith, Green, et al., 2008).

Increase Bystanders' Perceived Control to Help

According to the **TPB**, for help to occur, bystanders must also feel competent and able to help. As we know, often bystanders are unprepared to handle emergency situations. For example, when encountering a health-related emergency such as a cardiac arrest or stroke, bystanders are often reluctant to intervene, partly because they lack competence. Intervention programs must help bystanders increase their perceived behavioral control (i.e., self-efficacy). In one study, bystanders from one American city who learned how to identify a stroke victim using the **FAST** acronym: Facial drooping, Arm weakness, Speech difficulties, and Time to call emergency services were much more likely to correctly identify stroke victims and get them the help they need (Kleindorfer, Miller, Moomaw, et al., 2007).

It is important to note that even though the **SMB** emphasizes situational processes, while the **TPB** focuses more on cognitive processes, there is some degree of overlap, particularly with respect to self-efficacy *(identified as Step 4 in **SMB** and perceived behavioral control in **TPB**)*. Thus, rather than seeing the **SMB** and **TPB** as competing models, it is better to view them as complimentary models that provide a more comprehensive framework for increasing bystander intervention (Casey, Lindhorst, & Storer, 2017). As one research team proposes, *"Incorporating the TPB with constructs from Latané and Darley's 5-stage model* [SMB] *may offer a more comprehensive mechanism for capturing the processes involved in evaluating bystander opportunities"* (Casey & Ohler, 2012, p. 74).

> ### "What Can I Do?"
>
> The takeaway message here is that you can apply the **TPB** to any bystander situation. To increase your intentions to help, you need to strengthen your personal attitudes toward doing the desired behavior, determine what other people are *actually* doing, and decide on a competent course of action. For example, to become a better bystander you can strengthen your attitude by learning about the seriousness of the problem, to increase the salience of subjective norms you can find out what people actually do (not simply what you think they do), and to increase perceived control you can learn some relatively simple strategies to feel more confident and competent when faced with an emergency situation.

Summary

In this chapter, we mapped various helping strategies to each step of the **SMB**. By counteracting these obstacles, people can be transformed from passive bystanders into active responders. We also looked at how the **TPB** can be applied to increase intention to help in emergency situations. In the remaining chapters, we will look at how we can apply the **SMB** and **TPB** models to increase the intention to help in specific emergency situations including: alcohol-related and health-related emergencies (Chapter 4), bullying/cyberbullying (Chapter 5), sexual assault (Chapter 6), and discrimination (Chapter 7). As we will see, the **SMB** and **TPB** can be extremely useful in turning passive bystanders into active responders. We will also look at how the **SMB** and **TPB** can help public health educators/researchers design more effective intervention programs.

References

Ajzen, I. (1991). The theory of planned behavior. *Organizational Behavior and Human Decision Processes, 50,* 179–211.

Ashburn-Nardo, L., Morris, K. A., & Goodwin, S. A. (2008). The confronting prejudiced responses (CPR) model: Applying CPR in organizations. *Academy of Management Learning & Education, 7,* 333–342.

Banyard, V. L. (2008). Measurement and correlates of prosocial bystander behavior: The case of interpersonal violence. *Violence and Victims, 23,* 83–97.

Banyard, V. L., Moynihan, M. M., Cares, A. C., & Warner, R. (2014). How do we know if it works? Measuring outcomes in bystander-focused abuse prevention on campuses. *Psychology of Violence, 4,* 101–115.

Banyard, V. L., Moynihan, M. M., & Plante, E. G. (2007). Sexual violence prevention through bystander education: An experimental evaluation. *Journal of Community Psychology, 35,* 463–481.

Beaman, A. L., Barnes, P. J., Klentz, B., & McQuirk, B. (1978). Increasing helping rates through information dissemination: Teaching pays. *Personality and Social Psychology Bulletin, 4,* 406–411.

Bennett, S., Banyard, V. L., & Garnhart, L. (2014). To act or not to act, that is the question? Barriers and facilitators of bystander intervention. *Journal of Interpersonal Violence, 29,* 476–496.

Berkowitz, A. (2009). *Response ability: Complete guide on bystander behavior.* Beck.

Berkowitz, A. D. (2010). Fostering healthy norms to prevent violence and abuse: The social norms approach. In K. L. Kaufman (Ed.), *The prevention of sexual violence: A practitioner's sourcebook* (pp. 147–171). NEARI Press.

Berry, D. R., Wall, C. S. J., Tubbs, J. D., et al. (2021). Short-term training in mindfulness predicts helping behavior toward racial ingroup and outgroup members. *Social Psychological and Personality Science, 14,* 60–71.

Bovill, H., & White, P. (2019). Ignorance is not bliss: A U.K. study of sexual and domestic abuse awareness on campus, and correlations with confidence and positive action in a bystander program. *Journal of Interpersonal Violence, 35,* 1694–1718.

Bryan, J. H., & Test, M. A. (1967). Models and helping: Naturalistic studies in aiding behavior. *Journal of Personality and Social Psychology, 6,* 400–407.

Burger, J. M., Bender, T. J., Day, L., et al. (2015). The power of one: The relative influence of helpful and selfish models. *Social Influence, 10,* 77–84.

Burn, S. M. (2009). A situational model of sexual assault prevention through bystander education. *Sex Roles, 60,* 779–792.

Burn, S. M. (2017). Appeal to bystander interventions: A normative approach to health and risk messaging. In R. Parrot (Ed.), *The encyclopedia of health and risk message design and processing* (pp. 140–155). Oxford University Press.

Casey, E. A., Lindhorst, T. P., & Storer, H. L. (2017). The situational-cognitive model of adolescent bystander behavior: Modeling bystander decision making in the context of bullying and teen dating violence. *Psychology of Violence, 7,* 33–44.

Casey, E. A., & Ohler, K. (2012). Being a positive bystander: Male antiviolence allies' experiences of stepping up. *Journal of Interpersonal Violence, 27,* 62–83.

Clark, R. D. III., & Word, L. E. (1974). Where is the apathetic bystander?: Situational characteristics of the emergency. *Journal of Personality and Social Psychology, 29,* 279–287.

Condon, P. (2019). Meditation in context: Factors that facilitate prosocial behavior. *Current Opinion in Psychology, 28,* 15–19.

Cramer, R., McMaster, M., Bartell, P., & Dragna, M. (1988). Subject competence and minimization of the bystander effect. *Journal of Applied Social Psychology, 18,* 1133–1148.

Czopp, A. M. (2008). When is a compliment not a compliment? Evaluating expressions of positive stereotypes. *Journal of Experimental Social Psychology, 44,* 413–420.

Darley, J. M., & Batson, C. D. (1973). From Jerusalem to Jericho: A study of situational and dispositional variables in helping behavior. *Journal of Personality and Social Psychology, 27,* 100–108.

Darwin, C. (1859). *The origin of species.* Murray.

Doane, A. N., Ehlke, S., & Kelley, M. L. (2020). Bystanders against cyberbullying: A video program for college students. *International Journal of Bullying Prevention, 2,* 41–52.

Dovidio, J. F., & Gaertner, S. L. (1999). Reducing prejudice: Combating intergroup biases. *Current Directions in Psychological Science, 8,* 101–105.

Epley, N., Kumar, A., Dungan, J., & Echelbarger, M. (2023). A prosociality paradox: How miscalibrated social cognition creates a misplaced barrier to prosocial action. *Current Directions in Psychological Science, 32,* 33–41.

Fischer, P., Krueger, J. I., Greitemeyer, T., et al. (2011). The bystander-effect: A meta-analytic review on bystander intervention in dangerous and non-dangerous emergencies. *Psychological Bulletin, 137,* 517–537.

Good Samaritan laws: What exactly do they protect? (2019, January). Retrieved from https://www.lhsfna.org/index.cfm/lifelines/january-2019/good-samaritan-laws-what-exactly-do-they-protect/

Karakashian, L. M., Walter, M. I., Christopher, A. N., & Lucas, T. (2006). Fear of negative evaluation affects helping behavior: The bystander effect revisited. *North American Journal of Psychology, 8,* 13–32.

Kilmartin, C., Smith, S., Green, A., et al. (2008). A real time social norms intervention to reduce male sexism. *Sex Roles, 59,* 264–273.

Kleindorfer, D. O., Miller, R., Moomaw, C. J., et al. (2007). Designing a message for public education regarding stroke: Does FAST capture enough stroke? *Stroke, 38,* 2864–2868.

Krieger, H., Serrano, S., & Neighbors, C. (2017). The role of self-efficacy for bystander helping behaviors in risky alcohol situations. *Journal of College Student Development, 58,* 451–456.

Latané, B., & Darley, J. M. (1970). *The unresponsive bystander: Why doesn't he help?* Appleton-Century-Crofts.

Levine, R. M., Prosser, A., Evans, D., & Reicher, S. D. (2005). Identity and emergency intervention: How social group membership and inclusiveness of group boundaries shape helping behavior. *Personality and Social Psychology Bulletin, 31,* 443–453.

Levine, R. V. (2003). The kindness of strangers. *American Scientist, 91*, 226–233.

McMahon, S., Postmus, J., & Koenick, R. (2011). Conceptualizing the engaging bystander approach to sexual violence prevention on college campuses. *Journal of College Student Development, 52*, 115–130.

Moriarty, T. (1975). Crime, commitment, and the responsive bystander. *Journal of Personality and Social Psychology, 31*, 370–376.

Myers, D. G. & Twenge, J. M. (2019). *Social psychology* (13th ed.). McGraw Hill.

Piliavin, J. A., & Piliavin, I. M. (1972). Effect of blood on reactions to a victim. *Journal of Personality and Social Psychology, 23*, 353–361.

Puryear, C., & Reysen, S. (2013). A preliminary examination of cell phone use and helping behavior. *Psychological Reports, 113*, 1001–1003.

Slater, M., Rovira, A., Southern, R., et al. (2013). Bystander responses to a violent incident in an immersive virtual environment. *PLoS ONE, 8*, e52766.

Tajfel, H. (1970). Experiments in intergroup discrimination. *Scientific American, 223*, 96–102.

Turner, J. C. (1985). Social categorization and the self-concept: A social cognitive theory of group behavior. *Advances in Group Processes: Theory and Research, 2*, 77–122.

van Bommel, M., van Prooijen, J. W., Elffers, H., & van Lange, P. A. M. (2012). Be aware to care: Public self-awareness leads to a reversal of the bystander effect. *Journal of Experimental Social Psychology, 48*, 926–930.

van Bommel, M., van Prooijen, J. W., Elffers, H., & van Lange, P. A. M. (2016). Booze, bars, and bystander behavior: People who consumed alcohol help faster in the presence of others. *Frontiers in Psychology, 7*, Article 128.

Confronting Alcohol- and Health-Related Emergencies

4

Key Terms in This Chapter 64

Problems When Encountering Alcohol-Related Emergencies 65

Confronting Alcohol-Related Emergencies 67
Applying SMB 67
Applying TPB 71

Problems When Encountering Health-Related Emergencies 75

Confronting Health-Related Emergencies 78
Applying SMB 78

Applying TPB 86

Summary 91

Key Terms in This Chapter

alcohol myopia theory: proposes that intoxication reduces attentional capacity and narrows people's visual fields (creates "tunnel vision")

cost-reward model: proposes that helping is more likely to occur when the costs for helping are low and when the costs for not helping are high

Covid-19 pandemic: an ongoing global pandemic of coronavirus disease caused by severe acute respiratory syndrome coronavirus 2 (SARS-CoV-2)

descriptive norms: what others *typically* do

injunctive norms: what others *ought* to do

medical amnesty policies: contracts designed to protect students seeking medical attention from illegal action such as underage possession of alcohol/drugs or intoxication

moral agency: belief in one's capacity to act in accordance with moral standards

pluralistic ignorance: incorrectly assuming that others are thinking and feeling the same as us

situational model of bystander intervention (SMB): proposes that bystanders typically go through a series of five decision-making steps before help will be given

social norm theory: proposes people will often follow culturally-based rules for acceptable behavior

sympathetic empathy: caring about another person's distress and wanting to help them in some way

theory of planned behavior (TPB): proposes that the intent to do a behavior depends on three antecedent factors: one's *personal attitude* toward the behavior, the perceived *subjective norms* that relevant others hold about the behavior, and the degree of *perceived behavioral control* (i.e., self-efficacy) one has to do the behavior

trending minority norms: normative messages that emphasize a minority norm is increasing in popularity

zero-tolerance policies: severe disciplinary actions in response to specific types of misbehavior, regardless of the context of the improper behavior

Problems When Encountering Alcohol-Related Emergencies

If one person had made a call. One, we'd have our son.
—Distraught mother's response after finding out her son died of alcohol poisoning as part of a fraternity hazing incident at an American college (see Schackner, 2020)

Defining the Problem

Much to the chagrin of many college professors (including myself), college students do not only come to the hallowed halls of higher education for intellectual pursuits; the social opportunities are equally as (or even more) important. For many students, these social events revolve around drinking, sometimes in excessive amounts. The statistics, for American college students at least, are quite sobering (pun intended). In one US survey, roughly 13 percent of students surveyed reported consuming *ten or more drinks* in one sitting during the previous two weeks (White & Hingson, 2014). Each year in the United States, nearly 20 percent of college students (24 percent of males, 13 percent of females) report suffering from significant alcohol-related problems such as "blacking out" (Slutske, 2005), and approximately 60,000 college-aged young adults are hospitalized with alcohol poisoning (White, Hingson, Pan, & Yi, 2011). Sadly, like the quote above, each year around 2,000 students attending American colleges die from alcohol-related incidents, many of which could have been prevented if a friend or peer had called 911 or notified campus authorities (Hingson, 2010).

Traditional Strategies

Those who were with the victim did not seek medical care for him, but instead "JanSported" him [the act of attaching a backpack to person to prevent them from rolling on their back and choking on their vomit]. They periodically checked on him for about a day before calling for help.
—Investigators presenting a timeline of events leading up to a student's alcohol poisoning death (see *"Investigators announce role of alcohol . . ."*)

As the quote above suggests, college students may underestimate the risks of excessive drinking and falsely assume the victim is not at risk or in need of medical attention. All too often, however, this lax response to severe alcohol intoxication can have deadly consequences.

Typically, residence life staff on college campuses have mandatory programs that address these inadequate responses, while emphasizing that binge drinking is a serious problem. Ironically, these programs can backfire because the message that *"Many students are BINGE-DRINKING"* may be misconstrued as *"Many students ARE binge-drinking"* (see Cialdini, 2003, for a similar example with littering). Not surprisingly, students often complain of receiving mixed messages from these types of programs (e.g., *"Res. Life tells us not to get wasted, but then say that everyone is getting wasted"*). This message can be counterproductive, because as we will see later in this chapter, the best predictor of how much a student typically drinks is their perception of how much they think their peers drink (Perkins, Haines, & Rice, 2005).

In response to hazing incidents and drinking-related deaths, many colleges have renewed their commitment to **zero-tolerance policies**—severe disciplinary actions in response to specific types of misbehavior, regardless of the context, rationale, or magnitude of the improper behavior. Although a zero-tolerance policy may sound like an effective deterrent, the research does not appear to support this policy, especially when looking at the bystanders present at these events (Parks, 2021). From a bystander's perspective, one problem with these policies is that they do not explicitly state what bystanders should do in these high-risk situations. Another flaw is they do not address the perceived costs of intervention which include: fear of loss of relationships, fear of retaliation, and fear that their fellow students may be suspended or expelled (Rowe, Wilcox, & Gadlin, 2009).

Unique Barriers

Beyond the general obstacles that inhibit helping in emergency situations (see Chapter 2), there is a unique set of barriers preventing bystanders from intervening in excessive drinking situations. Ironically, one common obstacle in these cases is the bystanders themselves may be too impaired to notice that a highly intoxicated person is in potential danger (Schipani-McLaughlin, Salazar, & Vivolo-Kantor, 2019). Another unique problem inherent in drinking scenarios is that bystanders often underestimate the risks of excessive drinking and falsely assume the victim is not at risk or in need of medical attention (Oster-Aaland, Lewis, Neighbors, et al., 2009). Bystanders also tend to be concerned of the perceived social costs of getting the victim in trouble, especially if the victim is a friend or somebody they know (Blavos, Glassman, Sheu, et al., 2014).

In the next section, we will look at how both bystanders and public health advocates can overcome these unique barriers when dealing with alcohol-related emergencies such as binge drinking and alcohol poisoning.

Confronting Alcohol-Related Emergencies

As with each type of emergency situation covered in this book, the obstacles preventing bystanders from helping in alcohol-related emergencies can be mapped onto the situation model of bystander intervention (**SMB**).

Applying SMB

Applying the **SMB** to alcohol-related emergencies, researchers determined that successfully moving through each stage significantly increased the likelihood that a student would intervene to prevent a person from driving while intoxicated. Consistent with the **SMB**, the data showed that while 65 percent of the bystanders who noticed the event intervened (Step 1), 73 percent of those who thought the situation was serious intervened (Step 2), and 82 percent of those who felt they had the ability to help reported intervening (Step 4). Notably, students from a large American university who did intervene (typically by taking away the driver's keys), were successful in stopping the intoxicated person from driving drunk 96 percent of the time! (Monto, Newcomb, Rabow, & Hernandez, 1994).

Recognize Symptoms of Alcohol Poisoning

To increase bystander intervention for alcohol poisoning, college health policymakers have begun focusing on the major obstacles inhibiting helping in these situations. In one study, the most common reason students from an American university gave for not helping a victim of alcohol poisoning was the belief that the impaired student was not truly at risk. Although students did recognize some of the prominent symptoms of alcohol poisoning (such as seizures, bluish skin color, inability to be awakened), they were less aware of other red flags (such as passing out, confusion, and slow breathing) (Oster-Aaland et al., 2009).

As mentioned previously, another impediment to recognizing alcohol poisoning is that, all too frequently, the bystanders themselves are too impaired to notice that a highly intoxicated person is, in fact, in real danger. According to the **alcohol myopia theory**, intoxication reduces attentional capacity and narrows people's visual fields (creates "tunnel vision"), thus increasing the chance they may not notice a life-threatening situation (Leone, Haikalis, Parrott, & DiLillo, 2018). Consistent with this theory, binge drinkers from a large American university when compared to casual drinkers, had significantly lower intentions to intervene and less positive outcome expectancies for intervening (Schipani-McLaughlin et al., 2019). These findings highlight, somewhat ironically, the need for bystander intervention programs to also address alcohol use within the bystanders themselves.

Correct Misconceptions about Alcohol Use and Abuse

Social norms are culturally-based rules for acceptable behavior such as holding doors for strangers and not talking with a mouth full of food. As we know, social norms have a big influence on our behavior. When making decisions about how to behave, we often take into account what most other people appear to be doing (Myers & Twenge, 2019). Typically, this strategy works relatively well. For example, let's say you have never eaten edamame (soybeans) in the pod before. Because they look quite similar to snap peas, your first inclination may be to eat the entire pod; however, after gradually coming to the realization that trying to eat the pod is like chewing on shoe leather, you may begin to take notice of how others are eating the edamame by simply squeezing the pod directly into their mouths. At this point, you promptly adjust your behavior to follow this more conventional (and much safer, based on personal experience) alternative. Looking to others for advice on how to behave works well in this situation, *but what happens when the other people are not displaying the correct behavior?*

In Chapter 2, we talked about **pluralistic ignorance**—the tendency to be influenced by inaccurate perceptions of how other people behave. In regards to college drinking norms, researchers have found widespread evidence of pluralistic ignorance. Generally speaking, students tend to believe that their peers are more comfortable with binge drinking than they are themselves. To illustrate, when researchers asked students from a large American university to rate on an 11-point scale *"How comfortable do you feel with the alcohol drinking habits of students here?"* the typical response was around a five, however, when those same students were asked *"How comfortable would you say the average student is with the alcohol drinking habits of students here?"* the typical response was around 7 (about two points higher) (Prentice & Miller, 1993). Based on **SMB**, students tend to overestimate their peers' acceptance of drunken behavior, so in theory, they may be more reluctant to intervene in a risky drinking situation because they presume, incorrectly, that most of their peers would not see it as problem. As the authors of the study eloquently state, *"Believing that others are still comfortable with alcohol, students will perpetuate that norm by continuing to adopt a nonchalant demeanor that masks their growing concerns"* (Prentice & Miller, 1993, p. 245).

Social norm interventions can reduce risky drinking behavior by persuading people that the majority of their peers do not engage in these high-risk behaviors (i.e., undermine pluralistic ignorance). To illustrate, a 5-year study at large American university designed to correct misperceived binge-drinking norms by distributing posters that emphasize actual norms and promoting healthy drinking behaviors, found that over time, perceptions that others drank heavily went down from *70 percent to 30 percent*, and more importantly, self-reported binge drinking decreased from *45 percent to 33 percent* (Haines & Spear, 1996). Likewise, a large-scale study based on 130 American colleges (over 75,000 students) found that although most students reported having 3–4 drinks at a typical party (actual drinking norm), many students overestimated the drinking norm (perceiving most students had six to seven drinks per event) (Perkins et al., 2005). Furthermore, the best predictor of how much a student actually drank was their *perceptions* of the drinking norm. Specifically, each drink they overestimated was associated with ½ drink more in personal consumption. Studies such as these show that by exposing students to actual drinking norms, pluralistic ignorance can be reduced. By changing the social norm of what constitutes dangerous levels of alcohol, bystander intervention programs can help students change this misconception and hopefully increase the likelihood they would now take dangerous drinking more seriously.

Show How Benefits of Helping Outweigh Risks

Based on the **cost-reward model**, one of the strongest predictors of whether a bystander intervenes during an event like alcohol poisoning is the perceived benefits they receive *(e.g., "I would feel good about myself")*. Unfortunately, for many students, the focus tends to be on the perceived social costs *(e.g., "I might get the person in trouble")* (Blavos et al., 2014). This implies that as perceived negative social consequences of bystander behavior increase, bystanders' intentions to intervene will decrease. To overcome this common barrier, students in high-risk drinking situations need to see how the benefits of helping outweigh the risks. In one study, peer-led bystander training used motivational "change talk" to address students' motivation to change apathetic bystander behavior. Deemed a success, researchers from an American university found that students' reports of perceived benefits of active bystander behavior increased (e.g., *"My friends will look up to me if I help"*), while concerns over social costs decreased (e.g., *"I could get them in trouble"*) (Anthenien, Neighbors, & Rosa, 2017).

To encourage students to call 911 or campus authorities during alcohol-related emergencies, many colleges and universities have begun instituting

"Good Samaritan" or **medical amnesty policies** that minimize or waive penalties (e.g., underage possession of alcohol) for students involved in these types of emergencies. When examining the effects of amnesty policies, several studies have found that students from American universities expressed less concern over getting an intoxicated person in trouble (Lewis & Marchell, 2006), and were more likely to report contacting residence life staff in the event of an emergency (Haas, Wickham, McKenna, et al., 2018). Although, medical amnesty policies do show promise in motivating students to call for direct assistance, some critics have argued that rather than sending a clear message that underage drinking is unacceptable, these policies may, instead, perpetuate reckless underage drinking. Although studies have not reported any projected increases, one research team responded to critics by stating that *"while it is true that judicially charging all students treated for emergencies could achieve a high rate of compliance, it is also possible that doing so without an amnesty provision might contribute to fewer students calling for medical assistance"* (Lewis & Marchell, 2006, p. 336). Consistent with this response, the **SMB** predicts that intervention will be far more likely when the costs to intervene are minimized.

Unfortunately, when students do decide to help a fellow student exhibiting signs of alcohol poisoning, they typically do not seek outside help, and when they do obtain outside help, they usually ask for help from a trusted friend or parent (Oster-Aaland et al., 2009). Because failure to seek medical assistance

Photo 4.1 © iStock/AndreyPopov.

in cases of alcohol poisoning can lead to fatal outcomes, bystander intervention programs should focus on the need to act quickly and call emergency responders. One proposed solution is to assign a "designated interventionist" (similar to a "designated driver" popularized in the 1980s) who is trained to act mindfully and take appropriate action during alcohol-related situations such as vomiting or passing out (Megehee, Strick, & Woodside, 2012).

Applying TPB

Let's look at how the **TPB** can be used to increase bystander intentions to help when encountering a drug (alcohol)-related emergency. According

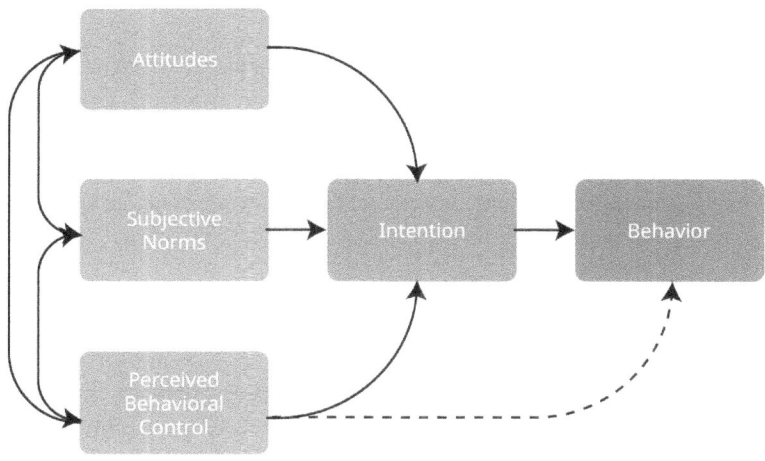

Figure 4.1 Theory of Planned Behaviour

the TPB, intentions to help are a product of three components: personal attitudes, subjective norms, and perceived behavioral control. For example, let's look at prescription drug abuse. Abuse of prediction stimulants such as Ritalin/Adderall remains a major problem on American college campuses, with approximately 15 percent of students admitting using prescription drugs for recreational purposes (Hall, Irwin, Bowman, et al., 2005).

Applying **TPB** to bystander intervention, researchers from an American university found that as student's personal attitudes *("It is my responsibility to intervene on behalf of a friend")* and perceptions of subjective norms *("My friends would also intervene")* toward helping became more positive, and perceived behavioral control *("I have confidence in my ability to conduct an intervention")* their intention to intervene on behalf of a friend engaging in excessive nonmedical use of prescription stimulants increased (LaBelle, 2018).

Strengthen Bystanders' Attitudes

Applying the **TPB** framework to bystander alcohol-related intervention, researchers from an American university looked at college students' willingness to intervene when a female friend is about to engage in an ambiguous drunken hookup. Compared to male participants, female participants indicated more favorable personal attitudes, stronger subjective norms toward intervening, and also reported higher perceived behavioral control (Savage, Menegatos, & Roberto, 2017).

Attitudes are generated by beliefs about behavioral outcomes and the valences of those outcomes. To strengthen attitudes about helping, especially for males, programs must increase men's sense of responsibility, their perceptions that an intervention would be helpful (i.e., emphasize positive outcomes), and that helping is appropriate and expected of them (Savage et al., 2017).

Emphasize Correct Subjective Norms

As we saw earlier in this chapter, students tend to overestimate their peers' acceptance of drunken behavior, so they may be more reluctant to intervene in a risky drinking situation because they presume, incorrectly, that most of their peers would not be phased by it. Social norm interventions, however, can reduce risky drinking behavior by showing people that the majority of their peers do see this behavior as potentially dangerous (i.e., undermine pluralistic ignorance). In particular, one longitudinal designed to correct misperceived binge-drinking norms by distributing posters emphasizing actual (more reality-based) norms was able to change perceived **descriptive norms** (what most others do) of alcohol intoxication from a highly inflated (70 percent) to a more realistic (30 percent) (Haines & Spear, 1996).

Correcting misconceptions about the dangers of alcohol abuse via posters is a good start toward increasing intentions, but ideally, these norms need to be acknowledged at the sociocultural level. An effective way to promote bystander intervention is to discuss social norms in a group setting where students can see first hand what their peers would do under similar circumstances. In one study, researchers examined what factors students at an American university consider when deciding whether to remove a female friend from an alcohol-fueled, high-risk sexual situation. After reading a scenario about watching their highly intoxicated friend "Jane" being coaxed to go to the bedroom of a male acquaintance, groups of students discussed with a trained facilitator what action, if any, they would take. For many students, relational concerns such as how well they knew Jane, how well they knew the guy in the scenario, and how close Jane was to the guy took precedence over potential health concerns such as an unwanted sexual encounter, unwanted pregnancy, and sexually transmitted diseases. In general, if they felt Jane was a close friend and she did not really know the guy, then most agreed that help was warranted; however, if they assumed the couple knew each other, then the willingness to help was much less likely. As the researchers conclude, *"Providing students with the opportunity to reflect on, discuss, and interpret their own and their peers' behaviors in situations involving both alcohol and sex, offers insights for both the participants and researchers about the social and/or relational norms that are part of the culture of college drinking"* (Menegatos, Lederman, & Hess, 2010, p. 385). Together these findings show the need to make **descriptive** ("actual") helping norms salient in binge-drinking situations and **injunctive** ("ought") helping norms more salient, especially in situations involving acquaintances and couples who know each other.

Increase Perceived Behavioral Control

Bystander intervention often requires some degree of communication with the impaired "victim," so it is important for bystanders to practice using direct communication strategies when encountering a high-risk drinking situation. In one study, students from an American university were presented with a common drinking scenario: an obviously intoxicated student feeling pressured by his peers to continue a drinking game. The most effective intervention strategies were to warn the group *("Dude, this guy doesn't seem okay. Let's let him sit out for a bit")* or to stop the guy from drinking by finding a substitute to take his place *("Why don't one of you guys take over")* (White & Hingson, 2014). Likewise, in a second study by the same research team, college students were presented with another drinking scenario: an obviously intoxicated female student is at risk for an unwanted sexual encounter with a male student. In this case, the most effective intervention strategies were to check in with the female *("Are you sure you want to do this?")*, warn the guy *("Yo dude, relax, she's obviously out of it")*, prevent them from being alone by walking between them *("Hey guys. Why don't you hang with us")* or disengage the guy by taking him aside *("Hey man, I haven't seen you in a long time. What's goin' on?").* Critically, these relatively simple communication strategies were deemed more effective than simply going in with the abstract (default) goal of *"make sure everyone is safe"* (White & Hingson, 2014). Thus, to increase students' degrees of self-efficacy, training programs should provide students with more practical and direct advice (e.g., stop the intoxicated victim from drinking more by removing him from the situation) rather than providing more abstract advice (e.g., try to keep him safe).

Together, these studies show that when designing programs to increase bystander intervention in response to alcohol-related emergencies, public health educators must boost attitudes (especially men's), subjective norms, and perceived behavioral control (and subsequent intentions) toward intervening. This would entail designing campaigns that appeal to men's sense of ethical responsibility toward their friends, emphasizing the actual norms regarding alcohol intoxication, and practicing direct communication strategies addressed above.

> ## "What Can Bystanders Do?"
>
> Based on research incorporating the **SMB** and **TPB**, there are several practical strategies you can do to transform yourself into an active responder if you are faced with an alcohol-related emergency including:
>
> - recognizing some of the lesser-known red flags such as passing out, confusion, and slow breathing
> - consulting with a sober person (if you happen to be intoxicated yourself) who may be better able to "read" the situation
> - undermining pluralistic ignorance by reminding yourself that your peers' "nonchalant demeanor" does not necessarily mean there is not a serious problem
> - avoiding diffusion of responsibility by reminding yourself to take action, especially when others are present
> - surrounding yourself with friends who believe it is important to intervene
> - practicing speaking up for the intoxicated person being pressured to drink more *("Hey, this guy doesn't seem okay. Let's let him sit out for a bit")*

"What Can Public Health Educators Do?"

Based on research incorporating the **SMB** and **TPB**, there are several additional practical strategies (beyond those listed above) that health practitioners can do when designing programs to get bystanders to confront alcohol-related emergencies including:

- identifying unique barriers such as bystanders' tendency to underestimate risks of excessive drinking and overestimate perceived social costs of getting the victim in trouble
- addressing alcohol use within the bystanders themselves (alcohol myopia)
- researching individual state Good Samaritan laws
- downplaying often ineffective zero-tolerance policies
- de-emphasizing the descriptive norm that "Many students BINGE-DRINK"
- undermining pluralistic ignorance by reminding people that binge drinking is not the norm
- providing young people with the opportunity to reflect on, discuss, and interpret their own and their peers' behaviors in a group setting
- designing programs with more practical/direct advice such as *"stop the intoxicated victim from drinking more by removing him from the situation"* rather than more vague/abstract advice such as *"try to keep the person safe"*

Problems When Encountering Health-Related Emergencies

You've heard the saying, "Fast friends.'"[close, devoted friends] *If you are having a stroke, that's exactly who you need nearby. Two out of three times, it's a bystander making the decision to call 911 or seek treatment on behalf of someone suffering a stroke.* (see *"Editorial: Needed: 'Stroke heroes'"*)

Defining the Problem

According to the American Heart Association, more than 350,000 out-of-hospital cardiac arrests in the United States happen each year and survival rates are generally less than 10 percent (Benjamin, Virani, Callaway, et al., 2018).

As the quote above suggests, bystanders are often the first line of defense before Emergency Medical Service (EMS) personnel arrive, however, in the vast majority of cardiac arrests, bystander CPR rates have remained relatively low, rarely exceeding 20 percent (Vaillancourt, Stiell, & Wells, 2008). This is unfortunate as bystander CPR and early defibrillation can drastically increase survival rates (Malta Hansen, Zinckernagel, Ersbøll, et al., 2017). According to recent stroke statistics, every forty seconds, someone in the United States has a stroke, and every 3.5 minutes, someone dies of stroke. Stroke is fatal in about ten to 20 percent of cases, and because the brain can only go a short time without oxygen, acting quickly is essential (Tsao, Aday, Almarzooq, et al., 2022). Although many people do call 9-1-1 when someone is suffering stroke emergencies, Emergency Medical Services (EMS) are only alerted in about half of acute stroke cases because many people are not aware of the symptoms of stroke or that treatment for stroke even exists (Corches, McBride, Robles, et al., 2020). According to the CDC (https://www.cdc.gov/epilepsy/index.html), about one out of ten people can expect to have a seizure during their lifetime. This means seizures are quite common, and chances are one day someone you know might experience a seizure.

Traditional Strategies

Traditional strategies to combat health-related emergencies typically involve encouraging people to get basic first aid skills or CPR-certified. The problem is that most adults do not get any training due in part that current methods for public CPR training and certification are burdensome (require 3 to 4 hours of training), expensive, and ineffective (Brown & Halperin, 2018). A potential, yet controversial method to increase CPR self-efficacy is to require mandatory CPR training. Even though most US states are required to offer training in CPR to HS students (Rapaport, 2017), to be effective CPR training must occur not at one point time, but across the lifespan. Currently, in the United States, there is no independent accrediting body to either enforce a mandate or assess CPR training courses to the public at large (Brown & Halperin, 2018).

By comparison, other countries outside the United States have introduced several national initiatives to strengthen bystander resuscitation attempts including: mandatory CPR training for staff in elementary schools or when acquiring a driver's license and wide-scale distribution of free CPR self-instruction training kits to the public. A nationwide Danish study designed to examine the impact of these policies over a ten-year period found that rates of bystander CPR more than doubled (from 20 percent to 45 percent), while both survival rates at thirty days (from 3.5 percent to 11 percent) and one-year survival rates more than tripled (from 3 percent to 10 percent) (Wissenberg, Lippert, Folke, et al., 2013). Although this strategy shows promise, mandatory programs may be seen by some as excessive and extremely costly to implement on a large-scale basis (see *CPR—should training become mandatory in the workplace?*). Nonetheless, while the idea of mandatory CPR training may sound particularly excessive, there is mounting evidence that it increases bystander CPR rates and could help victims from vulnerable populations (e.g., the elderly) who need it most.

Unique Barriers

Unlike alcohol poisoning which can be hard to recognize or diagnose, a person in cardiac arrest or suffering a seizure is relatively easy to spot. Although most bystanders who witness a health-related emergency are able to get through the initial steps of the SMB, other challenges remain. One common barrier is the expectation that someone with more experience else will act first, leading bystanders to diffuse responsibility to others. Predictably, bystanders in Australia were much less willing to administer CPR when in the presence of others than when alone (Johnston, Clark, Dingle, & FitzGerald, 2003). Another unique barrier is that bystanders fear they harm the victim while trying to help them, thus making matters worse. According to the American Heart Association, *"70% of Americans feel helpless to act in the event of a cardiac emergency because they either do not know how to effectively administer CPR or their training has lapsed"* (https://cprblog.heart.org/cpr-statistics/).

Another unique barrier is that, in many health-related emergencies (e.g., stroke or heart attack), the victims themselves may not know they need help and may be reluctant to ask for help (Teuschl & Brainin, 2010). This is especially true of elderly populations. Remarkably, a study from the UK found that not only are older people less confident in performing CPR, they also show less interest in becoming CPR-certified (Dobbie, Mackintosh, Clegg, et al., 2018). Relatedly, CPR training events targeting young people and family members of patients suffering from heart disease may be ineffective for increasing survival rates of cardiac arrest in part because they target the wrong population. For example, one large-scale Canadian study found that most cardiac arrest victims were in their late sixties, collapsed at home, and were witnessed by a person over the age of fifty-five (Vaillancourt, Kasaboski, Charette, et al., 2013).

While researching this book, the world has been dealing with the **Covid-19 pandemic**—an ongoing global pandemic of coronavirus disease caused by severe acute respiratory syndrome coronavirus 2 (SARS-CoV-2) (https://

en.wikipedia.org/wiki/COVID-19_pandemic). Recent studies using people from one American community show that levels of intervention such as heart attacks and strokes may be negatively impacted by the Covid-19 pandemic (Robles, Corches, Bradford, et al., 2021). Fortunately, as we will soon see, there are several ways bystanders can increase their willingness to intervene in health-related emergencies during the pandemic.

Confronting Health-Related Emergencies

Applying SMB

Many public health intervention programs have begun incorporating models of bystander intervention into their training for helping in health-related situations. In this section, we will look at how these programs can transform unresponsive bystanders to active responders when encountering incidents such as heart attacks, strokes, and seizures into active responders.

Get CPR Certified

Remarkably, one Canadian study found that a victim is nearly *4X* more likely to survive a cardiac arrest event when receiving cardiopulmonary resuscitation (CPR) from a bystander (Stiell, Wells, Field, et al., 2004). Another study estimated that, on average, for every thirty people who receive bystander CPR, one additional life could be saved (Sasson, Rogers, Dahl, & Kellermann, 2010). The fundamental problem is, in the vast majority of cardiac arrests, bystander CPR rates have remained relatively low, rarely exceeding 20 percent (Vaillancourt et al., 2008).

A common barrier to providing CPR is the uncertainty about how to perform CPR. According to the **SMB**, to overcome this barrier, people need to have the competence to perform the appropriate helping behavior. In one study, Scottish participants were given the following hypothetical scenario, *"Imagine that you are walking down the street and you see a person collapse. They are unconscious, not breathing and have no pulse. If you were the only person there, how likely or unlikely is it that you would give this person CPR?"* Predictably, respondents trained in CPR were *4X* more likely than untrained respondents to say they would be comfortable administering CPR (Dobbie et al., 2018).

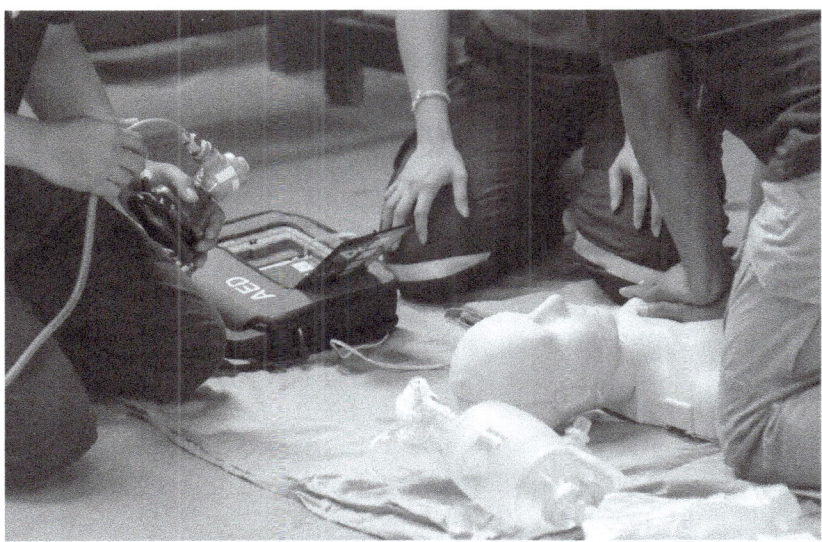

Photo 4.2 © iStock/NeagoneFo.

Fortunately there are some simple steps you can do to dramatically increase the chance of survival of a person experiencing a cardiac arrest by restoring the flow of blood and oxygen. According to the American Red Cross (https://www.redcross.org/take-a-class/cpr/performing-cpr/cpr-steps), first, ask the person *"Are you OK?"* to ensure that the person needs help, then call 911 for assistance. Place the person on their back and tilt their chin to open the airway and then check for breathing *(FYI: occasional gasping sounds do not equate to breathing)*. If there is no breathing begin CPR. Start by placing your hands, one on top of the other, in the middle of the chest. With your shoulders directly over your hands with elbows locked, use your body weight to help you administer compressions that are at least 2 inches deep and delivered at a rate of 120 compressions per minute. Deliver rescue breaths (see *hands-only CPR* alternative for untrained bystanders below) by pinching the person's nose shut and placing your mouth over the person's mouth to make a complete seal. Blow into the person's mouth to make the chest rise. Deliver two rescue breaths, then continue compressions. If the chest does not rise with the initial rescue breath, re-tilt the head before delivering the second breath. If the chest doesn't rise with the second breath, the person may be choking. After each subsequent set of thirty chest compressions, and before attempting additional breaths, look for an object in the mouth and, if seen, remove it. Keep performing cycles of chest compressions and breathing until the person exhibits signs of life, such as breathing, an automated external defibrillator is (AED) becomes available, or EMS or a trained medical responder arrives on scene.

It is also important to remember the caveat *"if you don't use it, you lose it."* That is, if you don't use these CPR skills regularly, you're likely to forget them. So, to maintain a high degree of competence (self-efficacy), you should also take online refresher courses to help you retain the information.

Learn Basic First Aid Training (Medical Crises)

In addition to CPR training, bystanders should also be encouraged to learn basic first aid training. First aid training not only increases frequency of helping, but it also provides a more direct form of helping. For example, in one study, subjects from a large American university overheard a worker they had earlier seen repairing a glass ceiling fixture "fall" off a ladder. If they went to investigate (most did), they saw the "victim" lying on the ground with "blood" spurting from his wound. Compared to an untrained group who tended to use indirect and less effective types of helping (e.g., calling out for help), those who had recently completed a course on first aid were far more likely to give correct and direct intervention (in this case, applying direct pressure to the wound and then soliciting outside help). Remarkably, the researchers estimate that *"In the untrained group, only 4 of 83 victims had a reasonable chance of survival. In the trained group, 32 of 80 victims had that chance. Thus, the effect of [first aid] training had a net value of saving as many as 28 lives."* (Shotland & Heinold, 1985, p. 354).

Direct intervention strategies can also be quite useful for people suffering a stroke. Strokes occur when there is poor blood flow to the brain. Time is essential in order to reduce the amount of cell death in the brain. To increase recognition of a stroke, bystanders must learn to recognize the major symptoms which include sudden weakness in the face (typically on one side), arm weakness (also typically on one side), trouble speaking or understanding speech, trouble seeing, and loss of balance (Wall, Beagan, O'Neill, et al., 2008). To help bystanders quickly identify the symptoms of a stroke, the **FAST** acronym (Face, Arm, Speech, Time) has been recommended. The acronym stands for **F**acial drooping, **A**rm weakness, **S**peech difficulties and **T**ime to call emergency services.[1] Specifically, to check for symptoms of a stroke, you should ask the potential victim: *"Can you smile?" "Can you raise*

---

1 A community-based health promotion program geared toward one African American community has incorporated the FAST acronym into a catchy, gospel-based song to encourage members to do something if they see someone having signs of a stroke (https://www.strokeready.com/).

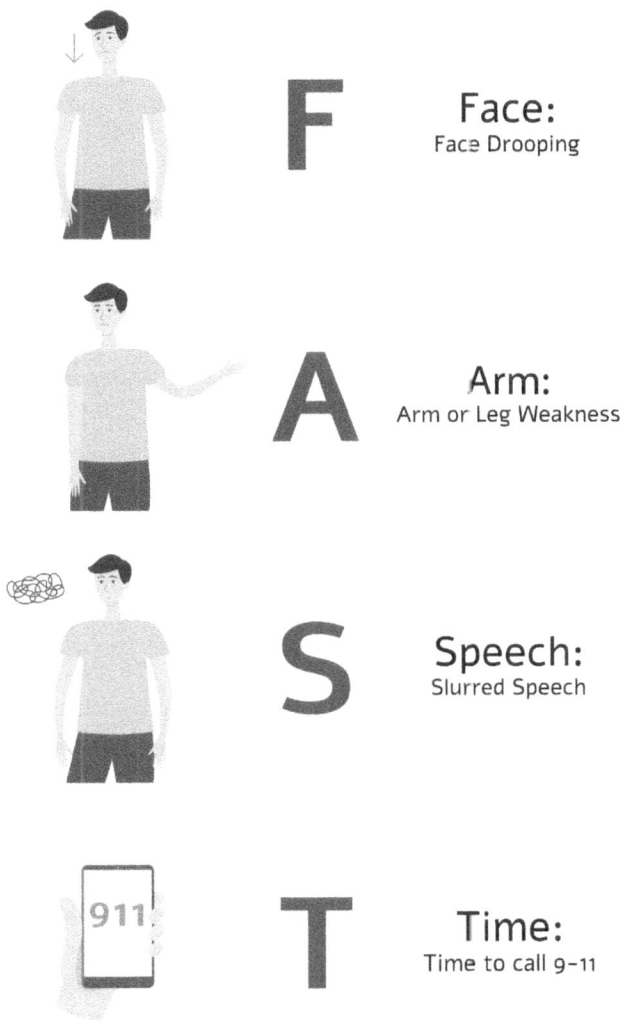

Warning signs of STROKE

Photo 4.3 © iStock/sabelskaya.

both arms?" and "Can you repeat a short sentence" such as "The sky is very blue today"). If the person has trouble following any of these behaviors, you should immediately call 911 as time is of the essence (every minute blood flow is interrupted can cause irreversible damage to brain cells).

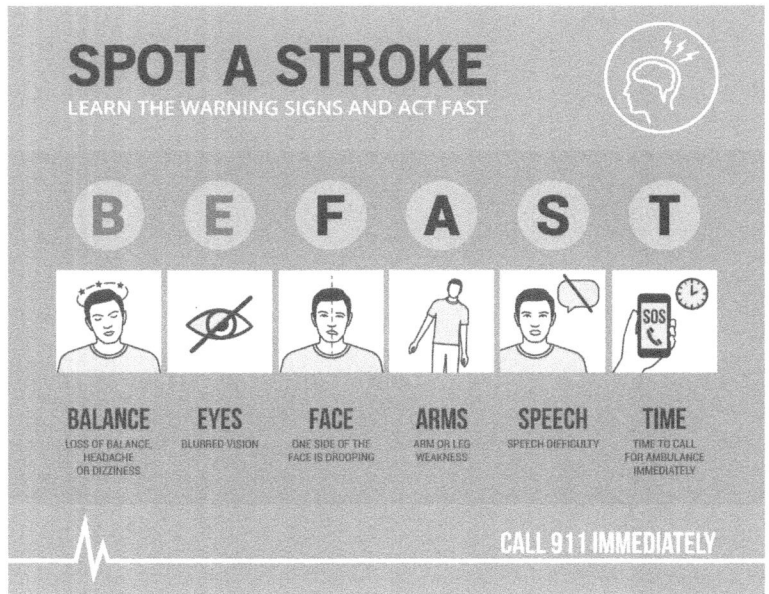

Photo 4.4 © iStock/elenabs.

The FAST campaign has successfully helped bystanders to identify a person having an acute stroke and, by definition (the T in FAST), quickly take direct action. One study based on 3,500 American stroke patients found the FAST message correctly identified almost 90 percent of the patients (Kleindorfer, Miller, Moomaw, et al., 2007). Although effective, some researchers suggest that FAST might not capture all the symptoms of a stroke. In one recent study using data from a stroke center in the United States, researchers found that a slight modification of the FAST acronym (**BE-FAST**), which includes the symptoms of **B**alance (gait/leg imbalances) and **E**yes (visual impairment) increased accuracy even more, to over 95 percent (Aroor, Singh, & Goldstein, 2017).

Direct forms of helping can also be effective for people suffering seizures. A seizure is a sudden, uncontrolled electrical disturbance in the brain often accompanied by uncontrollable shaking. According to the Centers for Disease Control and Prevention (https://www.cdc.gov/epilepsy/about/first-aid.htm), there are several do's and don'ts when dealing with a person having a seizure. The do's include easing the person to the floor, clearing the area around the person of anything hard or sharp, protecting their head, letting them shake, and then after the seizure stops, placing them on their sides to prevent them from choking. The don'ts include holding the person down to

EPILEPSY First Aid

Stay Safe Side

Do

1. Remain calm

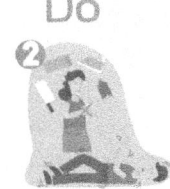
2. Keep the person safe from harmful objects

3. Look at a watch and time the seizure

4. Make the person as comfortable as possible

5. When seizure end Turn the person onto their side

6. If seizure more than 5 minutes call 911

7. Stay with them until they awake

Do Not

1. Do not panic

2. Do not restrain

3. Do not put anything in their mouth

Photo 4.5 © iStock/Start.

stop their movements, putting something in their mouth (*FYI: it's a myth that they might swallow their tongue*), and giving mouth-to-mouth breaths. According to the **Epilepsy Foundation** (epilepsy.com/firstaid), the acronym to help someone having a seizure is simple: **Stay. Safe. Side.** While attending to the seizure: **Stay** with the person until they are awake and alert; Keep the person **Safe** by putting something soft under their head (like a folded jacket); and turn the person onto their **Side** to make breathing easier. Call 911 if the seizure lasts longer than five minutes.

Acronyms are a great memory device.[2] With practice, learning these simple acronyms can greatly increase a bystander's sense of self-efficacy, and motivation to help. Public education campaigns could also market these simple strategies using PSAs to increase direct intervention when a person may be suffering from a stroke or seizure (Pepe, Zachariah, Sayre, & Floccare, 1998).

Reduce the Costs of Performing CPR

Willingness to perform CPR is often influenced by potential costs including the fear of making a mistake or dealing with unpleasant victim characteristics such as vomit, blood, saliva or disease (McCormack, Damon, & Eisenberg, 1989). Surprisingly, even physicians report being reluctant to perform mouth-to-mouth resuscitation on cardiac arrest victims in their community (Brenner, Van, & Cheng, 1997). Fortunately, the American Heart Association has come up with a practical solution to deal with these commonly cited costs/barriers: "hands-only CPR" that involves only chest compressions (thus, giving mouth-to-mouth resuscitation is no longer required)[3] (Bradley & Rea, 2011). To perform hands-only CPR, the responder simply pushes hard and fast in the center of the victim's chest at 120 bpm (recommended, somewhat ironically, to the beat of "Stayin Alive" by the Bee Gees) (see Heart.org/HandsOnly CPR). Ideally, this simplified method of CPR should increase bystander self-efficacy and reduce the perceived costs, thus increasing rate of responding.

Nonetheless, despite this simplified version of CPR, one potential setback to the hands-only (chest-compression) method may still exist. Researchers

---

2 For witnesses of drug overdoses, the somewhat lengthy, yet fitting acronym **SCARE ME** (Stimulate the victim; Call 911, Airway; Rescue breathing, Evaluate, Muscular injection of Naloxone; and Evaluate has been suggested as a potential life-saving strategy [Lankenau, 2013]).

3 In 2010, the CPR guidelines were updated with the concept of compression-only CPR as a simpler (and hygienic) option for *untrained bystanders*; rescue breadths are still part of CPR trained professionals (https://emergencycare.hsi.com/blog/rescue-breaths-are-they-gone-or-not).

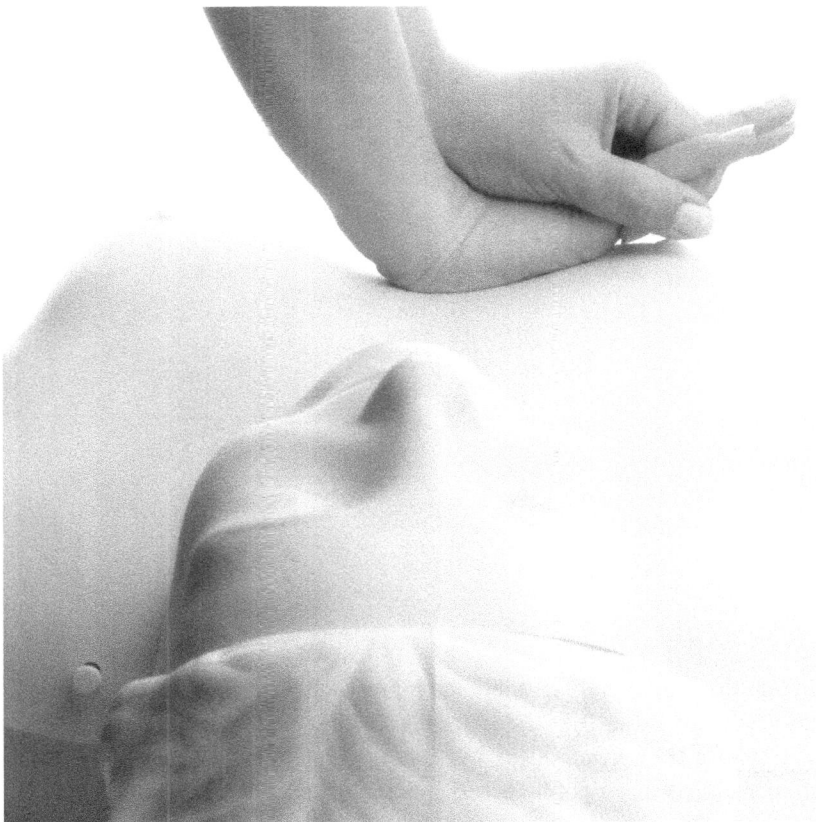

Photo 4.6 © iStock/fmajor.

using data from across the United States have found that when cardiac arrest occurs outside the home, women are *less* likely than men to receive CPR from a bystander; however, no gender differences were found for in-home CPR rates (Blewer, McGovern, Schmicker, et al., 2018). What might explain this peculiar finding? Apparently some bystanders, especially men, may be reluctant to touch the chest of a female stranger. Perhaps, they may feel uncomfortable or fear they could be accused of sexual harassment. In an attempt to overcome this obstacle, a breast attachment for the standard flat-chested CPR mannequin is now available. The hope is this new "womannequin," will reduce men's reluctance to touch the chest of a woman CPR victim, thus increasing her chance of survival (see *Women are less likely . . .*).

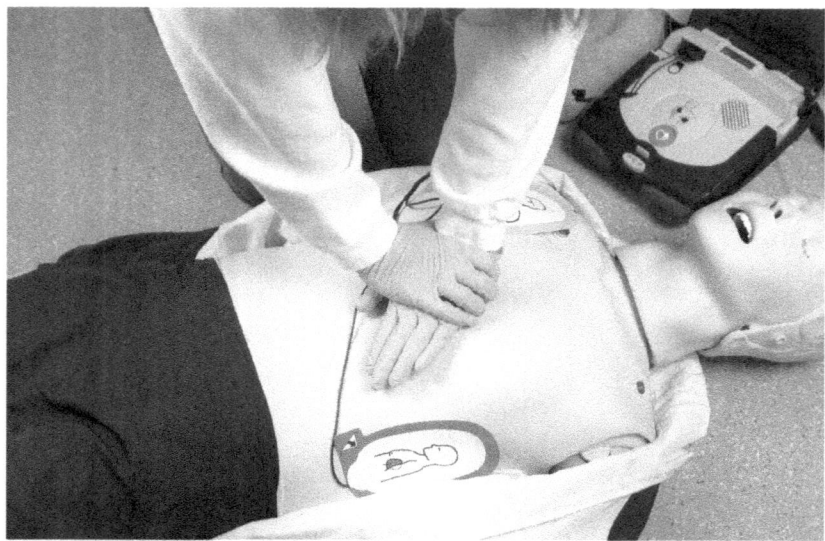

Photo 4.7 © iStock/ollo.

Utilize Mobile-Based Intervention Apps

In addition to calling 911, there are a growing number of smartphone apps that bystanders can use when faced with a medical health emergency. For example, *AED Locator* helps bystanders witnessing sudden cardiac arrest to locate the nearest public access automated extended defibrillator (AED). *BlueStar Savior* receives emergency requests in sudden cardiac arrest incidents and alerts the nearest trained volunteers so they can give CPR in the quickest possible time. *Stroke Detector* senses signs of stroke through a quick series of questions so the user can alert caregivers or EMS about the event and location (Gaziel-Yablowitz & Schwartz, 2018). Although these apps are not well known, with a little promotion they could provide a relatively, low-risk option for bystanders to increase their self-efficacy and provide more direct assistance.

Applying TPB

A recent study on students from an American university found that **TPB** accounted for 50 percent of the variance in intention to perform CPR (Magid, Ranney, & Risica, 2021). In lay terms, this means that certain components of the model were strong predictors of whether a bystander will administer

Photo 4.8 © iStock/almagami.

CPR. In this case, personal attitudes and subjective norms toward performing CPR were the strongest predictors of intention to perform CPR. These findings suggest that bystander CPR trainings should emphasize the positive outcomes (by strengthening personal attitudes) and social norms (by aligning subjective norms with positive attitudes) associated with performing CPR in a health-related emergency.

Strengthen Attitudes by Building Sympathetic Empathy and Moral Agency

To become more active responders when encountering health-related emergencies, bystanders must develop strong positive attitudes toward helping others, especially strangers. One way to strengthen attitudes is to develop **sympathetic empathy**—caring about another person's distress and wanting to help them in some way (Brazil, Volk, & Dane, 2022). Likewise, bystanders must also develop strong attitudes about moral responsibility and **moral agency**—belief in one's capacity to act in accordance with moral standards (Thornberg, Daremark, Gottfridsson, & Gini, 2020). To strengthen sympathetic empathy and moral agency, public health interventions can target attitudinal beliefs by reminding people, especially those who spend time with the elderly, that basic CPR training could save someone's life and significantly increase the likelihood of surviving a cardiac arrest (Magid et al., 2021). In one large-scale national survey done in Canada, respondents with positive beliefs about CPR training including: CPR has been made much simpler, CPR is highly effective and could save a life before EMS arrives, and CPR should be administered even after calling 9-1-1 showed an increased willingness to help those suffering from cardiac arrest (Vaillancourt et al., 2013). These strategies should also be targeted toward older populations who are often reluctant to complete CPR training.

Emphasize Trending Minority Norms

As a rule of thumb, if most people are doing the correct behavior (in this case helping), **descriptive** norms ("most people would help") should be emphasized. As we saw previously, if students are reminded that, contrary to their beliefs, most of their peers would intervene in an alcohol-related emergency, then they should be more likely to follow the group norm. *But what do we do if most people are not currently doing the correct behavior?* In terms of CPR, communicating the descriptive norms *("Did you know most people would not perform CPR in a health-related emergency")* may backfire by establishing a non-helping norm (Cialdini, Demaine, Sagarin, et al., 2006). Because bystander CPR rates have remained relatively low (Vaillancourt et al., 2008), especially in elderly populations who are more likely to need to use CPR, there needs to be a better strategy to target this population.

Fortunately, the answer may lie in emphasizing a different set of social norms. In contrast to descriptive norms which focus on how people currently behave, **trending minority norms** emphasize that a minority norm is increasing in popularity (i.e., on the rise). For example, students from an American university told that the percentage of students conserving water while brushing their teeth is trending upward *("Did you know: 48% of students now conserve water when brushing teeth, which is up from 37% from last year")* were more likely to conserve water compared to students given a static norm *("Did you know: 48% of students conserve water when brushing teeth")* (Mortensen, Neel, Cialdini, et al., 2019). This research implies that portraying a behavior as increasing in popularity can increase compliance, even to norms held by a minority. Social norm interventions could adapt this strategy by showing that the percentage of elderly people learning CPR is on the rise. This could potentially help to increase CPR rates in this vulnerable population.

Increase Bystanders' Perceived Behavioral Control

Earlier in this section, we discussed how to increase self-efficacy by learning basic first training in medical crises. In this section, we will show how to increase perceived behavioral control by learning basic first aid training for those suffering from acute mental health crises. Mental health first aid training teaches bystanders how to provide help to a person in a mental health crisis (e.g., suicidal, psychotic episode) until appropriate professional help arrives (similar to giving CPR until the medics get there) (Kitchener & Jorm, 2002; Morgan, Ross, & Reavley, 2018). According to **National Alliance of Mental Illness** (U.S.: https://www.nami.org/Blogs/NAMI-Blog/December-2018/Please-Don-t-React-Respond) and the **Mental Health Foundation** (UK: https://www.mentalhealth.org.uk/explore-mental-health/articles/how-support-someone-mental-health-problem), there are many online resources a person can use to increase their competence during a mental health crisis. These include avoiding: minimizing the problem *("it could be worse")*, discrediting the problem *("it's all in your head")* or trying to diagnose the person's problem *("sounds like you have panic disorder")*. Instead, it is better to listen without making judgments, use validating language (e.g., *I'm really sorry you are going through this")* and reframe global, negative statements (e.g., *"I'm a failure")* into something more positive (e.g., *"No, you had a setback. But it's a lesson learned, and now you can try again")*.

Despite these helpful online resources, research shows that the majority of the public (bystanders) have poor mental health literacy and are ill-prepared to handle mental health crises. Indeed, one study found only a small percentage of students from an American university believed they could recognize a friend at suicide risk, and most were not aware of campus mental health support resources (King, Vidourek, & Strader, 2008). Compounding the problem is the finding that most youth and adults who died by suicide communicated warning signs of their intentions to their family and friends, yet the vast majority of these confidants did not alert teachers or emergency personnel (Kalafat, Elias, & Gara, 1993). Relatedly, American adult participants responding to a person in suicidal crisis were significantly less comfortable and less likely to access emergency services in comparison to someone suffering a heart attack (Rudd, Goulding, & Carlisle, 2013).

To help bystanders increase self-efficacy in mental health crises, public health educators have begun developing mental health training programs that incorporate the **SMB and TPB.** One such program is the **ALGEE** Action Plan: Action Plan: **A**ssess for risk; **L**isten and communicate nonjudgmentally;

Give support; Encourage the person to seek professional help; and Encourage self-help (Kitchener & Jorm, 2002).

Several studies also show that suicide prevention training enhance a community's intervention readiness, confidence, and intent to respond to mental health crises. For example, in one study, a mental health course improved Australian adults' ability to recognize mental disorders (such as depression and schizophrenia), helped to change their incorrect beliefs about treatment to be more like those of health professionals,[4] and increased their confidence in providing help to someone with a mental disorder (Kitchener & Jorm, 2002). Likewise, Australian adults taking a training showed higher levels of detecting and responding to suicide risk readiness, confidence, and intent than a control group (Hill, Somerset, Schwarzer, & Chan, 2021). In support of these separate findings, a meta-analysis evaluating mental health first aid training programs showed moderate improvements in mental health first aid knowledge, recognition of mental disorders and beliefs about effective treatments (Morgan et al., 2018).

As noted earlier in this section, levels of intervention for heart attacks and strokes may be negatively impacted by the Covid-19 pandemic. Fortunately, in combining both **TPB** and **SMB**, there are several ways bystanders can increase their willingness to intervene in health-related emergencies during the pandemic. These include: understanding that strokes/heart attacks/self-harm are always considered an emergency (even during a pandemic); fear of exposure to the virus in an ambulance is unwarranted; and the level of hospital care given the patient will not be diminished or superseded by Covid-19 (Robles et al., 2021). Armed with this knowledge, bystanders can feel more motivated to help when faced with time-sensitive medical situations, even during a world-wide pandemic.

> ## "What Can Bystanders Do?"
>
> Based on research incorporating the **SMB** and **TPB**, there are several practical strategies you can do (besides calling 911) to transform yourself into an active responder the next time you are faced with a health-related emergency including:
>
> - getting trained in CPR and basic first aid so you can feel competent providing assistance before medical personnel arrive

---

4 For depression, there is a professional consensus that psychiatrists, clinical psychologists, antidepressants, counseling, and cognitive behavior therapy are helpful, while for schizophrenia there is a professional consensus that psychiatrists, clinical psychologists, antipsychotics and admission to a ward are helpful (Kitchener & Jorm, 2002).

- when performing chest compressions (if untrained) simply push hard and fast in the center of the victim's chest at 120 bpm (to the beat of "Stayin Alive" by the Bee Gees)
- downloading mobile-based intervention apps such as *BlueStar Savior* (cardiac arrest) and *Stroke Detector*
- learning health-related acronyms to help in medical emergencies (FAST/BE-FAST for strokes) and mental health emergencies (ALGEE for suicidal thoughts)
- never losing sight that strokes/cardiac arrest/suicidal thoughts are still a crisis in need of immediate attention, despite occurring during a world-wide pandemic (Covid-19)

"What Can Public Health Educators Do?"

Based on research incorporating the **SMB** and **TPB**, there are several additional practical strategies (beyond those above) that health practitioners can do when designing programs to get bystanders to confront health-related emergencies including:

- explaining how most state Good Samaritan laws protect bystanders acting in good faith
- utilizing simple tip sheets to help bystanders develop action plans such as FAST for strokes, Stay/Safe/Side for seizures, and ALGEE for mental health crises
- developing short refresher courses with hands-on practice for the lay rescuer
- working with elderly populations to learn basic first aid as many medical emergencies happen inside the home (often with other elderly people present)

Summary

In this chapter, we looked at how passive bystanders can become more active responders when faced with alcohol- and health-related emergencies. For each emergency situation, there is a unique set of barriers preventing bystanders from helping. For bystanders faced with alcohol-related emergencies, we addressed strategies at the situational (**SMB**), cognitive (**TPB**), and legal level (**medical amnesty policies**). For bystanders faced with health-related emergencies such as heart attacks, seizures, and strokes, we looked at relatively simple, yet effective strategies at the situational and cognitive level, and the need to be extra vigilant when dealing with a world-wide (Covid-19) pandemic. In the next chapter, we will examine strategies bystanders can use to counteract the obstacles they face when confronting the challenging social problems of bullying and cyberbullying.

References

Anthenien, A. M., Neighbors, C., & Rosa, J. (2017). Training first-year college students to intervene in alcohol-related emergencies: Addressing bystander beliefs and perceived consequences of intervening. *Journal of Alcohol and Drug Education, 61,* 17–36.

Aroor, S., Singh, R., & Goldstein, L. B. (2017). BE-FAST (Balance, eyes, face, arm, speech, time): Reducing the proportion of strokes missed using the fast mnemonic. *Stroke, 48,* 479–481.

Benjamin, E. J., Virani, S. S., Callaway, C. W., et al. (2018). Heart disease and stroke statistics—2018 update: A report from the American Heart Association. *Circulation, 137,* e67–e492.

Blavos, A. A., Glassman, T., Sheu, J. J., et al. (2014). Using the Health Belief Model to predict bystander behavior among college students. *Journal of Student Affairs Research and Practice, 51,* 420–432.

Blewer, A. L., McGovern, S. K., Schmicker, R. H., et al. (2018). Gender disparities among adult recipients of bystander cardiopulmonary resuscitation in the public. *Circulation: Cardiovascular Quality and Outcomes, 11,* e004710.

Bradley, S. M., & Rea, T. D. (2011). Improving bystander cardiopulmonary resuscitation. *Current Opinion in Critical Care, 17,* 219–224.

Brazil, K. J., Volk, A. A., & Dane, A. V. (2022). Is empathy linked to prosocial and antisocial traits and behavior? It depends on the form of empathy. *Canadian Journal of Behavioral Science, 55,* 75.

Brenner, B. E., Van, D. C., & Cheng, D. (1997). Determinants of reluctance to perform CPR among residents and applicants: The impact of experience on helping behavior. *Resuscitation, 35,* 203–11.

Brown, L. E., & Halperin, H. (2018). CPR training in the United States: The need for a new gold standard (and the gold to create it). *Circulation Research, 123,* 950–952.

Cialdini, R. B. (2003). Crafting normative messages to protect the environment. *Current Directions in Psychological Science, 12,* 105–109.

Cialdini, R. B., Demaine, L. J., Sagarin, et al. (2006). Managing social norms for persuasive impact. *Social Influence, 1,* 3–15.

Corches, C. L., McBride, A. C., Robles, M. C., et al. (2020). Development, adaptation and scale-up of a community-wide, health behavior theory-based stroke preparedness intervention. *American Journal of Health Behavior, 44,* 744–755.

CPR – Should training become mandatory in the workplace? (2018, October 31). Retrieved from https://www.penningtonslaw.com/news-publications/latest-news/2018/cpr-should-training-become-mandatory-in-the-workplace

Dobbie, F., Mackintosh, A. M., Clegg, G., et al. (2018). Attitudes towards bystander cardiopulmonary resuscitation: Results from a cross-sectional general population survey. *PLoS One, 3,* e0193391.

"Editorial: Needed: 'stroke heroes'" (2016, May 11). St. Joseph News-Press (MO).

Gaziel-Yablowitz, M., & Schwartz, D. G. (2018). A review and assessment framework for mobile-based emergency intervention apps. *ACM Computing Surveys, 51,* 1–32.

Haas, A. L., Wickham, R. E., McKenna, K., et al. (2018). Evaluating the effectiveness of a medical amnesty policy change on college students' alcohol consumption, physiological consequences, and helping behaviors. *Journal of Studies on Alcohol and Drugs, 79,* 523–531.

Haines, M. P., & Spear, S. F. (1996). Changing the perception of the norm: A strategy to decrease binge drinking among college students. *Journal of American College Health, 45,* 134–140.

Hall, K. M., Irwin, M. M., Bowman, K. A., et al. (2005). Illicit use of prescribed stimulant medication among college students. *Journal of American College Health, 53,* 167–174.

Hill, K., Somerset, S., Schwarzer, R., & Chan, C. (2021). Promoting the community's ability to detect and respond to suicide risk through an online bystander intervention model-informed tool: A randomized controlled trial. *Crisis: The Journal of Crisis Intervention and Suicide Prevention, 42,* 225–231.

Hingson, R. W. (2010). Magnitude and prevention of college drinking and related problems. *Alcohol Research and Health, 33,* 45–54.

"Investigators announce role of alcohol, parties in McCrae Williams' death." (2017, September 22). Retrieved from https://www.lafayettestudentnews.com/blog/2017/09/22/investigators-announce-role-of-alcohol-parties-in-mccrae-williams-death

Johnston, T. C., Clark, M. J., Dingle, G. A., & FitzGerald, G. (2003). Factors influencing Queenslanders' willingness to perform bystander cardiopulmonary resuscitation. *Resuscitation, 56,* 67–75.

Kalafat, J., Elias, M., & Gara, M. A. (1993). The relationship of bystander intervention variables to adolescents' responses to suicidal peers. *Journal of Primary Prevention, 13,* 231–244.

King, K. A., Vidourek, R. A., & Strader, J. L. (2008). University students' perceived self-efficacy in identifying suicidal warning signs and helping suicidal friends find campus intervention resources. *Suicide and Life-Threatening Behavior, 38,* 608–617.

Kitchener, B. A., & Jorm, A. F. (2002). Mental health first aid training for the public: Evaluation of effects on knowledge, attitudes and helping behavior. *BMC Psychiatry, 2,* 1–6.

Kleindorfer, D. O., Miller, R., Moomaw, C. J., et al. (2007). Designing a message for public education regarding stroke: Does FAST capture enough stroke? *Stroke, 38,* 2864–2868.

LaBelle, S. (2018). College students' intent to intervene when a peer is engaging in nonmedical use of prescription stimulants: An application of the theory of planned behavior. *Substance Use & Misuse, 53,* 1108–1116.

Lankenau, S. E., Wagner, K. D., Silva, K., et al. (2013). Injection drug users trained by overdose prevention programs: Responses to witnessed overdoses. *Journal of Community Health, 38,* 133–141.

Leone, R. M., Haikalis, M., Parrott, D. J., & DiLillo, D. (2018). Bystander intervention to prevent sexual violence: The overlooked role of bystander alcohol intoxication. *Psychological Violence, 8,* 639–647.

Lewis, D. K., & Marchell, T. C. (2006). Safety first: A medical amnesty approach to alcohol poisoning at a U.S. university. *International Journal of Drug Policy, 17,* 329–338.

Magid, K. H., Ranney, M. L., & Risica, P. M. (2021). Using the theory of planned behavior to understand intentions to perform bystander CPR among college students. *Journal of American College Health, 69*(1), 47–52.

Malta Hansen, C., Zinckernagel, L., Ersbøll, A. K., et al. (2017). Cardiopulmonary resuscitation training in schools following 8 years of mandating legislation in Denmark: A nationwide survey. *Journal of the American Heart Association, 6,* e004128.

McCormack, A. P., Damon, S. K., & Eisenberg, M. S. (1989). Disagreeable physical characteristics affecting bystander CPR. *Annals of Emergency Medicine, 18,* 283–285.

Megehee, C. M., Strick, S. K., & Woodside, A. G. (2012). Overcoming bystander apathy and non-intervention in alcohol-poisoning emergency situations: Advancing field testing of training-for-intervention theory via thought experiments. *International Journal of Business and Economics, 11,* 93–103.

Menegatos, L., Lederman, L. C., & Hess, A. (2010). Friends don't let Jane hook up drunk: A qualitative analysis of participation in a simulation of college drinking-related decisions. *Communication Education, 59,* 374–388.

Monto, M. A., Newcomb, M. D., Rabow, J., & Hernandez, A. C. R. (1994). Do friends let friends drive drunk? Decreasing drunk driving through informal peer intervention. In P. J. Venturelli (Ed.), *Drug use in America: Social, cultural and political perspectives* (pp. 183–192). Jones & Bartlett.

Morgan, A. J., Ross, A., & Reavley, N. J. (2018). Systematic review and meta-analysis of Mental Health First Aid training: Effects on knowledge, stigma, and helping behaviour. *PloS One, 13,* e0197102.

Mortensen, C. R., Neel, R., Cialdini, R. B., et al. (2019). Trending norms: A lever for encouraging behaviors performed by the minority. *Social Psychological and Personality Science, 10,* 201–210.

Myers, D. G., & Twenge, J. M. (2019). *Social psychology* (13th ed.). McGraw Hill.

Oster-Aaland, L., Lewis, M. A., Neighbors, C., et al. (2009). Alcohol poisoning among college students turning 21: Do they recognize the symptoms and how do they help? *Journal of Studies on Drugs and Alcohol, 16,* 122–130.

Parks, G. S. (2021). The failure of zero-tolerance policies in addressing hazing. *Penn State Law Review, 126,* 1.

Pepe, P. E., Zachariah, B. S., Sayre, M. R., & Floccare, D. (1998). Ensuring the chain of recovery for stroke in your community. *Academic Emergency Medicine, 5,* 352–358.

Perkins, H. W., Haines, M. P., & Rice, R. (2005). Misperceiving the college drinking norm and related problems: A nationwide study of exposure to prevention information, perceived norms and student alcohol misuse. *Journal of Studies on Alcohol, 66*, 470–478.

Prentice, D. A., & Miller, D. T. (1993). Pluralistic ignorance and alcohol use on campus: Some consequences of misperceiving the social norm. *Journal of Personality and Social Psychology, 64*, 243–256.

Rapaport, L. (2017, November, 20). *"Many U.S. schools don't teach CPR even when states require it."* Reuters News.

Robles, M. C., Corches, C. L., Bradford, M., et al. (2021). Understanding and informing community emergency cardiovascular disease preparedness during the COVID-19 pandemic: Stroke ready. *Journal of Stroke and Cerebrovascular Diseases, 30*, 105479.

Rowe, M., Wilcox, L., & Gadlin, H. (2009). Dealing with—or reporting—"unacceptable" behavior. *Journal of the International Ombudsman Association, 2*, 52–64.

Rudd, M. D., Goulding, J. M., & Carlisle, C. J. (2013). Stigma and suicide warning signs. *Archives of Suicide Research, 17*, 313–318.

Sasson, C., Rogers, M. A., Dahl, J., & Kellermann, A. L. (2010). Predictors of survival from out-of-hospital cardiac arrest: A systematic review and meta-analysis. *Circulation: Cardiovascular Quality and Outcomes, 3*, 63–81.

Savage, M. W., Menegatos, L., & Roberto, A. J. (2017). When do friends prevent friends from hooking up intoxicated? An examination of sex differences and hypothetical intoxication in peer interventions. *Archives of Sexual Behavior, 46*, 1819–1829.

Schackner, B. (2020, January 12). *"'Breathe, Nolan, Breathe': To save a life, WVU asks 'Would you?'"* Pittsburgh Post-Gazette (PA).

Schipani-McLaughlin, A., Salazar, L. F., & Vivolo-Kantor, A. M. (2019). The relationship between binge drinking and prosocial bystander behavior among college men. *Journal of American College Health, 67*, 570–574.

Shotland, R. L., & Heinold, W. D. (1985). Bystander response to arterial bleeding: Helping skills, the decision-making process, and differentiating the helping response. *Journal of Personality and Social Psychology, 49*, 347–356.

Slutske, W. S. (2005). Alcohol use disorders among us college students and their non-college-attending peers. *Archives of General Psychiatry, 62*, 321–327.

Stiell, I. G., Wells, G. A., Field, B., et al. (2004). Advanced cardiac life support in out-of-hospital cardiac arrest. *New England Journal of Medicine, 351*, 647–656.

Teuschl, Y., & Brainin, M. (2010). Stroke education: Discrepancies among factors influencing prehospital delay and stroke knowledge. *International Journal of Stroke, 5*, 187–208.

Thornberg, R., Daremark, E., Gottfridsson, J., & Gini, G. (2020). Situationally selective activation of moral disengagement mechanisms in school bullying: A repeated within subjects experimental study. *Frontiers in Psychology, 11*, 1101–1113.

Tsao, C. W., Aday, A. W., Almarzooq, Z. I., et al. (2022). Heart disease and stroke statistics—2022 update: A report from the American Heart Association. *Circulation, 145*, e153–e639.

Vaillancourt, C., Kasaboski, A., Charette, M., et al. (2013). Barriers and facilitators to CPR training and performing CPR in an older population most likely to witness cardiac arrest: A national survey. *Resuscitation, 84*, 1747–1752.

Vaillancourt, C., Stiell, I. G., & Wells, G. A. (2008). Understanding and improving low bystander CPR rates: A systematic review of the literature. *Canadian Journal of Emergency Medicine, 10*, 51–65.

Wall, H. K., Beagan, B. M., O'Neill, J., et al. (2008). Addressing stroke signs and symptoms through public education: The Stroke Heroes Act FAST campaign. *Preventing Chronic Disease, 5*, A49.

White, A. M., Hingson, R. W., Pan, I. J., & Yi, H. Y. (2011). Hospitalizations for alcohol and drug overdoses in young adults ages 18–24 in the United States, 1999–2008: Results from the nationwide inpatient sample. *Journal Studies on Alcohol and Drugs, 72*, 774–786.

White, A., & Hingson, R. (2014). The burden of alcohol use: Excessive alcohol consumption and related consequences among college students. *Alcohol Research: Current Reviews, 35*, 201–218.

Wissenberg, M., Lippert, F. K., Folke, F., et al. (2013). Association of national initiatives to improve cardiac arrest management with rates of bystander intervention and patient survival after out-of-hospital cardiac arrest. *Journal of the American Medical Association, 310*, 1377–1384.

Women are less likely than men to receive CPR in public. A new product is designed to change that. (2019, June 5). Retrieved from https://www.cnn.com/2019/06/05/health/female-cpr-dummy-women-cardiac-arrest/index.html

Confronting Bullying and Cyberbullying in Schools

5

Key Terms in This Chapter 98

Problems When Encountering Bullying and Cyberbullying 99

Confronting School Bullying and Cyberbullying 104
Applying SMB 105
Applying TPB 108

Evidence-Based Anti-Bullying Bystander Intervention Programs 115
Steps to Respect ® 115
Second Step ® 116
Olweus Bullying Prevention Program (OBPP) 116
KiVa 117
"Media Heroes" 117
Friendly ATTAC 118

Summary 119

Key Terms in This Chapter

active listening skills: the skill to respond genuinely to the needs and feelings of those seeking help

affective empathy: an emotional reaction by an observer to the affective state of another

bullying: typically involves repeated acts of physical, verbal, relational, and more recently, online (i.e., "cyberbullying") intimidation intended to cause physical or psychological harm against a less powerful peer

cognitive empathy: ability to understand what a person is thinking without getting involved

critical mass: the critical group size for initiating social change

cyberbullying: repeatedly sending or posting electronic messages or images (e.g., insults, threats, embarrassing photos) intended to harass, humiliate, or inflict harm on another person

descriptive norms: what others *typically* do

injunctive norms: what others *ought* to do

moral agency: belief in one's capacity to act in accordance with moral standards

moral disengagement: allows people to remain passive in helping situations without any feelings of remorse or guilt

moral distress: occurs when people recognize the morally appropriate thing to do, yet fail to intervene because of external constraints such as loyalty to the perpetrator

situational model of bystander intervention (SMB): proposes that bystanders typically go through a series of five decision-making steps before help will be given

theory of planned behavior (TPB): proposes that the intent to do a behavior depends on three antecedent factors: one's *personal attitude* toward the behavior, the perceived *subjective norms* that relevant others hold about the behavior, and the degree of *perceived behavioral control* (i.e., self-efficacy) one has to do the behavior

zero-tolerance policies: severe disciplinary actions in response to specific types of misbehavior, regardless of the context of the improper behavior

Problems When Encountering Bullying and Cyberbullying

It appears that Phoebe's death on Jan. 14 followed a torturous day for her, in which she was subjected to verbal harassment and threatened physical abuse . . . It was common knowledge . . . the actions or inactions of some adults at the school are troublesome.

—Local District Attorney from US city reacting to the suicide of a fifteen-year-old student who was tormented repeatedly by a group of bullies from her school allegedly while the school knew about the abuse (Crimaldi, 2010)

Defining the Problem

Bullying in school settings typically involves repeated acts of physical, verbal, relational, and more recently, online (i.e., "cyberbullying") intimidation intended to cause physical or psychological harm against a less powerful peer. Bullying often takes place in a social (group) context where perpetrators are reinforced for their aggressive behavior from their peers, resulting in increased social status or popularity (Hawkins, Pepler, & Craig, 2001).

Photo 5.1 © iStock/SolStock.

Photo 5.2 © iStock/monkeybusinessimages.

As shown in the quote above, even though many people perceive bullying as a harmless "rite of passage" or a natural part of life that "builds character," the effects of bullying can be devastating. Victims of school bullying often report feeling humiliated, anxious, and develop a strong dislike of school. Youth who are bullied often feel alone and ashamed especially when there are others around who witness the event. Class participation also tends to decline and school avoidance increases among children who are victims of bullying (Frey, Hirschstein, Edstrom, & Snell, 2009).

According to a 2019 survey conducted by the Center for Disease Control and Prevention (CDC), bullying continues to be a significant problem in American high schools, with 20 percent of youth reporting being bullied *in the past year* (see https://www.cdc.gov/healthyyouth/data/yrbs/index.htm). It is also well documented that the prevalence of bullying peaks during early adolescence (particularly in middle school), not coincidentally at the same time that bullying becomes more accepted by peers (Wang, Iannotti, & Nansel, 2009). Indeed, when American students (grades 1–12) were asked to complete the following statement: *"When I see someone being teased or hit, I think _____,"* older students were *five times more* likely than younger students to say "they deserved it" (35 percent vs 7 percent) (Davis & Davis, 2007). These findings imply children often learn to passively accept various forms of bullying.

Photo 5.3 © iStock/Egoitz Bengoetxea Iguaran.

Jumping off the gw bridge sorry

> —Tyler Clementi's last post before committing suicide after finding out his college roommate secretly videotaping and "outing" him for being intimate with another male student (see Hill, 2010)

In one tragic case of cyberbullying, a student attending an American college deceitfully used a webcam to spy on his male roommate while engaging in intimacy with another male student. Despite the fact that many students watched the illicit live video feed, nobody intervened on behalf of the violated student (Byers, 2013). Tragically, as the harrowing quote from Tyler Clementi above shows, once he learned that his roommate planned to use the webcam footage for others "entertainment," he posted on Facebook that he was going to jump off the George Washington Bridge shortly before he committed suicide.

Cyberbullying is commonly defined as repeatedly sending or posting electronic messages or images (e.g., insults, threats, false rumors, embarrassing photos) intended to harass, humiliate, or inflict harm on another person (Tokunaga, 2010). As in traditional bullying, cyberbullying takes place in a social (group) context where perpetrators expect rewards for their cyberbullying acts from their peers, such as increased social status or popularity (DeSmet, Bastiaensens, Cleemput, et al., 2018). Unlike traditional bullying, however, cyberbullies can remain anonymous, cyberbullying is often harder for authorities (parents, teachers, police) to detect, and the incidents are typically witnessed by much larger audiences (Allison & Bussey, 2016). Thus, cyberbullying's potential for anonymity, difficulty in detection, and viral reach to people outside the victim's social circle make it suitable for people to use as a tool to harm or intimidate their enemies.

In terms of prevalence, approximately 20–40 percent of all American youths report having experienced cyberbullying at least once in their lives, with a peak occurring among those in the 12–15-year age range (Tokunaga, 2010). Similarly, studies conducted in European countries show that approximately 10 percent of children and adolescents reported that they had been cyberbullied *within the past year* (Bastiaensens, Van Cleemput, Vandebosch, et al., 2019). With the popularity of the internet, cyberbullying also appears on the rise. Indeed, Canadian school-aged children were $2X$ as likely to take part in cyberbullying than schoolyard bullying, presumably because many see it as a "victimless crime" that does not cause any serious harm (Law, Shapka, Hymel, et al., 2012).

Like traditional bullying, cyberbullies are typically motivated to gain dominance within the group. To achieve this goal, cyberbullies are dependent on the members of their peer group (i.e., bystanders) to reinforce their behavior (Salmivalli, Voeten, & Poskiparta, 2011). By taking sides with the bully or by defending the victim, bystanders have the power to either protect or endanger the perpetrator's goal of achieving status and power. Unfortunately, similar to traditional bullying, the vast majority of youth from North American (Allison & Bussey, 2016) and Scandinavian (Bastiaensens et al., 2019) countries who reported witnessing incidents of cyberbullying typically avoid getting involved.

Traditional Strategies

The classic approach—pile kids into an auditorium and lecture them on the dangers of bullying, perhaps including a sad story about its effects along the way—doesn't appear to really work. (Singal, 2016)

For most bystanders faced with school bullying and cyberbullying, their lack of help does not appear to be the result of apathy. In fact, numerous studies show a that a large number of students find bullying and name-calling unpleasant to witness, disapprove of bullying, and express admiration for peers who intervene (Hawkins et al., 2001; Padgett & Notar, 2013). Yet, despite the fact that most adolescents generally sympathize with the victims and disapprove of bullying, the vast majority are reluctant to intervene or to inform adults.

To counteract this problem, schools typically display signs and posters condemning bullying combined with mandatory assemblies addressing the dangers of bullying, but as the quote above implies, even though these actions are well-intentioned, there is little evidence to suggest adopting **zero-tolerance policies** reduce bullying in any measurable way. While it seems intuitive that removing disruptive students from school will make schools safer, an APA task force concluded that zero-tolerance policies have not been shown to improve school climate, and suspension/expulsion have not proven to be an effective means of improving student behavior (and may even run counter to best practices for child development) (see *American Psychological Association Zero Tolerance Task Force, 2008*). Furthermore, a meta-analysis on schools across the United States showed that anti-bullying programs had no benefit in reducing instances of bullying, and instead led to *increases* in covert forms of bullying such as ostracizing, shunning, and intimidating the victim, and even cyberbullying (Borgwald & Theixos, 2013).

Although done with good intentions to protect victims of bullying, these "one-size-fits-all" disciplinary strategies have not fared well. Oversimplified simple messages like *"Bullying will not be tolerated"* or signs at the front of a school reading *"This is a bully-free zone"* are not likely to be effective when bullying often increases social status and respect for the perpetrator. Indeed, Finnish students judged to be the "coolest," were rated by other kids as more likely to *"start fights or push other kids around"* and *"spread nasty rumors about other kids"* (Juvonen, Schacter, Sainio, & Salmivalli, 2016). Notably, this behavior also tends to be bi-directional such that popular kids bully more, and those who bully increase in popularity.

Furthermore, from a bystander's perspective, these policies do not adequately address the barriers inhibiting helping. In addition to not adequately addressing subtle forms of bullying, these policies neither explicitly state what a bystander should do in these social situations nor do they address the perceived costs of intervention such as loss of valued relationships, fear of retaliation, and concern that their fellow students may be suspended or expelled (Borgwald & Theixos, 2013). For anti-bullying programs to work, *"students must develop an awareness of the problem, a willingness to report bullying, and a sense of security in the knowledge that protection and support are available from teachers, administrators, and other peers"* (Craig & Pepler, 1998, p. 57).

Unique Barriers

Beyond the general obstacles that inhibit helping in emergency situations (see Chapter 2), there is a unique set of barriers preventing bystanders from confronting a bullying scenario. These obstacles include: bullying at school typically occurs in unsupervised settings like playgrounds, bathrooms, buses or online where adults are not present; most bullying involves verbal attacks for a relatively short duration, so many bystanders may simply not notice it; bullying involves a vicious cycle in which bystanders may reinforce the bullying behavior; and often the bullies are popular or have high status, so bystanders might be concerned about damaging their own reputation if they intervene (Jenkins, Fredrick, & Nickerson, 2018; Salmivalli et al., 2011).

Beyond these barriers, there are additional barriers a bystander must contend with when encountering a cyberbullying event such as: cyberbullying may not occur in real time (i.e., "live"), so cyber-bystanders may incorrectly assume that the situation has been resolved and their help is no longer needed; helpful cues like facial expression, body language, and tone of voice are missing in online communications, so cyber-bystanders may lack the relevant information to interpret whether the problem warrants intervention; and unlike traditional bullying, cyberbullies can also remain anonymous making direct intervention difficult (Allison & Bussey, 2016).

Confronting School Bullying and Cyberbullying

As with each type of emergency situation covered in this book, the obstacles preventing bystanders from helping in bullying scenarios can be mapped onto the **SMB** (See Figure 1.1). Consistent with the **SMB** theoretical framework, researchers looking at high school bullying at an American school confirmed that the five steps are sequential: noticing the event was related to interpreting the event as an emergency, viewing the event as an emergency was a significant predictor of accepting responsibility for helping, accepting responsibility was subsequently highly predictive of knowing how to help, which in turn had the strongest relationship with taking sufficient action (Nickerson, Aloe, Livingston, & Feeley, 2014). Furthermore, a study using sophisticated analysis (structural equation modeling) on college students from an American university found that the **SMB** accurately predicted bystanders' responses to cyberbullying (Karasavva & Mikami, 2024).

In this chapter, we will look at how bystanders and public health intervention programs can overcome these unique barriers when confronting bullying/cyberbullying by applying both the **SMB** and **TPB** models.

Applying SMB

Recognize Warning Signs of Bullying

Bullying at school typically occurs in unsupervised settings like playgrounds, bathrooms, and buses. In one observational study done on Canadian school playgrounds, more than six episodes of bullying occurred *per hour*. Verbal aggression was observed in half of the observations, while physical or both physical/verbal aggression were observed in the other half. Typically, the bullying was direct (e.g., hitting someone or hurtful name-calling), but in about 25 percent of the cases the bullying was indirect (e.g., saying something mean or spreading a nasty rumor) (Craig & Pepler, 1998).

Because these acts often go unnoticed, observational studies show that teachers and staff often fail to intervene. In fact, given the brevity of these episodes (most last less than twenty seconds) and the high prevalence of verbal attacks (presumably outside of earshot), Canadian researchers estimated that school staff were unaware of bullying in about 80 percent of the incidents! (Charach, Pepler, & Ziegler, 1995). Remarkably, however, most staff when surveyed reported that they consistently intervene in bullying episodes on the playground, while children report (accurately it appears) that adults rarely intervene (Pepler, Craig, Ziegler, & Charach, 1993). Furthermore, when looking at various bullying vignettes, students from a large American university were much less likely to intervene or punish bullies when they displayed relational bullying (e.g., social ostracism/shunning) than physical or verbal forms of bullying (Bauman & Del Rio, 2006).

It's a safe bet that if adults fail to notice the vast majority of the bullying episodes, or worse, fail to intervene, we can assume that many children are doing the same. In support of this assumption, researchers estimate that in 80–90 percent of bullying incidents on school grounds peer bystanders were present, yet they actively intervened under 20 percent of the time (Hawkins et al., 2001; O'Connell, Pepler, & Craig, 1999). In fact, one observational study conducted on a Canadian school playground found that bullies were seldom punished for their aggressive behavior as peers and teachers were observed intervening in only about 10 percent and 4 percent of the episodes, respectively (Craig & Pepler, 1998). Another large-scale study looking at more than fifty videotaped segments of bullying on the playground of Canadian schools found slightly more encouraging results—25 percent of bystanders came to the aid of the victim, however, on the downside, they also found that over half passively watched, and the remaining 20 percent actually supported the bully in some way (O'Connell et al., 1999).

Unless bystanders are taught to recognize some of the subtler signs of bullying, anti-bullying intervention at both the individual and programmatic levels are bound to fail. For change to occur, bystander interventions need to help student/staff/teacher bystanders to recognize the subtler signs of bullying such as social ostracism, intimidation, and spreading nasty rumors. All parties need to be educated about the consequences of spreading rumors and the damage relational bullying creates. They also need to understand that their passivity is often perceived by victims as acting in collusion with bullies, which may inadvertently reinforce the bully by giving the message that bullying is both tolerated and acceptable (Jenkins et al., 2018).

View Bullying as a Social System

To reduce bullying in schools, interventions should view bullying as a social system, rather than a simple interaction between a victim and a tormentor. After all, the typical bullying situation consists of the victim, bully, and multiple bystanders (or potential allies). Peer groups must understand that bystander roles range from active participation to passive neutrality to active defense of students who are victimized (Byers, 2013). Typically the more bystanders present to reinforce the bully, the more frequent bullying occurs, which in turn, reinforces the bullying behavior (Salmivalli et al., 2011). Thus, contrary to public opinion, bullies do not typically have low social status, rather they are perceived as popular by classmates, in part due to their displays of social control and power (Aboud & Joong, 2008). Experts point out the rewards of bullying contribute to the vicious cycle of bullying where the *"bully and the bystanders become a deadly combination committed to denigrating the target further."* (Coloroso, 2011, p. 38).

To help bystanders, programs must show how the group dynamics maintain the status quo for bullying. In one study, Italian researchers found that students made aware that cyberbullying involves group dynamics that typically reinforce rather than punish the bully were more amenable to using strategies that discourage aggressive behaviors online (Guarini, Menin, Menabo, & Brighi, 2019).

Build Supportive Communities (Culture)

To counter bullying, interventions should also focus more holistically on changing the school culture. As an example, children from a large American school system who felt a sense of connection to the school (e.g., *"My teachers care about me"; "I feel like I am a part of this school"*) reported *less* bullying and were more likely to seek help from staff when bullied (Lindstrom Johnson, Waasdorp, Debnam, & Bradshaw, 2013). In the same study, victimized students with positive school environments *("Adults at this school try to stop bullying"; "Students at this school try to stop bullying")* were more likely to seek support from teachers. Based on a National Education Association (NEA) survey, other strategies to change the bullying culture include: urging teachers/staff/students to speak up against bullying, especially in places with a strong code of silence (such as middle school), encouraging teachers and staff to avoid excusing or dismissing the behavior *("I'm sure he didn't mean it"),* infusing anti-bullying messages in the curriculum, encouraging adults and students to become partners in bullying prevention, and posting trained educators in "hot spots" where bullying is most likely to occur (Bradshaw, Waasdorp, O'Brennan, & Gulemetova, 2013, Ttofi & Farrington, 2011).

Encourage Popular Peer-Led Intervention

Another problem with standard anti-bullying programs is that adolescents rarely take their cues for how to behave from authority figures. Peer influence is a much stronger predictor, and if popular peers are doing the bullying (and oftentimes they are), then most students will fail to intervene when they see their high-status peers engaging in this behavior (Juvonen et al., 2016). To counteract this problem, some intervention programs have begun using peer-led intervention strategies. In one large study based on over fifty American schools, popular students (defined as socially well-connected) were used to spread anti-bullying messages by posting hashtag slogans on social network sites and distributing orange wristbands with the intervention logo (a tree) as a reward to students who stood up to inappropriate behavior. By encouraging a small set of students to take a public stance against typical forms of conflict at their school, this intervention reduced overall levels of conflict by an estimated 30 percent (Paluck, Shepherd, & Aronow, 2016). Likewise, Italian researchers found cyberbullying prevention programs utilizing peer-led interventions reduced the amount of cyberbullying. They attributed the success to the fact that *"Peer-led models grow out of the spontaneous willingness of children and adolescents to help one another and create roles and structures where students can be trained and helped to act in a responsible, sensitive, and empathic way towards other pupils"* (Menesini, Nocentini, & Palladino, 2012, p. 315). Many experts also support the idea of mobilizing high-status peers to intervene as it might make it easier for others to also help (Pöyhönen, Juvonen, & Salmivalli, 2010). Training peer mediators should also incorporate **active listening skills**—the skill to respond genuinely to the needs and feelings of those seeking help. Peer mediators will be most effective if they receive proper training in words of support, the tone of their voice, and their confidence that the problem can be resolved (Cowie & Smith, 2012).

Increase Online Accountability and Peer Support

As we have seen in previous chapters, not accepting personal responsibility is a strong predictor of a bystander's willingness to intervene. Diffusion of responsibility is especially common in online interactions like cyberbullying. Indeed, German university students who read about a severe incident of cyberbullying were less likely to help in the presence of a large number of bystanders (Obermaier, Fawzi, & Koch, 2014). Based on these findings, one can predict that willingness to intervene will be moderated by whether or not bystanders are visible to the victim (Brody & Vangelisti, 2016). To test this hypothesis, 400 online American participants were exposed to derogatory comments about another "user" (e.g., *"When will you get it into your head that nobody likes your stupid ass"*). Although most bystanders did not intervene, those who received viewer notifications alerting them that "others can see they read the offensive post" were more likely to indirectly intervene (i.e., flag the user) (DiFranzo, Taylor, Kazerooni, et al., 2018). Thus, making users feel more accountable via public surveillance can increase a sense of personal responsibility, leading to greater likelihood of providing help to a cyberbullying victim. The researchers do point out that making digital behavior more transparent does raise potential ethical concerns regarding privacy and consent to share personal information, however, they also mention that existing social media platforms such as LinkedIn allow paying customers to see who has visited their profile page making it impossible to anonymously "lurk" on a premium user.

With cyberbullying, teachers and parents are deemed less adequate as social support providers by youth because the victims fear that adults will not take their problem seriously, try to help in an inappropriate way (e.g., parents restricting the victim's internet access), or will take actions that can aggravate the problem (e.g., contacting the bully's parents). Online peers, however, can provide victims with simple messages of emotional support *("I feel your pain"; "There are plenty of people who stand by your side")* (Bastiaensens et al., 2019). For many bystanders, however, in-person messages are favored over sending online messages. For example, based on focus groups of Belgian adolescents, bystanders preferred to handle cyberbullying offline and in-person to comfort the victim (DeSmet, Veldeman, Poels, et al., 2014).

Applying TPB

Let's look at how the **TPB** can be used to increase bystander intentions to help when involved in a bullying scenario.

Theory of Planned Behavior

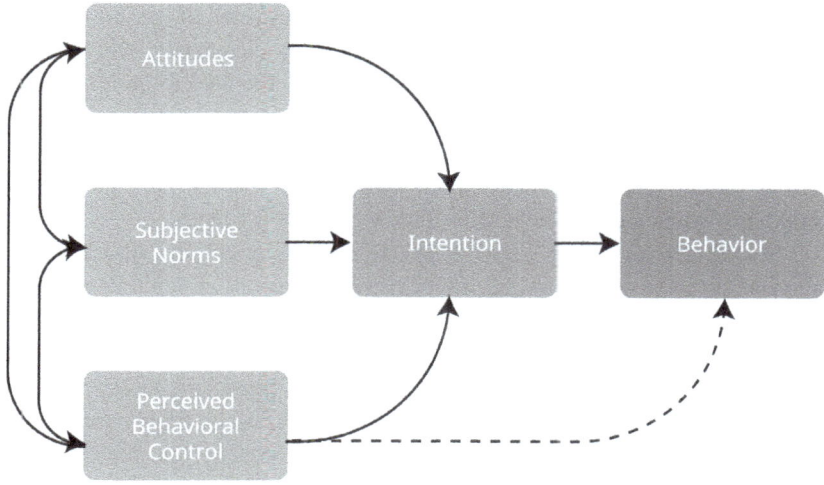

Figure 5.1 Theory of Planned Behavior

Strengthen Attitudes by Building Moral Agency and Empathy

To become active responders, bystanders must have strong attitudes about moral responsibility and believe that all people (even strangers) deserve help during an emergency. This sense of **moral agency**, however, depends on the belief in one's capacity to act in accordance with moral standards (Thornberg, Daremark, Gottfridsson, & Gini, 2020). Unfortunately, when it comes to bullying, researchers often find a disconnect between a bystander's attitudes and their behavior. This gap between internal standards and prosocial behavior can be explained by two complementary processes: moral disengagement and moral distress.

Moral disengagement permits bystanders to remain passive without any feelings of remorse or guilt (e.g., blaming the victim for their mistreatment or distorting the negative impact) (Bandura, 1999). For example, unresponsive Danish adolescents who witnessed peers being bullied showed significantly higher acceptance of moral disengagement than active responders (Obermann, 2011). To counteract the tendency for moral disengagement, anti-bullying educators should develop programs that inhibit moral disengagement and facilitate the development of moral agency (Brüggemann, Forsberg,

Colnerud, et al., 2019). To increase moral agency, teachers should engage students in discussions about moral issues such as what it means to be a caring and responsible person and encourage students to reflect upon and discuss the problems with weak excuses. Moral agency can also be addressed through positive role modeling. For example, American elementary and middle school students who reported that their teachers responded to bullying with strong victim support were less inclined to morally disengage and less likely to bully (Thornberg, Wänström, & Hymel, 2019). Thus, teachers showing strong collective efficacy to stop peer aggression might in turn encourage students to enhance their own self-efficacy and moral agency.

Moral distress may occur when bystanders recognize the morally appropriate thing to do, yet fail to intervene because of external constraints such as loyalty to the bully or lack of self-efficacy (Brüggemann et al., 2019). Often bystanders experience guilt due to conflicted motives of feeling sympathy for the victim and guilt for not helping them. Unlike the need to reduce moral disengagement in bystanders, however, some experts argue that intervention programs should *increase* students' proneness to feel morally distressed in order to provide more motivation to defend victims of peer aggression. The logic behind this is that *"Students who have experienced moral distress in the past (when they behaved as passive bystanders) are more likely to anticipate moral distress if they do not intervene, and this anticipated moral distress may work as a moral compass that guides decision-making in morally salient social situations"* (Gini, Thornberg, & Pozzoli, 2020, p. 43)

In elementary schools, although many interventions have been successful at changing knowledge and attitudes about bullying, they typically do not result in significant reductions in bullying behavior (Wang & Goldberg, 2017). To reduce bullying in predominantly Hispanic elementary schools in the United States, researchers initiated a class-wide intervention that uses children's storybooks with bullying situations (e.g., *"Bullying B.E.A.N.S.," "Say Something," "Juice Box Bully"*) to encourage awareness about bullying, teach appropriate problem solving and social skills, and decrease moral disengagement. Notably, teachers were asked to initiate conversations around moral disengagement that were done to raise awareness that bullying cannot be justified under any circumstance (e.g., *"Is it okay to blame the person who is getting bullied like the story character did?"* or *"He always says he is 'just kidding' instead of admitting 'I am being mean.' Is this ok?"*). Each conversation was then followed by a writing activity (e.g., creating a class poster of anti-bullying strategies) to strengthen connections with themes from the books. Compared to the control classrooms, students receiving the intervention significantly decreased their use of moral disengagement mechanisms that justified bullying behavior and those classes also showed decreases in student-reported bullying (including physical, verbal, and relational forms) (Wang & Goldberg, 2017).

Not surprisingly, bystanders who join in on the bullying have little empathy for the victim and are probably more concerned with their social status, yet even passive bystanders with some degree of empathy often fail to get involved (Pöyhönen, Juvonen, & Salmivalli, 2012). Building empathy is an important part of any anti-bullying program. Indeed, consistent with **SMB**, American middle school students scoring high on empathy were more likely to view the bullying as a problem, interpret it as an situation requiring help, accept responsibility for helping, know what to do, and act on those decisions (Jenkins & Nickerson, 2017).

Empathy training includes raising awareness about the harmful consequences of bullying for the victim and having people imagine how they would feel if they were being bullied (Spivak, Lipsey, Farran, & Polanin, 2015). To increase active responding, interventions should build empathy that allow bystanders to take on the perspective of the victim. Two common types of empathy are cognitive and affective empathy. **Cognitive empathy** is defined as the ability to understand what a person is thinking or feeling without getting emotionally involved oneself (e.g., *"I can listen to others"*) while **affective empathy** is defined as an emotional reaction by an observer to the affective state of another (e.g., *"I am sensitive to other people's feelings, even if they are not my friends."*) (Walters & Espelage, 2021).

In one study, Polish high school students watched a short video of the emotional impact of being cyberbullied. To induce empathy, the students were instructed to *"identify with the situation depicted in the video and to focus on those aspects that reflected the victim's emotions and behavior."* Compared to a control group, those induced to experience affective empathy were much *less* willing to forward a hurtful message to another student. One caveat, however, was the empathy training only worked in the short-term; those who had to make the decision to forward the cruel message a week later were no less likely to send the message than a control group (Barlińska, Szuster, & Winiewski, 2015). There is some evidence, however, that long-term interventions promoting affective empathy can have longer lasting effects. In one study, German students were given a 10-week empathy training course (incorporating stories, news items, videos, plays) and then asked to reflect on the victim's thoughts and feelings. Compared to a control group, the intervention group showed larger reductions in bullying over time (Schultze-Krumbholz, Schultze, Zagorscak, et al., 2016). One explanation for the success of affective empathy may be due to a reduction in pro-bullying beliefs. Indeed, researchers found that pro-bullying beliefs *("If other students are being teased too much, it's not my problem")* successfully mediated the relationship between affective empathy and bystander intervention in American middle school students (Walters & Espelage, 2021).

Programs that teach affective empathy can also be implemented in younger children. Elementary school children can learn the basic ingredients of empathy which allow them to: determine the emotional state of another person, perceive situations from the perspective of others, and accurately respond emotionally to another person (Kahn & Lawhorne, 2003). One effective way to do this is through exposing children to age-appropriate books such as *The 100 Dresses* or *Bridge to Terabithia* where the characters are bullied and the writers provide vivid descriptions of how the victims feel and respond (e.g., sadness, fear, or anger) (Davis & Davis, 2007).

There is no doubt that small displays of empathy can have a big impact. When asked what is the best thing another student can do to help them, targets of bullying consistently mentioned peers who showed empathy by reassuring them it is not their fault, calling them at home, or spending time with them after they had been mocked (Bazelon, 2013). As one expert on bullying stressed, *"We effectively stop bullying early in by limiting the rewards of bullying behavior and empowering the empathetic majority to fulfill their positive potential as active bystanders"* (Davis & Davis, 2007, p. 4).

Emphasize Correct Subjective Norms

People often take their cues from what other people do. These social norms are often defined as **descriptive norms** (what others typically do) and **injunctive norms** (what others ought to do). Typically, these norms are aligned, for example, students know they should not talk on their cell phone during class (injunctive norm) and the vast majority of students do not engage in this behavior (descriptive). With bullying behavior, however, there is an interesting paradox—most students believe bullying is wrong, yet wrongly assume most of their peers do not feel the same way. These misperceptions can exacerbate the bullying behavior because bystanders may falsely assume others do not find it problem. Furthermore, the inaction of bystanders who privately condone bullying sends a message to bullies of implicit approval (Bastiaensens, Vandebosch, Poels, et al., 2014; Kubiszewski, Auzoult, Potard, & Lheureux, 2019). Indeed, American schoolchildren who overestimated peers' approval of bullying reported lower levels of defending the victim and higher levels of joining in on the bullying (Sandstrom, Makover, & Bartini, 2012). In contrast, however, a study on Italian school children found that those who believe their classmates share their anti-bullying views reported less fear of rejection and were more willing to intervene if necessary (Pozzoli & Gini, 2013).

To increase bystander intervention, anti-bullying educators must make the correct **subjective norms**—the norms that relevant others hold about the behavior—prominent. In one study, Australian researchers looking at elementary and secondary school children found that many expected that their friends and/or family would not be supportive of intervention and would prefer that they "stay out of it." They also tended to be dismissive of what teachers expected of them in regard to interpersonal relations with peers (Rigby, 2005). In terms of intervention strategies, this implies that the *"direct communicating of expectations of teachers regarding bullying behavior (e.g., by policy statements exhorting children not to bully) is likely to have little or no effect on how students interact"* (Rigby, 2005, p. 159). Together these studies demonstrate that perceived social norms are often better predictors of helping than student's self-reported beliefs (Kubiszewski et al., 2019).

Providing people with accurate information about their peers' views on bullying (i.e., *"most peers also think bullying is wrong")* is an effective way to correct their misperceptions, and subsequently increase helping. When discussing social norms, educators should clarify misperceptions of injunctive norms (e.g., *"Did you know that sometimes your classmates have private beliefs that don't match their public behaviors?"),* as well as providing accurate descriptive norms (e.g., *Did you know nine out of ten students at your school believe that helping a victim of bullying is the right thing to do?")* (Sandstrom et al., 2012). Indeed, American middle school students shown a pie chart depicting that most students think it is wrong to exclude others or spread nasty rumors reported significantly lower levels bullying and victimization (Perkins, Craig, & Perkins, 2011). As the researchers state. *"Bullying and victimization in schools are inherently relational processes, relying on domination, subjugation, and bystander apathy, all presumably shaped by peer norms"* (Perkins et al., 2011, p. 705). Social norm interventions should also focus on the relationship of bystanders. Often the bystanders are good friends rather than mere acquaintances. People are more likely to follow the descriptive norms of their reference group. So to counteract this, interventions must also address the need to take action, even when your close friends do not (Bastiaensens et al., 2014).

Besides reminding people of the actual descriptive norms, another strategy to facilitate helping is to get a dedicated minority to adopt the norm. Using an online methodology to establish social norms, researchers found that a committed minority of just 25 percent of the population triggered a turning point resulting in changing the original social norm. Applying the dynamics of **critical mass**—the critical group size for initiating social change—interventions designed to overturn the current acceptability of online bullying behavior (i.e., make bystander engagement the new norm) by a committed minority may help to change the social norm from passive observing to active responding (Centola, Becker, Brackbill, & Baronchelli, 2018).

Increase Perceived Behavioral Control (Self-Efficacy)

Let's face it, for many of us, confronting a bully or confronting someone who said something offensive takes a level of self-confidence that many of us lack. Often when faced with these challenges, the default is to avoid conflict and any feelings of social awkwardness (Dungan, Munguia Gomez, & Epley, 2022). Although building empathy toward the victim of bullying can increase active responding, bystanders may still remain passive if they believe their help will not alleviate the problem (Pöyhönen et al., 2012) or if they lack the competence to intervene (Gini, Albiero, Benelli, & Altoe, 2008). On the bright side, people with high self-efficacy in these situations tend to help more. Indeed, in one study, Finnish children who scored high in bystander self-efficacy for confronting a bully (e.g., *"Trying to make the others stop the bullying would be very easy for me"*) were more likely to intervene than those low in self-efficacy (Pöyhönen et al., 2010). Likewise, Italian researchers found that adolescents having high levels of social self-efficacy (e.g., *"being able to make new friends"* or *"being able to express personal opinions in a group"*) were more likely to be defend their peers against bullies (Gini et al., 2008).

A large American survey conducted by the National Education Association found that the majority of educators lack training in the appropriate response to bullying (Bradshaw et al., 2013). One possible solution involves incorporating role-playing exercises and assertiveness training into the curriculum so students can learn concrete skills to raise their confidence in bullying situations. To be effective, however, these programs must go beyond the ineffective advice such as telling the bully to "stop being mean." Fortunately, there are many relatively simple and concrete strategies programs can use to increase self-efficacy. For example, rather than asking closed questions such as *"Bullying hurts people, right?"* asking more open-ended questions such as *"How might you stand up for somebody who is being treated badly?"* encourages students to see that there is more than one right answer (Bradshaw et al., 2013). To increase assertiveness and initiative in younger children, students from American elementary schools were taught a three-step response ("stop, walk, talk") when they encounter bullying behavior. If they see someone being bullied they say "stop," if bullying continues they are told to "walk" away, and then go "talk" to the teacher (Ross & Horner, 2009). Furthermore, older students taught that offering help indirectly (e.g., comforting the victim, reporting the incident to a moderator) rather than directly facing the bully, showed a greater confidence to intervene (Jenkins & Nickerson, 2017; Karasavva & Mikami, 2024).

Evidence from a multi-national meta-analysis of twelve school-based programs (approximately 13,000 students) that focused on self-efficacy training, indicated that overall the programs were successful at defending the target of bullying, often stopping the bullying within ten seconds! (Polanin, Espelage, & Pigott, 2012).

For older adolescents and adults, cyberbullying behaviors can often turn sexual in nature (e.g., unwanted sexual images, calling people "sluts," revenge porn). One group of researchers recently developed a cyberbullying bystander video grounded in the **TPB**. Specifically, the video showed examples of cyberbullying followed by interviews with students expressing their disapproval of cyberbullying and how bystanders can make a difference (attitudes), their approval of supporting victims and disapproval of doing nothing (subjective norms), and advice for how they would want others to respond (perceived behavioral control). Relative to a control group watching video dealing with student drinking, students from an American university reported they would be more likely to help the victim of cyberbullying (Doane, Ehlke, & Kelley, 2020).

Evidence-Based Anti-Bullying Bystander Intervention Programs

What follows are evidenced-based bystander anti-bullying programs that have been shown to be successful in (a) increasing active responding when encountering a bullying situation, and (b) changing the social climate of bullying.

Steps to Respect ®

The program **Steps to Respect** ® (https://www.cfchildren.org/resources/previous-programs/) is a research-based, comprehensive bullying prevention program designed to help young children confront behavior like bullying. The program is designed to decrease school bullying problems in multiple ways such as addressing student social-emotional skills that directly counter bullying and support social competence. To accomplish this, the program provides scenarios for students to practice using assertive language and posture to refuse bullying (e.g., standing up straight, facing the person, and using a strong and respectful voice). One longitudinal study done in US schools showed 2-year declines (of 20–30 percent) in playground bullying after students were trained using the Steps to Respect program (Frey et al., 2009).

Second Step ®

For older children, programs such as **Second Step ®** (https://www.secondstep.org/bullying-prevention) have incorporated self-reflection exercises to increase self-efficacy and empathy. In one activity, students write two brief paragraphs: In the first, they describe what could happen if someone was being bullied and nobody helped, and in the second, they describe what would happen differently if the bystanders acted responsibly and helped stop the bullying. For another activity, students in pairs are given a hypothetical scenario (e.g., *"Mitsu recently moved here from Japan. She is very quiet and doesn't speak much English. Cyndi and Tom tease her in a mean way about not speaking much: 'What's wrong with you? Are you mute?' Now they've gotten several classmates to call her 'Mute' instead of 'Mitsu'"*). With your partner, decide what you would do to help stop the bullying if you were a bystander. Older students increase efficacy by learning ways to shift the focus away from the victim, using humor to redirect the conversation, walking with the target of bullying to reduce future bullying interactions, and checking in with the person who was bullied to let them know they care.

Olweus Bullying Prevention Program (OBPP)

For very young children, it is recommended that school-based bullying prevention efforts focus on engaging children in proactive strategies that promote an inclusive school climate during playground activities (e.g., *"We don't say 'you can't' play"*) (Flaspohler, Elfstrom, Vanderzee, et al., 2009). For older children, the **Olweus Bullying Prevention Program (OBPP)** developed in Norway is a comprehensive, school-wide program designed to reduce bullying and achieve better peer relations among students in elementary, middle, and junior high school grades. Although, the program does not directly address bystander intervention, the program does emphasize a restructuring of the school environment at multiple levels including: at the school level (establish a bullying prevention coordinating committee), at the classroom level (enforce school-wide rules against bullying), at the individual level (ensure that all staff intervene at the time when bullying is observed), and at the community level (develop school—community partnerships to support the school's program) A whole-school approach requires all parties (school, parents, pupils, peers) be involved. To be effective the program must include staff training, behavioral monitoring via surveys, school-wide rules, parental involvement, and classroom activities (Olweus & Limber, 2010). Though quite sophisticated to implement, several large-scale studies from schools across the world provide compelling evidence of the program's effectiveness (Ttofi & Farrington, 2011).

KiVa

KiVa ("Kiusaamista Vastaan," translation "Against Bullying"; https://www/kivaprogram.net) is an anti-bullying program developed in Finland specifically designed to improve the school climate by changing bystander (both peer and teacher) responses to bullying. Like the Olweus program, the KiVA program is a whole-school intervention that addresses individual, classroom, and school-level factors. The curriculum consists of ten lessons that are delivered over twenty hours by trained classroom teachers. The students engage in discussions, group work, and role-playing exercises. Moreover, students practice their knowledge and skills (e.g., choosing safe strategies to support victims, dealing with group pressure to join in bullying) with a computer game depicting various scenarios in virtual school hallways and lunchrooms. Each lesson is constructed around a central theme, and one rule is associated with that theme; after the lesson is delivered, the students adopt that rule as a class rule. At the end of the year, all the rules are combined into a contract, which all students then sign. For recess, special vests are given to the playground helpers to enhance their visibility and remind students that the school takes bullying seriously. Findings show that the KiVa program has been found to be particularly effective in creating a caring school climate among students and reducing the harm associated with bullying and victimization (Juvonen et al., 2016).

"Media Heroes"

Using the **TPB** to curb cyberbullying, German researchers developed a program **("Media Heroes"** in English) that focuses on strengthening attitudes toward cyberbullying by raising middle school student's awareness concerning the impact of cyberbullying on the victim, and by changing existing subjective norms by making students aware that even though they may view others' behavior as dismissive, that may not represent the actual group norms (Wölfer, Schultze-Krumbholz, Zagorscak, et al., 2014).

Friendly ATTAC

To increase active responding to defend against cyberbullying, some antibullying programs have turned to gaming. **Friendly ATTAC** (Adaptive Technological Tools Against Cyberbullying), developed by researchers from Belgium, is a highly interactive digital game designed to help adolescents deal with cyberbullying issues. By means of highly personalized virtual experience scenarios, the game provides players with immediate feedback in a safe and anonymous environment. As described by the lead designer,

> *The game . . . resembles a hate page, that . . . has been constructed on a social networking site by someone to make fun of pupils at school by posting their pictures and calling them ugly. The player in the story is transferred from the future to this school, to solve this problem by talking to students, responding to cyberbullying by using positive bystander behavior to end the cyberbullying and get the "ugly people page" removed.* (DeSmet et al., 2018, p. 338)

Feedback was used to show the players whether they chose the correct behavior, why it was a good/bad option, and how they might better prepare for future bullying events. Belgian middle schoolers assigned to the play the game showed significant improvements in self-efficacy, prosocial skills, and willingness to engage in proactive behavior. Further, these students expressed more confidence they could resist social pressure to join in the bullying, take the initiative to defend the target, as well as comfort the target (DeSmet et al., 2018).

"What Can Bystanders Do?"

Based on research incorporating the **SMB** and **TPB**, there are several practical strategies you can do to become an active responder the next time you are faced bullying/cyberbullying scenario including:

- recognizing the subtler signs of bullying that others may miss such as social ostracism, intimidation, and the spreading of nasty rumors

- understanding that bystander passivity is often perceived by victims as acting in collusion with bullies, which may inadvertently reinforce the bully
- realizing that you need to intervene when you witness relational bullying (e.g., social ostracism/spreading rumors), and not just physical forms of bullying
- avoiding diffusion of responsibility by reminding yourself to take action, especially when others are present
- inhibiting moral distress by becoming moral agents and building empathy toward victims

"What Can Public Health Educators Do?"

Based on research incorporating the **SMB** and **TPB**, there are several additional practical strategies (beyond those above) that health practitioners can do when designing programs to get bystanders to confront bullying/cyberbullying including

- viewing bullying as a social system that creates a vicious cycle in which passive bystanders may unwittingly reinforce the bully, thus increasing bullying behavior
- downplaying zero-tolerance policies that are typically ineffective and may even increase in covert forms of bullying such as ostracizing, spreading rumors, and even cyberbullying
- urging teachers/staff/students to speak up against bullying, especially in places with a strong code of silence (such as bathrooms, playgrounds, buses)
- encouraging teachers and staff to avoid excusing the behavior *("I'm sure he didn't mean it")*
- mobilizing high-status peers to intervene
- developing programs that inhibit moral disengagement and facilitate the development of moral agency and affective empathy
- designing programs to increase online accountability and support

Summary

Peer bystanders are in unique position to send the message to bullies that they are responsible for their actions and the targets are not to blame. Unlike bullies, most bystanders want to reduce bullying, and unlike targets, they have the power to do so. When bystanders intervene on behalf of the victim, they can successfully lessen victimization. Unless the necessary steps of the **SMB** and **TPB** are taken into consideration, however, anti-bullying intervention at both the individual and programmatic level is bound to fail. For change to occur, school administrators should consider implementing programs that address, among other things, the unique barriers to bullying/cyberbullying, viewing bullying as a social system, increasing empathy and self-efficacy, and emphasizing social norms (descriptive and injunctive) and escalating intentions to help by strengthening personal attitudes, subjective norms and perceived behavioral control. In the next chapter, we will examine effective strategies bystanders and public health professionals can use to combat sexual assault.

References

Aboud, F. E., & Joong, A. (2008). Intergroup name-calling and conditions for creating assertive bystanders. In S. R. Kevy & M. Killen (Eds.), *Intergroup attitudes and relations in childhood through adulthood* (pp. 249–260). Oxford University Press.

Allison, K. R., & Bussey, K. (2016). Cyber-bystanding in context: A review of the literature on witnesses' responses to cyberbullying. *Children and Youth Services Review, 65*, 183–194.

American Psychological Association Zero Tolerance Task Force. (2008). Are zero tolerance policies effective in the schools? An evidentiary review and recommendations. *American Psychologist, 63*, 852–862.

Bandura, A. (1999). Moral disengagement in the perpetration of inhumanities. *Personality and Social Psychological Review, 3*, 193–209.

Barlińska, J., Szuster, A., & Winiewski, M. (2015). The role of short- and long-term cognitive empathy activation in preventing cyberbystander reinforcing cyberbullying behaviour. *Cyberpsychology, Behavior and Social Networking, 18*, 241–244.

Bastiaensens, S., Van Cleemput, K., Vandebosch, H., et al. (2019). "Were you cyberbullied? Let me help you." Studying adolescents' online peer support of cyberbullying victims using thematic analysis of online support group fora. In H. Vandebosch & L. Green (Eds.), *Narratives in research and interventions on cyberbullying among young people*. Springer International Publishing.

Bastiaensens, S., Vandebosch, H., Poels, K., et al. (2014). Cyberbullying on social network sites. An experimental study into bystanders' behavioral intentions to help the victim or reinforce the bully. *Computers in Human Behavior, 31*, 259–271.

Bauman, S., & Del Rio, A. (2006). Preservice teachers' responses to bullying scenarios: Comparing physical, verbal and relational bullying. *Journal of Education Psychology, 98*, 219–231.

Bazelon, E. (2013). *Sticks and stones: Defeating the culture of bullying and rediscovering the power of character and empathy.* Random House. https://www.youtube.com/watch?v=tUHDxBaOi3Q

Borgwald, K., & Theixos, H. (2013). Bullying the bully: Why zero-tolerance policies get a failing grade. *Social Influence, 8,* 149–160.

Bradshaw, C. P., Waasdorp, T. E., O'Brennan, L., & Gulemetova, M. (2013). Teachers' and education support professionals' perspectives on bullying and prevention: Findings from a National Education Association (NEA) survey. *School Psychology Review, 42,* 280–297.

Brody, N., & Vangelisti, A. L. (2016). Bystander intervention in cyberbullying. *Communication Monographs, 83,* 94–119.

Brüggemann, A. J., Forsberg, C., Colnerud, G., et al. (2019). Bystander passivity in health care and school settings: Moral disengagement, moral distress, and opportunities for moral education. *Journal of Moral Education, 48,* 199–213.

Byers, D. (2013). Do they see nothing wrong with this?: Bullying, bystander complicity, and the role of homophobic bias in the Tyler Clementi case. *Families in Society: The Journal of Contemporary Social Services, 94,* 251–258.

Centola, D., Becker, J., Brackbill, D., & Baronchelli, A. (2018). Experimental evidence for tipping points in social convention. *Science, 360,* 1116–1119.

Charach, A., Pepler, D. J., & Ziegler, S. (1995). Bullying at school: A Canadian perspective. *Education Canada, 35,* 12–18.

Coloroso, B. (2011). Bully, bullied, bystander . . . and beyond: Help students choose a new role. *Education Digest: Essential Readings Condensed for Quick Review, 77,* 36–39.

Cowie, H., & Smith, P. K. (2012). Peer support as a means of improving school safety and reducing bullying and violence. In B. Doll, W. Pfohl, & J. Yoon (Eds.), *Handbook of youth prevention science* (pp. 179–193). Routledge.

Craig, W. M., & Pepler, D. J. (1998). Observations of bullying and victimization in the schoolyard. *Canadian Journal of School Psychology, 13,* 41–59.

Crimaldi, L. (2010, March 29). *"DA: School knew of brutal bullying of Phoebe Prince."* Boston Herald (MA).

Davis, S., & Davis, J. (2007). *Empowering bystanders in bullying prevention, grades K–8.* Research Press.

DeSmet, A., Bastiaensens, S., Cleemput, K., et al. (2018). The efficacy of the Friendly Attac serious digital game to promote prosocial bystander behavior in cyberbullying among young adolescents: A cluster-randomized controlled trial. *Computers in Human Behavior, 78,* 336–347.

DeSmet, A., Veldeman, C., Poels, K., et al. (2014). Determinants of self-reported bystander behavior in cyberbullying incidents amongst adolescents. *Cyberpsychology, Behavior, and Social Networking, 17,* 207–215.

DiFranzo, D., Taylor, S. H., Kazerooni, F., et al. (2018). Upstanding by design: Bystander intervention in cyberbullying. *In Proceedings of the 2018 CHI Conference on Human Factors in Computing Systems.*

Doane, A. N., Ehlke, S., & Kelley, M. L. (2020). Bystanders against cyberbullying: A video program for college students. *International Journal of Bullying Prevention, 2,* 41–52.

Dungan, J. A., Munguia Gomez, D. M., & Epley, N. (2022). Too reluctant to reach out: Receiving social support is more positive than expressers expect. *Psychological Science, 33,* 1300–1312.

Flaspohler, P. D., Elfstrom, J. L., Vanderzee, K. L., et al. (2009). Stand by me: The effects of peer and teacher support in mitigating the impact of bullying on quality of life. *Psychology in the Schools, 46,* 636–649.

Frey, K. S., Hirschstein, M. K., Edstrom, L. V., & Snell, J. L. (2009). Observed reductions in school bullying, nonbullying aggression, and destructive bystander behavior: A longitudinal evaluation. *Journal of Educational Psychology, 101,* 466–481.

Gini, G., Albiero, P., Benelli, B., & Altoe, G. (2008). Determinants of adolescents' active defending and passive bystanding behavior in bullying. *Journal of Adolescence, 31,* 93–105.

Gini, G., Thornberg, R., & Pozzoli, T. (2020). Individual moral disengagement and bystander behavior in bullying: The role of moral distress and collective moral disengagement. *Psychology of Violence, 10,* 38–47.

Guarini, A., Menin, D., Menabo, L., & Brighi, A. (2019). RPC teacher-based program for improving coping strategies to deal with cyberbullying. *International Journal of Environmental Research and Public Health, 16,* 948–961.

Hawkins, D. L., Pepler, D. J., & Craig, W. M. (2001). Naturalistic observations of peer interventions in bullying. *Social Development, 10,* 512–527.

Hill, K. (2010, September 30). Tyler Clementi turned to a gay message forum for help before his suicide. *Forbes.* Retrieved from https://www.forbes.com/sites/kashmirhill/2010/09/30/tyler-clementi-turned-to-a-gay-message-forum-for-help-before-his-suicide/?sh=4f8350424550

Jenkins, L. N., Fredrick, S. S., & Nickerson, A. (2018). The assessment of bystander intervention in bullying: Examining measurement invariance across gender. *Journal of School Psychology, 69,* 73–83.

Jenkins, L. N., & Nickerson, A. (2017). Bystander intervention in bullying: Role of social skills and gender. *Journal of Early Adolescence, 39,* 141–166.

Juvonen, J., Schacter, H. L., Sainio, M., & Salmivalli, C. (2016). Can a school-wide bullying prevention program improve the plight of victims? Evidence for risk × intervention effects. *Journal of Consulting and Clinical Psychology, 84,* 334–344.

Kahn, W. J., & Lawhorne, C. V. (2003). *Empathy: The critical factor in conflict-resolution and culture of civility.* University of West Chester.

Karasavva, V., & Mikami, A. (2024). I'll be there for you? The bystander intervention model and cyber aggression. *Cyberpsychology: Journal of Psychosocial Research on Cyberspace, 18,* 1–25.

Kubiszewski, V., Auzoult, L., Potard, C., & Lheureux, F. (2019). Witnessing school bullying: To react or not to react? An insight into perceived social norms regulating self-predicted defending and passive behaviors. *Educational Psychology, 39,* 1174–1193.

Law, D. M., Shapka, J. D., Hymel, S., et al. (2012). The changing face of bullying: An empirical comparison between traditional and internet bullying and victimization. *Computers in Human Behavior, 28,* 226–232.

Lindstrom Johnson, S., Waasdorp, T. E., Debnam, K., & Bradshaw, C. P. (2013). The role of bystander perceptions and school climate in influencing victims' responses to bullying: To retaliate or seek support? *Journal of Criminology, 2013,* 1–10.

Menesini, E., Nocentini, A., & Palladino, B. E. (2012). Empowering students against bullying and cyberbullying: Evaluation of an Italian peer-led model. *International Journal of Conflict and Violence, 6,* 314–321.

Nickerson, A. B., Aloe, A. M., Livingston, J. A., & Feeley, T. H. (2014). Measurement of the bystander intervention model for bullying and sexual harassment. *Journal of Adolescence, 37,* 391–400.

O'Connell, P., Pepler, D., & Craig, W. (1999). Peer involvement in bullying: Insights and challenges for intervention. *Journal of Adolescence, 22,* 437–452.

Obermaier, M., Fawzi, N., & Koch, T. (2014). Bystanding or standing by? How the number of bystanders affects the intention to intervene in cyberbullying. *New Media & Society, 18,* 1491–1507.

Obermann, M. L. (2011). Moral disengagement among bystanders to school bullying. *Journal of School Violence, 10,* 239–257.

Olweus, D., & Limber, S. P. (2010). Bullying in school: Evaluation and dissemination of the Olweus Bullying Prevention Program. *American Journal of Orthopsychiatry, 80,* 124–134.

Padgett, S., & Notar, C. E. (2013). Bystanders are the key to stopping bullying. *Universal Journal of Educational Research, 1,* 33–41.

Paluck, E. L., Shepherd, H., & Aronow, P. M. (2016). Changing climates of conflict: A social network experiment in 56 schools. *Proceedings of the National Academy of Science, 113,* 566–571.

Pepler, D. J., Craig, W. M., Ziegler, S., & Charach, A. (1993). A school-based antibullying intervention: Preliminary evaluation. In D. Tattum (Ed.), *Understanding and managing bullying* (pp. 76–91). Heinemann Books.

Perkins, H. W., Craig, D. W., & Perkins, J. M. (2011). Using social norms to reduce bullying: A research intervention among adolescents in five middle schools. *Group Processes & Intergroup Relations, 14,* 703–722.

Polanin, J. R., Espelage, D. L., & Pigott, T. D. (2012). A meta-analysis of school-based bullying prevention programs' effects on bystander intervention behavior. *School Psychology Review, 41,* 47–65.

Pöyhönen, V., Juvonen, J., & Salmivalli, C. (2010). What does it take to stand up for the victim of bullying? The interplay between personal and social factors. *Merrill-Palmer Quarterly, 56,* 143–163.

Pöyhönen, V., Juvonen, J., & Salmivalli, C. (2012). Standing up for the victim, siding with the bully or standing by? Bystander responses in bullying situations. *Social Development, 21,* 722–741.

Pozzoli, T., & Gini, G. (2013). Why do bystanders of bullying help or not? A multidimensional model. *The Journal of Early Adolescence, 33,* 315–340.

Rigby, K. (2005). Why do some children bully at school? The contributions of negative attitudes towards victims and the perceived expectations of friends, parents and teachers. *School Psychology International, 26,* 147–161.

Ross, S. W., & Horner, R. H. (2009). Bullying prevention in positive behavior support. *Journal of Applied Behavior Analysis, 42,* 747–759.

Salmivalli, C., Voeten, M., & Poskiparta, E. (2011). Bystanders matter: Associations between reinforcing, defending, and the frequency of bullying behavior in classrooms. *Journal of Clinical Child and Adolescent Psychology, 40,* 668–676.

Sandstrom, M., Makover, H., & Bartini, M. (2012). Social context of bullying: Do misperceptions of group norms influence children's responses to witnessed episodes? *Social Influence, 8,* 196–215.

Schultze-Krumbholz, A., Schultze, M., Zagorscak, P., et al. (2016). Feeling cybervictims' pain—The effect of empathy training on cyberbullying. *Aggressive Behavior, 42*, 147–156.

Singal, J. (2016, January 6). *Want to end bullying? Get the popular students to help.* Retrieved from http://nymag.com/scienceofus/2016/01/end-bullying-get-the-cool-kids-to-help.html

Spivak, A. L., Lipsey, M. W., Farran, D. C., & Polanin, J. R. (2015). Protocol: Practices and program components for enhancing prosocial behavior in children and youth: A systematic review. *Campbell Systematic Reviews, 11*, 1–105.

Thornberg, R., Daremark, E., Gottfridsson, J., & Gini, G. (2020). Situationally selective activation of moral disengagement mechanisms in school bullying: A repeated within subjects experimental study. *Frontiers in Psychology, 11*, 1101–1113.

Thornberg, R., Wänström, L., & Hymel, S. (2019). Individual and classroom social-cognitive processes in bullying: A short-term longitudinal multilevel study. *Frontiers in Psychology, 10*, 1752.

Tokunaga, R. S. (2010). Following you home from school: A critical review and synthesis of research on cyberbullying victimization. *Computers in Human Behavior, 26*, 277–287.

Ttofi, M. M., & Farrington, D. P. (2011). Effectiveness of school-based programs to reduce bullying: A systematic and meta-analytic approach. *Journal of Experimental Criminology, 7*, 27–56.

Walters, G. D., & Espelage, D. L. (2021). Cognitive/affective empathy, pro-bullying beliefs, and willingness to intervene on behalf of a bullied peer. *Youth & Society, 53*, 563–584.

Wang, C., & Goldberg, T. S. (2017). Using children's literature to decrease moral disengagement and victimization among elementary school students. *Psychology in the Schools, 54*, 918–931.

Wang, J., Iannotti, R. J., & Nansel, T. R. (2009). School bullying among adolescents in the United States: Physical, verbal, relational and cyber. *Journal of Adolescent Health, 45*, 368–375.

Wölfer, R., Schultze-Krumbholz, A., Zagorscak, P., et al. (2014). Prevention 2.0: Targeting cyberbullying@ school. *Prevention Science, 15*, 879–887.

Confronting Sexual Misconduct

6

Key Terms in This Chapter 126

Problems When Encountering Sexual Misconduct 127

Confronting Sexual Misconduct 130
Applying SMB 131
Applying the TPB 134

Evidence-Based Bystander Intervention Programs for Sexual Misconduct 139
Bringing in the Bystander® 140
Green Dot 141
Know Your Power® 141
"It's Your Place" 142
Men's Workshop 142
"Mentors in Violence Prevention" (MVP) 143

TakeCARE 143

Single-User Virtual Reality Training 143

Booster Sessions 144

Summary 146

Key Terms in This Chapter

#MeToo movement: a social movement against sexual assault, in which people (mainly women) publicize their experiences of sexual abuse or sexual harassment

alcohol myopia: intoxication reduces attentional capacity and narrows people's visual fields (creates "tunnel vision")

benevolent sexism: a form of gender bias in which women are seen as virtuous, pure, and in need of protection by men

cost-reward model: proposes that helping is more likely to occur when the costs for helping are low and when the costs for not helping are high

hegemonic masculinity: rigid social practices that promote the dominant position of men and the subordination of women

moral (civil) courage: willingness to protect moral standards, even in the face of potential social risks

sexual assault: deliberate or repeated sexual advances or contact without the explicit consent of the recipient

situational model of bystander intervention (SMB): proposes that bystanders typically go through a series of five decision-making steps before help will be given

theory of planned behavior (TPB): proposes that the intent to do a behavior depends on three antecedent factors: one's *personal attitude* toward the behavior, the perceived *subjective norms* that relevant others hold about the behavior, and the degree of *perceived behavioral control* (i.e., self-efficacy) one has to do the behavior

Problems When Encountering Sexual Misconduct

Defining the Problem

So, yeah, I am sorry. Sorry and ashamed. Because, in the end, I was complicit. I didn't say shit. I didn't do shit. Harvey was nothing but wonderful to me. So I reaped the rewards and I kept my mouth shut. And for that, once again, I am sorry. But you should be sorry, too. With all these victims speaking up . . . To tell their tales. Shouldn't those who witnessed it from the sidelines do the same?.. Doesn't being a bystander bring with it the responsibility of telling the truth, however personally disgraceful it may be?

—Scott Rosenberg, admonishing himself and other passive bystanders for not speaking out about Harvey Weinstein's long history of sexual misconduct (see Fleming, 2017)

Harvey Weinstein, a once powerful American film producer and media mogul, became the poster child for the **#MeToo movement**—a social movement against sexual abuse, sexual harassment, and rape culture, in which people (mainly women) publicize their experiences of sexual abuse or sexual harassment (see *Leading with empathy . . .*). Over a 30-year period, more than 100 woman (most of them actresses, models, and former employees) accused Weinstein of sexual misconduct and sexual assault (Sand, 2017). Weinstein's trial and conviction led to a global trend coined the "Weinstein effect" in which rich and powerful men accused of sexual misconduct were now being held accountable for their actions and swiftly removed from their positions of power (see *"Powerful men confronted . . ."*).

By many accounts, including the quote above, Weinstein's abusive behavior was an "open secret." According to one source, sixteen former or current executives and assistants connected with Weinstein said they had witnessed or had been informed of Weinstein's non-consensual sexual advances toward women (Farrow, 2017). Sadly, with wide-ranging complicity, the vast majority who became aware did nothing to stop the abuse. As one reporter lamented, *"It should not be the responsibility of victims alone to speak out against those who harass or abuse. That responsibility should be shared by those who become aware of allegations of this nature. What is tragically clear is that in these situations many do nothing."* (Aslam, 2017).

Sexual assault involves deliberate or repeated sexual advances or contact without the explicit consent of the recipient. Forms of sexual misconduct or assault can be verbal (e.g., making sexual comments), physical (e.g., fondling, assault), or online (e.g., posting pornographic images) (https://rainn.org/articles/sexual-assault). According to the **Rape, Abuse, & Incest National Network (RAINN)**, approximately 300,000 people living in the United States are sexually assaulted each year (https://rainn.org/articles/sexual-assault). Research shows that, relative to males, females are overwhelmingly the victims of sexual assault. Indeed, studies show that while attending college in the United States, approximately 40 percent of female and 4 percent of male students report experiencing unwanted sexual contact, the vast majority committed by an acquaintance (Fedina, Holmes, & Backes, 2018; Sundstrom, Ferrara, DeMaria, et al., 2018). Further, the consequences of sexual victimization can be extremely detrimental as survivors often have difficulty maintaining personal relationships, returning to work or school, and regaining a sense of normalcy (Basile, Smith, Kresnow, et al., 2022).

Although most assaults occur in private, research shows that nearly one-third of these assaults take place in public settings (e.g., workplaces, schools, bars), with the bystander default of not getting involved (Planty, 2002). Indeed, in one study examining over sixteen million EMS calls, compared to medical emergencies such as cardiac arrest, bystander intervention was least likely to occur during sexual assaults (Faul, Aikman, & Sasser, 2016).

Traditional Strategies

Historically, sexual assault prevention programs depict men as potential perpetrators and women as potential victims. Studies have shown this method can lead to defensiveness in men and victim-blaming toward women (Banyard, Moynihan, Cares, & Warner, 2014). Traditionally, intervention programs have also segregated men and women. Men's programs tend to focus on defining sexual assault and debunking the rape myths (e.g., *"no really means yes"; "women who dress provocatively are "'asking for it'"*), while women's programs tend to focus on self-protection strategies to avoid unwanted sexual advances (e.g., *"don't walk alone at night"; "always watch your drink")* or self-defense training (e.g., biting, scratching, using a weapon, martial arts). While these efforts can be helpful, they unduly place the responsibility on the target/victim, any change in attitudes tends to be short-lived, and most importantly, these programs typically do not stop sexual assaults from occurring (Breitenbecher, 2000; Katz & Moore, 2013).

As we will see, bystander intervention programs can help to discourage defensiveness and victim-blaming by depicting sexual violence as a community problem, rather than an individual problem (Lonsway, Banyard, Berkowitz, et al., 2009; Tabachnick, 2009). As one intervention expert states, *"A bystander focus creates less defensiveness because people are approached as potential allies rather than as potential victims or potential perpetrators"* (Burn, 2009, p. 780). Thus, by treating potential bystanders as part of the solution to sexual assault, rather than part of the problem, prevention programs may limit the risk of defensiveness or backlash that is common among participants.

Unique Barriers

Beyond the general obstacles that inhibit helping in emergency situations (see Chapter 2), there is a unique set of barriers preventing bystanders from confronting a sexual assault. Like binge-drinking scenarios, bystanders may be too impaired themselves to notice or identify sexual violence occurring around them. For example, one male bystander expounded, *"When you're drunk, the environment you're in is already kind of weird . . . [Risk] becomes part of the scenery almost and just people aren't able to distinguish between what's right and what's wrong"* (Oesterle, Orchowski, Moreno, & Berkowitz, 2018, p. 1214). The problem with **alcohol myopia** seems especially relevant to men. Researchers from one American university found that males who had been drinking were less likely to intervene in a sexual assault scenario, especially when they knew the perpetrator, while for female students, alcohol consumption did not affect bystander intervention (Fleming & Wiersma-Mosley, 2015). Thus, cues about sexual assault may be camouflaged by the campus drinking culture, especially for males (McMahon & Banyard, 2012).

Another barrier when encountering a sexual assault is the bystander's concern over the perceived social costs of getting the alleged perpetrator in trouble, especially if the offender is a friend or somebody they know (Blavos, Glassman, Sheu, et al., 2014). As you might expect, studies typically show that people are more likely to protect their friends than strangers, and the more serious the crime (e.g., excessive drinking, assault) the more likely they are to cover for their friend (Weidman, Sowden, Berg, & Kross, 2020). Thus, for some bystanders at least, loyalty to friends may influence whether they respond to apparent moral violations.

In addition to loyalty, another unique barrier to confronting sexual assault is the strong sociocultural norms for men to not interfere with another man's sexual advances (i.e., "c*ckblocking"). Due to this powerful norm, men tend to show "respect" for other mens right to engage in sexual behavior and will typically not intervene unless the victim has already been physically harmed in some way (Oesterle et al., 2018; Wrightson-Hester, Allan, & Allan, 2022).

Victim-blaming is another unique barrier to sexual assault. Unlike other potential emergencies, bystanders of sexual assault may see the victim as responsible for their predicament, especially in cases where the victim was intoxicated or dressed provocatively (Burn, 2009; Workman & Freeburn, 1999). Men are often socialized to believe rape myths such as women have "secret rape fantasies," women who dress provocatively are "asking for it," and women are socialized to give "token resistance" (so "no really means yes") (Burt, 1980). Acceptance of these rape myths, allows men to effectively transfer accountability from the perpetrator to the victim of sexual assault. Predictably, rape myth acceptance is also associated with lower intention to intervene in hypothetical sexual assault situations (Bannon, Brosi, & Foubert, 2013). Another form of victim-blaming can occur in people (men and women) who endorse **benevolent sexism**—women are seen as virtuous, pure, and in need of protection by men. Consistent with this construct, male students from an American university who scored high in benevolent sexism were *less* likely to intervene during a sexual assault scenario in which a female was drunk and flirtatious (Yule, Hoxmeier, Petranu, & Grych, 2020). One plausible explanation was that these men perceive women who are drinking and acting provocatively (i.e., impurely) as less deserving of their protection. Effective bystander education programs should provide space for people to discuss victim-blaming beliefs, with the goal of debunking common rape myths and countering benevolent sexist beliefs (Robinson, Casiano, & Elias-Lambert, 2022; Yule et al., 2020).

Confronting Sexual Misconduct

They were kicking her in her head and they were beating her up, and ripping her clothes off; it's something you can't get out your mind. I feel like I could have done something but I don't feel like I have any responsibility for anything that happened.
—Quotes from one bystander[1] of a gang rape outside school grounds during a high school homecoming dance (see Vega, 2009).

As the quote above illustrates, bystanders may not always intervene during a sexual assault. In this section, we will look at how both bystanders can overcome and public health advocates can help people overcome the various obstacles that bystanders face when confronted with sexual misconduct.

---

1 Reportedly as many as twenty bystanders watched the assault without calling 911 to report it (see *"Police: As many as 20 . . ."*).

Applying SMB

As with each type of emergency situation covered in this book, the obstacles preventing bystanders from helping in sexual assault scenarios can be mapped onto the **Situational Model of Bystander Intervention (SMB)**. Using an **SMB** theoretical framework, researchers looking at sexual assault at an American high school found support that the five steps are indeed sequential: noticing the event was related to interpreting the event as an emergency, viewing the event as an emergency was a significant predictor of accepting responsibility for helping, accepting responsibility was subsequently highly predictive of knowing how to help, which in turn had the strongest relationship with taking sufficient action (Nickerson, Aloe, Livingston, & Feeley, 2014). Likewise, African American adolescents asked to speculate about how they might respond to a vignette in which a male friend physically abuses his girlfriend, cited many of the obstacles highlighted by **SMB** including: *"It is none of my business"* (step 1), *"It didn't seem that severe"* (step 2), *"I did not have anything to do with it"* (step 3), *"I wouldn't want to give wrong advice"* (step 4), and *"If he's crazy enough to hurt her, he can hurt me too"* (step 5) (Weisz & Black, 2008).

Despite these challenges, bystanders are still one of the best lines of defense to prevent sexual assault from occurring. Because bystanders are often present during the pre-assault phase, public health researchers have recently begun designing training programs to promote bystander intervention in these types of high-risk settings (Bennett, Banyard, & Garnhart, 2014; Berkowitz, 2009; Burn, 2017). As one intervention researcher contends, *"Programs intended to promote bystander intervention in situations at-risk for sexual assault may be more effective if they address the barriers identified by a situational model of bystander intervention"* (Burn, 2009, p. 791).

Recognize Early Warning Signs

Many experts view sexual assault from a feminist perspective in which sexual assault occurs on a continuum based on patriarchal power and control (Brownmiller, 1975). To help bystanders become more mindful of potential sexual assault incidents, intervention programs should address the full continuum of behaviors from relatively low-risk behaviors (e.g., ogling, sexually degrading language, catcalling) to high-risk markers leading up to the assault (e.g., using alcohol to render victims vulnerable to attack, physically isolating victims, and sharing with peers their plans of sexual misconduct) (McMahon & Banyard, 2012). Although many of the behaviors at the lower end of the continuum are not necessarily illegal, they are seen as contributing to a culture of violence that supports and tolerates the more severe forms of violence against women such as unwanted sexual contact and assault. Unfortunately, people typically ignore many of the early warning signs. For example, although students from an American university were more likely to recognize the importance of intervening in situations that appear high risk to the victim (e.g., check in with my female friend who looks drunk when she goes to a room with a guy she just met), they were less likely to identify bystander opportunities deemed trivial (e.g., challenge a male friend who uses degrading language such as "they're all sluts" when referring to women) (McMahon, Postmus, & Koenick, 2011). Thus, bystander intervention programs must address the warning signs of sexual abuse before it happens. As one expert warns, *"If we limit our interventions to a culminating 'event,' we miss multiple opportunities to do something or say something before someone is harmed."* (Tabachnick, 2009, p. 10).

Programs should also encourage bystanders to be vigilant of sexual assault across different social groups. For some groups, sexual assault/ harassment may be less likely to be noticed as victims are typically portrayed as young, white, physically attractive, and traditionally feminine, despite the fact that women of color, queer women, and less stereotypically feminine women are especially likely to experience sexual harassment (Kaiser, Bandt-Law, Cheek, & Schachtman, 2022). Bystanders must realize that sexual assault is also common in the LGBT+ community. In one study, compared to heterosexual men and women, both bisexual and gay American adults experienced more sexual violence and unwanted sexual harassment (Chen, Walters, Gilbert, & Patel, 2020). Cases such as these might be especially difficult for heterosexual, cisgender bystanders to spot, in part, because they might have less experience with the dynamics of these relationships.

Reduce Ambiguity

Compared to men, women's greater risk of sexual assault may make the risk of sexual assault more salient to them, thereby increasing the chance of noticing the situation and interpreting it as dangerous (Burn, 2009). This implies that the ambiguity inherent in many high-risk situations may adversely affect intervention, especially in men. As we know, real-world incidents of sexual assault and harassment can be highly nuanced and complex to suss out. Sexual harassment can often be disguised as flattery, which puts the burden on women to gracefully accept harassment, leaving the bystanders confused on whether to actively intervene (Porat, Gantman, Green, et al., 2024). This is especially true during the pre-assault phase where no clear crime or victim has been determined. As one research team states, *"In contrast to many emergency situations, many of the situations in which male allies are encouraged to take a stand involve disrespectful, sexist remarks or conduct by a male peer—circumstances that may be difficult to interpret and in which there may be no clear, immediate victim"* (Casey & Ohler, 2012, p. 66).

Ambiguity makes intervention difficult. For example, if the alleged victim knows the assailant or does not explicitly call out for help, this may signal to the onlooker that the person is in no apparent danger. In support of this theory, a majority of participants reported they would call the police if they heard a woman call for help; however, far less said they would call if they simply heard lots of yelling (Lazarus & Signal, 2013). Thus, unless a victim of assault is actually calling out for help, bystanders may not perceive the person as a "true" victim.[2] In addition to discussing signs during a sexual assault, programs need to properly address specific red flags at the pre-assault phase such as physically isolating the person from their friends, plying the person with alcohol, or taking a clearly intoxicated person back to their room (Hoxmeier, Flay, & Acock, 2016). Studies show that the more bystanders learn about the various phases of sexual violence the greater their intent to intervene, presumably because they are now better able to identify when others are at risk (Banyard, 2008).

Promote Social Solidarity

Imagine this scenario: At a house party, you see a young man approach an intoxicated woman who just spilled her drink on her lap. After "helping" her clean up, he whispers something in her ear. He then ushers the woman, who by this point is swaying back and forth, up the stairs to a bedroom. *Would you intervene in this potential party rape scenario?* Based on one study using this scenario, the answer depends on how well you know the victim. If she is a friend or somebody you know, you will probably be more likely to help than if she is a complete stranger, presumably because you will feel more responsibility and empathy toward your friend (Katz, Olin, & Rich, 2014).

Fortunately, we know from previous research that social categories of in-group/out-group members can be flexible. Remember, in a previous study we saw how widening the net from "Manchester football fan" to the more inclusive category of "football fan" increased helping (Levine, Prosser, Evans, & Reicher, 2005). Interestingly, this recategorization occurs not only at the social level, but the neurological level too. Indeed, studies using brain scans show that our brains are wired to adopt collective identities (to be

---

2 **Circle of 6** (http://www.circleof6app.com/) is a phone app that allows a user to alert up to six of their friends if they are in a potentially harmful situation. If a person needs help, one quick tap will send a message such as *"Call and pretend you need me. I need an interruption."*

"groupish") (van Bavel, Packer, & Cunningham, 2011). Further, our brains continuously update and revise how we see "us" vs. "them" leading to deeper levels of processing to those who were previously identified as out-group members (which, as we know, could increase the motivation to help these "new" in-group members).

These studies show that to increase help toward strangers victimized by sexual violence, programs must promote a sense of social solidarity with unfamiliar peers. To accomplish this, a group of researchers from an American university campus designed a poster campaign utilizing a context that is recognizable to students. The goal of these posters is to strengthen identification within peer group members (i.e., recognize themselves in others) by promoting a sense of comradery at the community level (Potter, Moynihan, & Stapleton, 2011). Ideally, increasing a sense of responsibility to unknown peers by promoting the power of community should have a beneficial effect on individual actions.

Emphasize Costs of Not Intervening

According to the **cost-reward model** (Piliavin & Piliavin, 1972), helping is more likely to occur when both the costs for helping are low *and* the costs for *not* helping are high. In support of this model, students from an American college who had participated in a bystander intervention program on sexual assault were more likely to value the benefits of helping (e.g., *"If I intervene, I can prevent someone from being hurt"*) and the costs to not intervene (e.g., *"If I don't do anything, that person is going to get hurt"*) over the costs to intervene (e.g., *"Intervening might cost me a friendship"*) (Banyard, Moynihan, & Plante, 2007). Likewise, self-identified anti-violence male advocates from the United States reported being motivated more by the consequences of *not* taking action. As one participant reflected, *"If you see something going on, you need to intervene, because if you don't, you don't know what's going to happen. And if something bad happens, you own part of it"* (Casey & Ohler, 2012, p. 77). Based on these findings, programs should emphasize the costs of not helping (e.g., the impact could be devastating) and how they outweigh the costs of helping (e.g., possibly escalating the problem).

Applying the TPB

Let's look at how the **Theory of Planned Behavior (TPB)** can be used to increase bystander intentions to help when confronting a sexual assault scenario.

Strengthen Attitudes by Building Moral Courage and Empathy

To become active responders, bystanders must have strong attitudes about moral responsibility and believe that all people (even strangers) deserve help during an emergency. Unfortunately, for many, it is easier to imagine standing up against sexual misconduct than to actually do it. If you want to be the kind of person who speaks up, it may take more than just good intentions; bystanders need to have the **moral courage**—willingness to protect moral standards, even in the face of potential social risks (e.g., *"I would stand up for a just or rightful cause even if the cause is unpopular and it would mean criticizing important others"*) to speak up (Goodwin, Graham, & Diekmann, 2020). To demonstrate, in one study, adult American participants took part in an online discussion with two other "discussants." During the introductions, the female discussant indicated that she liked to play volleyball and surf at the beach, to which the male discussant responded: *"I can't wait to see your hot ass on the beach."* Although, most people claim they would report sexual harassment if they witnessed it, only a small number of people in this study actually did. Importantly, those high on moral courage were more likely to report and confront sexual harassment (Goodwin et al., 2020). Thus, people with strong attitudes about moral responsibility may be less threatened by associated risks, and subsequently more likely to act in ways consistent with their principles and values (Baumert, Halmburger, & Schmitt, 2013).

Empathy training can also strengthen attitudes to intervene during a sexual assault. Because women tend to identify and empathize more with sexual assault survivors (Burn, 2009), programs should focus on fostering empathy in men. To accomplish this, one researcher developed the "Men's Workshop" (see below for details), which provides men with the opportunity to describe the impact of sexual assault on women in their lives and discuss alternative explanations for men's perceptions of false accusations of assault (Berkowitz, 1994, 2010).

Correct Misperceptions of Norms of Masculinity

Norms have a powerful influence on behavior; however, as we have seen repeatedly, norms can often be misperceived (underestimated or overestimated), and these miscalculations may lead people to follow an incorrect norm. For sexual assault, these distorted norms are much more prevalent in men than women. Indeed, studies consistently find that the single strongest predictor of whether or not a man intervenes to prevent a sexual assault is what *he thinks* other men would do (Fabiano, Perkins,

Berkowitz, et al., 2003; Mainwaring, Gabbert, & Scott, 2023).[3] To best use the **TPB**, programs need to correct the distorted view that the majority of men do not want to get involved in sexual assault situations nor consider the situation a crisis. To support this prediction, male students from an American college who attended an intervention program that addressed, among other things, discrepancies between actual and perceived norms regarding sexist attitudes showed more accurate perceptions of their peers' sexist attitudes/rape myths, which in turn, influenced their willingness to intervene in misogynistic situations (Kilmartin, Smith, Green, et al., 2008).

Although norm interventions about sexism/rape myths are a good start, programs must also challenge other deep-seated masculinity norms, specifically in regard to powerful social norms preventing men from blocking another man's "sexual conquest." Based on interviews of male students across American colleges, when men are looking to "score" the social pressure to enable them is high, while showing sensitivity and concern to the female target is often construed as weakness (Carlson, 2008; Deitch-Stackhouse, Kenneavy, Thayer, et al., 2015). In one vivid example, male college students who overheard a misogynistic (vs. non-sexist) comment made in front of a female student were *less* likely to stop a sexually explicit video they had control over, even though the woman had clearly expressed her wishes not want to watch it (Leone & Parrott, 2019).

To overcome these powerful norms, programs must encourage men to speak out against sexual violence so they can see sexual assault as a transgression of (rather than obedience to) the social norms of masculinity (Katz, Heisterkamp, & Fleming, 2011). Similarly, men must learn to avoid perpetuating **hegemonic masculinity**—rigid social practices that promote the dominant position of men and the subordination of women (Leone & Parrott, 2019). These rigid social practices include any behaviors indicating sexual entitlement, power, control, acceptance of interpersonal violence, hypermasculinity, and male peer groups that glorify sexual conquest (Lonsway et al., 2009). To help men overcome rigid norms of masculinity, training programs should emphasize that helping in these cases is heroic (not weak or unmanly), while also showing how "locker-room talk" can perpetuate misogynistic peer norms that deter men from actively responding to sexual assault scenarios (Leone & Parrott, 2019).

---

3 Furthermore, colleges with the largest misperceived drinking norms reported the highest rates of sexual assaults involving alcohol (Fleming & Wiersma-Mosley, 2015).

Increase Perceived Behavioral Control (Self-Efficacy)

Studies consistently show that bystanders lack the competence to help in sexual assault situations. As exemplified by one passive bystander, *"What would be helpful and useful would be tools . . . to where I may not always be able to put my sentences together or remember a word that I'm thinking of . . . to have the tools, to have a go-to sentence, to have some quick answers to some of the most-asked questions"* (Casey & Ohler, 2012, p. 74).

Intervention programs should include an assortment of tools that bystanders can use across the various phases of sexual assault. Simple actions can often be effective, such as approaching the victim and saying *"You're coming with us. It's not safe for you to be here"* or telling the instigator *"Sorry, she's too intoxicated to provide consent"*[4] (Burn, 2009; Cares, Banyard, Moynihan, et al., 2015). In one study, students from an American university asked to generate a "bystander plan" with concrete helping strategies reported higher bystander self-efficacy to stop an assault (e.g., *"How confident are you that you could ask a stranger who looks very upset at a party if they need help?"*) than control subjects (Banyard et al., 2007). Regarding the post-assault phase, Australian adult community members with high self-efficacy (e.g., *"I know a place where women can go for help"*) were also more likely to intervene (Lazarus & Signal, 2013).

Combine SMB and TPB

The **SMB** and the **TPB** have areas of overlap, particularly related to the role of self-efficacy, and the strengths of each model (namely their focus on situational or cognitive processes, respectively) also complement each other. As one research team contends, *"Incorporating the TPB with constructs from Latané and Darley's 5-stage model [SMB] may offer a more comprehensive mechanism for capturing the processes involved in evaluating antiviolence bystander opportunities"* (Casey & Ohler, 2012, p 74). Thus, synthesizing these theories should provide a more comprehensive framework for improving bystander intervention.

In support of combining these theories, American adolescents were given a scenario on dating violence that culminates with a boy intimidating his

---

4 A popular video (https://youtu.be/oQbei5JGiT8) with over 10 million views uses a "tea" metaphor to explain sexual consent. Some excerpts include: *"If you are struggling with consent, just imagine instead of initiating sex, you're making them a cup of tea."* . . . *"If they want a cup tea, then make it. If they do not want tea, don't make them drink tea and don't get annoyed at them for not wanting tea."* . . . *"Some people may change their mind about tea, so don't make them drink the tea."* . . . *"If they are unconscious don't ask them if they want tea."*. . . *"Whether it's tea or sex, consent is everything."*

on-again off-again girlfriend by screaming that *"she is a slut and is nothing without him."* Focus groups found that students endorsed common concerns consistent with both the **SMB** and **TPB**. The researchers suggest that to model effective bystander decision-making, bystander-based prevention programs need to address bystander concerns such as: *"What do you think might happen if a student confronted the man?" "What good things might come out of it?" "Whose opinion would influence you the most about what you would decide to do?"* and *"What do you think is the single most important thing that adults need to understand about what factors impact student's willingness to intervene in relationship violence?"* (Casey, Lindhorst, & Storer, 2017).

Strengthen Intentions Using Revised TPB

In general, bystanders who report greater perceived behavioral control, more supportive subjective norms, and more positive attitudes about helping tend to show a greater intent to intervene when confronted with a sexual assault scenario (Hoxmeier et al., 2016). Typically, women also report stronger attitudes, subjective norms, and perceived behavioral control to engage in bystander intervention in high-risk sexual situations (Hackman, Branscum, Rush Griffin, et al., 2022).

To further predict intentions to help, a revised version of the **TPB** (Fishbein & Ajzen, 2010) may be useful. According to the revised model (referred to as the **reasoned action approach**; **RAA**), the three antecedent factors that determine the intention to do a behavior can each be split into two components: personal attitudes include an instrumental (*"how practical is the behavior?"*) and experiential component (*"how do I feel about doing the behavior?"*); social norms include a descriptive (*"what do other people typically do?"*) and injunctive (*"what should other people do?"*) component; and the degree of self-efficacy can be broken down into autonomy (*"how responsible do I feel to do the behavior?"*) and capacity (*"how confident am I that I can do the behavior?"*)

Let's apply this revised **RAA** model to predict whether a bystander would intervene during a sexual assault. To increase the likelihood of becoming an active responder, a bystander must believe that: *"My intervening to prevent sexual assault would be good for the community"* (instrumental attitude), *"My intervening to prevent sexual assault would make me feel good about myself"* (experiential attitude), *"Most of my peers would intervene to prevent sexual assault"* (descriptive norm), *"Most of my peers think people should intervene to prevent sexual assault"* (injunctive norm), *"Intervening to prevent sexual assault is my responsibility"* (autonomy), and *"Even if it is* *difficult, I still think I could intervene to prevent sexual assault"* (capacity) (Lukacena, Reynolds-Tylus, & Quick, 2019).

It is also important to realize that certain components may be stronger predictors of whether someone intervenes to stop a sexual assault. As we know, men's perceptions of their peers' attitudes about sexual assault are often stronger predictors of whether they will help a potential victim than their own attitudes (Brown & Messman-Moore, 2010). Further, researchers found that instrumental attitudes, descriptive norms, and capacity for self-efficacy were the strongest predictors of helping during a sexual assault (Lukacena et al., 2019). This implies that when designing an effective bystander intervention program, it would be best to include narratives of students who successfully intervened and how they believed it helped the college community, highlight that the number of students actively responding is on the rise, and provide training that increases a sense of responsibility and confidence.

Evidence-Based Bystander Intervention Programs for Sexual Misconduct

Broadly speaking, bystander intervention programs aim to reframe sexual assault as a community issue, empower bystanders to be active responders who stand up to prevent sexual assault, and seek to change social norms that contribute to the prevalence of sexual violence. To increase efficacy, these programs provide bystanders with strategies for intervening in a variety of situations ranging from hearing a friend tell an inappropriate joke about sexual assault to witnessing an individual attempting to take a visibly intoxicated person to a secluded location (Banyard et al., 2014). Key strategies used in many of these programs include: a shift in focus from top-down enforcement to active bystander responding, using a social media marketing approach, and correcting misconceptions of common "hooking up" norms (Wooley & Stubbs, n.d.).

Several meta-analyses have found that bystander intervention programs (e.g., **"Bringing in the Bystander," MVP, Green Dot**) have been successful at changing attitudes and behavioral intentions. For example, one program conducted with American college students reported higher bystander efficacy (e.g., *"I feel confident I would walk a friend who has had too much to drink home from a party")* and greater willingness to help others at risk (e.g., *"I would be more willing to think through the pros and cons of different ways I might help if I see an instance of sexual violence")* relative to untrained controls. Although there was evidence that these programs also increased actual bystander helping behaviors (e.g., *"I said something when I heard someone say 'she deserved to be raped'"*), these effects tended to be smaller. Based on their findings, the researchers concluded that, *"bystander education programs for sexual assault prevention offer a positive, empowering solution to a difficult, controversial problem,"* however they also warned, *"it remains unclear to what degree bystander education truly prevents sexual assaults"* (Katz & Moore, 2013, p. 1065). Likewise, a team of British researchers concluded that bystander programs *"can change norms and attitudes (around 'rape myths' and the acceptability of perpetrator behavior), and self-reported feelings of efficacy, empowerment, willingness to intervene, and intentions to intervene. However, the evidence that this actually impacts on real-life intervention; or is responsible for a reduction in sexual assaults and violence, is much less strong"* (Levine, Philpot, & Kovalenko, 2020, p. 279). To deal with this problem, behavioral problems may require more behavioral solutions such as changing physical features of the environment (e.g., introducing more common social spaces to reduce sexual violence on campus) (Porat et al., 2024). Thus, more research is needed to determine whether the skills learned in bystander programs are effectively being used in actual bystander intervention situations (Evans, Burroughs, & Knowlden, 2019).

Taking that into account, what follows are evidenced-based bystander programs that have been shown to be effective in increasing the *willingness* to intervene in real-world sexual assault situations.

Bringing in the Bystander®

The **Bringing in the Bystander®** program (https://www.soteriasolutions.org/bringing-in-the-bystander) trains bystanders how to safely intervene when confronting sexual and relational violence. The objectives of the program include: identifying the range of unacceptable sexual behaviors, gaining an understanding of situational factors that inhibit/facilitate appropriate bystander intervention, and increasing bystander responsibility (Banyard et al., 2014). In one study, sorority members from an American university participating in the program showed higher self-efficacy, a greater likelihood to intervene as a bystander, and an increased sense of responsibility to intervene in comparison to a control group (Moynihan, Banyard, Arnold, et al., 2011). A larger, systematic review also found consistent evidence of effectiveness for in-person programs such as Bringing in the Bystander (Mujal, Taylor,

Fry, et al., 2019). Combining the Bring the Bystander program with the **TPB**, Chinese college students showed positive changes in subjective norms and self-efficacy, which, in turn, led to increased bystander intervention intention and actual behavior (Chen, Huang, & Jiang, 2022). Currently, more than 500 colleges and organizations across the world have used this program.

Green Dot

The **Green Dot** program (https://alteristic.org/services/green-dot/) is a bystander intervention training designed to prevent sexual and dating violence on college campuses. The Green Dot program seeks to empower potential bystanders to actively engage in both proactive responses (e.g., defusing the situation before things escalate), and reactive responses (e.g., immediately supporting victims). The program also incorporates the three D's of intervention (Direct, Delegate, Distract). **Direct** involves calmly letting the harasser know that what they are doing is wrong (e.g., *"She looks upset. Why don't you leave her alone?"*); **Delegate** involves asking others to join in helping; and **Distract** involves safely de-escalating the problem, often by creating a diversion (Coker, Fisher, Bush, et al., 2015).[5] Relative to people who did not get the Green Dot training, college students from the United States (Coker et al., 2015) and New Zealand employees at a healthcare facility (Kuntz & Searle, 2023) reported significantly lower victimization rates and displayed more bystander behaviors when confronting real cases of sexual assault.

Know Your Power®

Know Your Power® (https://www.unh.edu/research/prevention-innovations-research-center/evidence-based-initiatives/know-your-powerr-bystander-social-marketing-campaign) is a social marketing campaign designed to raise awareness about sexual and relationship violence by using posters of college students modeling active bystander behaviors in high-risk situations (Potter, 2012). One important focus of the program is to create posters that strengthen identification within peer group members (i.e., recognize themselves in others) (Potter et al., 2011). Researchers implementing this social marketing campaign on an American university campus found that posters made

---

5 *One female student recommends using the "tampon trick" for disrupting an awkward interaction by telling the target she has the tampon she asked for earlier (Koumpilova, 2019).

descriptive norms more salient and were effective in increasing student's willingness to get involved in sexual violence on campus (Potter, 2012).

"It's Your Place"

Using the **TPB** as a conceptual framework, **"It's Your Place"** is a large-scale social marketing campaign tested on one American college campus. The campaign uses multiple channels to increase bystander intervention including posting flyers on campus with sexual assault reporting locations, placing posters on campus with messages such as *"It's your place to prevent sexual assault: You're not ruining a good time"*, contacting local businesses to display the It's Your Place logo on their store windows, and distributing postcards with QR codes linked to social media (#ItsYourPlace). To strengthen attitudes and perceived behavioral control, the link includes daily campaign messages, testimonials, a series of scenarios showing how a situation may escalate to a sexual assault without proper bystander intervention, and safe and appropriate ways to intervene. Compared to students unfamiliar with the campaign, students familiar with the campaign showed an increased willingness (about 10 percent more) to prevent a sexual assault from occurring (Sundstrom et al., 2018).

Men's Workshop

The **Men's Workshop** (https://cultureofrespect.org/program/mens-workshop/) is a bystander intervention education programs geared toward providing accurate descriptive and injunctive norms regarding sexual violence. In order to undermine traditional conceptions of masculinity, men are encouraged to share their discomfort with aspects of the male gender role script and work together to generate alternatives that are more positive and appropriate (Berkowitz, 2010). After participating in this program, first-year college men from an American university were more likely to believe they would choose to actively respond to high-risk sexual situations that they would have ignored previously (Gidycz, Orchowski, & Berkowitz, 2011). One systematic review on bystander training programs found evidence of effectiveness for in-person programs that used active learning exercises such as Men's Workshop (Mujal et al., 2019), while another review found bystander training programs geared toward men helped men to see that masculinity is not incompatible with helping others and was also effective in reducing rape-supportive attitudes (Katz & Moore, 2013).

"Mentors in Violence Prevention" (MVP)

The MVP program (https://mvpstrat.com/about/) is designed to raise awareness about the level of men's violence against women and empower them to intervene. The program encourages male student athletes and leaders to be role models in violence prevention. Educational programs led by student leaders involve skits/discussions with the goal of: dissociating masculinity from dominance, dispelling myths about rape, and modeling acceptable forms of social interaction (Katz, 1995; O'Brien, 2001). By focusing on men as potential bystanders rather than as potential perpetrators of sexual violence, MVP helps to reduce defensiveness in men while also emphasizing that *"when men don't speak up or take action in the face of other men's abusive behavior toward women, that constitutes implicit consent of such behavior"* (Katz, 1995, p. 168).

TakeCARE

TakeCARE is a video bystander program that uses relevant scenarios to help prevent sexual violence on college campuses. In one scenario, bystanders are trained to discourage a friend from "hooking up" with someone who is clearly intoxicated. The narrator uses the phrase "TakeCARE" where CARE stands for successful bystander behavior: C—*Confident* that they can help their friends avoid risky situations, A—*Aware* that their friends could get hurt in these types of situations, R—*Responsible* for helping, and, E—*Effective* in how they help. Students from two large American universities who participated in TakeCARE reported more prosocial attitudes about sexual violence, engaging in more bystander behavior on behalf of friends, and greater self-efficacy, compared to students in the control group. (Jouriles, McDonald, Rosenfield, et al., 2016). Although program effects diminished over time, meaningful changes persisted for at least three months following program participation (Jouriles, Krauss, Vu, et al., 2018).

Single-User Virtual Reality Training

Since **#MeToo**, companies have begun incorporating bystander intervention training using new technology such as single-user 360-degree immersive virtual reality. Some advantages of this method is that it provides learners a safe place to make mistakes without facing ridicule from coworkers, and it provides a virtual reality that can help future bystanders recognize contextual nuances that might otherwise be hard to detect (Rawski, Foster, & Bailenson, 2022). In one study, students from an American university using immersive VR technology watched as a man took lurid pictures of a woman without her consent. A bystander then modeled various response options (e.g., confronting the harasser, offering support to the target). Students using the immersive technology reported an increased willingness to intervene in future sexual harassment incidents (Rawski et al., 2022).

Booster Sessions

Several systematic reviews on the effectiveness of bystander intervention programs have found that although the programs tend to show a significant impact on bystander attitudes and willingness to help, whether they actually make a lasting change on a bystander's behavior has not been well established (Evans et al., 2019; Katz & Moore, 2013). In addition, reviews have found that the positive effects of bystander intervention programs may diminish over time (Kettrey & Marx, 2019). To establish whether the programs lead to actual changes in behavior, researchers need to look at post-intervention bystander behavior. To establish successful long-term outcomes, one solution may be to add booster sessions.

In one study, researchers administered a follow-up (booster) session 2 months after implementing the prevention program. For the booster session, participants watched a powerful skit performed by a campus theater troupe depicting a survivor of sexual assault asking for help from other actors with blindfolds who ignore her request. Following this skit, the facilitator led participants in an open-ended discussion about what they remembered from the prevention program. Results from the booster session revealed that students increased prosocial attitudes toward preventing sexual violence and also were considerably more aware of the community-wide social marketing campaign (e.g., images displayed on academic buildings, dining facilities, residence hall lobbies, bathroom stalls) that was happening concurrently (Banyard, Potter, Cares, et al., 2018).

> ### "What Can Bystanders Do?"
> Based on research incorporating the **SMB** and **TPB**, there are several practical strategies you can do to become an active responder the next time you encounter a potential sexual assault scenario including:

- understanding that sexual assault may be camouflaged by the campus drinking culture
- avoiding victim-blaming, especially in cases where the victim was intoxicated
- becoming educated about rape myths such as women have "secret rape fantasies," women who dress provocatively are "asking for it," and women are socialized to give "token resistance"
- realizing that sexual assault is also common in the LGBT+ community
- learning to identify red flags at the pre-assault phase such as: physically isolating the person from their friends, plying the person with alcohol, or taking a clearly intoxicated person back to their room
- proactively preventing a sexual assault by never leaving a friend alone at a party even if she insists everything will be OK or reminding male friends that if a person is intoxicated or wasted they cannot grant consent to have sex
- practicing simple messages when confronting the instigator such as *"That's not cool"* or *"Sorry, she's too intoxicated to provide consent"*
- realizing that intervening to prevent sexual assault is your responsibility, even when nobody else seems concerned

"What Can Public Health Educators Do?"

Based on research incorporating the **SMB** and **TPB**, there are several additional practical strategies (beyond those above) that health practitioners can do when designing programs to get bystanders to confront sexual assault scenarios including:

- avoid creating defensiveness and victim-blaming by depicting sexual violence as a community problem, rather than an individual (often male) problem
- approaching people as potential allies rather than as potential victims or potential perpetrators
- debunking common rape myths and countering benevolent sexist beliefs

- addressing the full continuum of behaviors from relatively low-risk behaviors (e.g., ogling, sexually degrading language) to high-risk markers leading up to the assault (e.g., physically isolating victims, sharing with peers their plans of sexual misconduct)
- emphasizing the costs of not helping (e.g., the impact could be devastating) and how they outweigh the social costs of helping (e.g., awkwardness)
- developing moral courage, even in the face of potential social risks
- correcting the misperception that most men do not want to get involved in sexual assault situations
- challenging deep-seated masculinity norms such as men should not block another man's "sexual conquest"
- emphasizing to men that helping in these cases is heroic (not weak or unmanly)
- showing men how "locker-room talk" can perpetuate misogynistic peer norms that deter other men from actively responding to sexual assault scenarios
- adding booster sessions to establish successful long-term outcomes of bystander intervention

Summary

Bystanders are in the unique position to help people encountering sexual misconduct. When bystanders proactively intervene on behalf of the target, they can successfully prevent a sexual assault from occurring. To become an active responder, bystanders must learn to recognize warning signs of sexual assault and become aware of unique barriers that preclude helping. Bystanders also need to know that sexual assault may be camouflaged by the campus drinking culture as well as powerful masculinity norms. For positive change to occur, bystander programs must avoid creating defensiveness and victim-blaming, debunk common rape myths and benevolent sexist beliefs, challenge deep-seated masculinity norms such as men should not block another man's "sexual conquest," and strengthen intentions to intervene. Currently, there are many evidence-based bystander intervention programs effectively incorporating the **SMB** and **TPB** models. In the next chapter, we will examine effective strategies bystanders and diversity educators can use to combat various forms of discrimination.

References

Aslam, F. (2017, October 29). *Harvey Weinstein and the bystander effect: How sexual predators persist in a conspiracy of silence.* Retrieved from https://www.hongkongfp.com/2017/10/29/harvey-weinstein-bystander-effect-sexual-predators-persist-conspiracy-silence/

Bannon, R. S., Brosi, M. W., & Foubert, J. D. (2013). Sorority women's and fraternity men's rape myth acceptance and bystander intervention attitudes. *Journal of Student Affairs Research and Practice, 50,* 72–87.

Banyard, V. L. (2008). Measurement and correlates of prosocial bystander behavior: The case of interpersonal violence. *Violence and Victims, 23,* 83–97.

Banyard, V. L., Moynihan, M. M., Cares, A. C., & Warner, R. (2014). How do we know if it works? Measuring outcomes in bystander-focused abuse prevention on campuses. *Psychology of Violence, 4,* 101–115.

Banyard, V. L., Moynihan, M. M., & Plante, E. G. (2007). Sexual violence prevention through bystander education: An experimental evaluation. *Journal of Community Psychology, 35,* 463–481.

Banyard, V., Potter, S. J., Cares, A. C., et al. (2018). Multiple sexual violence prevention tools: Doses and boosters. *Journal of Aggression, Conflict and Peace Research, 10,* 145–155.

Basile, K. C., Smith, S. G., Kresnow, M., et al. (2022). *The national intimate partner and sexual violence survey: 2016/2017 Report on sexual violence.* National Center for Injury Prevention and Control, Centers for Disease Control and Prevention.

Baumert, A., Halmburger, A., & Schmitt, M. (2013). Interventions against norm violations: Dispositional determinants of self-reported and real moral courage. *Personality and Social Psychology Bulletin, 39,* 1053–1068.

Bennett, S., Banyard, V. L., & Garnhart, L. (2014). To act or not to act, that is the question? Barriers and facilitators of bystander intervention. *Journal of Interpersonal Violence, 29,* 476–496.

Berkowitz, A. D. (1994). A model acquaintance rape prevention program for men. In A. D. Berkowitz (Ed.), *Men and rape: Theory, research and prevention programs in higher education* (pp. 35–42). Jossey-Bass.

Berkowitz, A. D. (2009). *Response ability: Complete guide on bystander behavior.* Beck.

Berkowitz, A. D. (2010). Fostering healthy norms to prevent violence and abuse: The social norms approach. In K. L. Kaufman (Ed.), *The prevention of sexual violence: A practitioner's sourcebook* (pp. 147–171). NEARI Press

Blavos, A. A., Glassman, T., Sheu, J. J., et al. (2014). Using the Health Belief Model to predict bystander behavior among college students. *Journal of Student Affairs Research and Practice, 51,* 420–432.

Breitenbecher, K. H. (2000). Sexual assault on college campuses: Is an ounce of prevention enough? *Applied and Preventative Psychology, 9,* 23–52.

Brown, A. L., & Messman-Moore, T. L. (2010). Personal and perceived peer attitudes supporting sexual aggression as predictors of male college students' willingness to intervene against sexual aggression. *Journal of Interpersonal Violence, 25,* 503–517.

Brownmiller, S. (1975). *Against our will: Men, women, and rape.* Simon and Schuster.

Burn, S. M. (2009). A situational model of sexual assault prevention through bystander education. *Sex Roles, 60,* 779–792.

Burn, S. M. (2017). Appeal to bystander interventions: A normative approach to health and risk messaging. In R. Parrot (Ed.), *The encyclopedia of health and risk message design and processing* (pp. 140–155). Oxford University Press.

Burt, M. R. (1980). Cultural myths and supports of rape. *Journal of Personality and Social Psychology, 38,* 217.

Cares, A. C., Banyard, V. L., Moynihan, M. M., et al. (2015). Changing attitudes about being a bystander to violence: Translating an in-person education program to a new campus. *Violence Against Women, 21,* 165–187.

Carlson, M. (2008). I'd rather go along and be considered a man: Masculinity and bystander intervention. *Journal of Men's Studies, 16,* 3–17.

Casey, E. A., Lindhorst, T. P., & Storer, H. L. (2017). The situational-cognitive model of adolescent bystander behavior: Modeling bystander decision making in the context of bullying and teen dating violence. *Psychology of Violence, 7,* 33–44.

Casey, E. A., & Ohler, K. (2012). Being a positive bystander: Male antiviolence allies' experiences of stepping up. *Journal of Interpersonal Violence, 27,* 62–83.

Chen, H., Huang, Q., & Jiang, M. (2022). Empowering Chinese college students to prevent sexual assault in post-MeToo era: An empirical study of the bystander intervention approach. *Journal of Interpersonal Violence, 37,* 449–472.

Chen, J., Walters, M. L., Gilbert, L. K., & Patel, N. (2020). Sexual violence, stalking, and intimate partner violence by sexual orientation, United States. *Psychology of Violence, 10,* 110–119.

Coker, A. L., Fisher, B. S., Bush, H. M., et al. (2015). Evaluation of the Green Dot bystander intervention to reduce interpersonal violence among college students across three campuses. *Violence Against Women, 12,* 1507–1527.

Deitch-Stackhouse, J., Kenneavy, K., Thayer, R., et al. (2015) The influence of social norms on advancement through bystander stages for preventing interpersonal violence. *Violence Against Women, 21,* 1284–1307.

Evans, J. L., Burroughs, M. E., & Knowlden, A. P. (2019). Examining the efficacy of bystander sexual violence interventions for first-year college students: A systematic review. *Aggression and Violent Behavior, 48,* 72–82.

Fabiano, P., Perkins, H. W., Berkowitz, A. D., et al. (2003). Engaging men as social justice allies in ending violence against women: Evidence for a social norms approach. *Journal of American College Health, 52,* 105–112.

Farrow, R. (2017, October 10). From aggressive overtures to sexual assault: Harvey Weinstein's accusers tell their stories. *The New Yorker.*

Faul, M., Aikman, S. N., & Sasser, S. M. (2016). Bystander intervention prior to the arrival of emergency medical services: Comparing assistance across types of medical emergencies. *Prehospital Emergency Care, 20,* 317–323.

Fedina, L., Holmes, J. L., & Backes, B. L. (2018). Campus sexual assault: A systematic review of prevalence research from 2000 to 2015. *Trauma, Violence, & Abuse, 19,* 76–93.

Fishbein, M., & Ajzen, I. (2010). *Predicting and changing behavior: The reasoned action approach.* Psychology Press.

Fleming, M., (2017, October 16). 'Beautiful Girls' scribe Scott Rosenberg on a complicated legacy with Harvey Weinstein. Retrieved from https://deadline.com/2017/10/scott-rosenberg-harvey-weinstein-miramax-beautiful-girls-guilt-over-sexual-assault-allegations-1202189525/

Fleming, W. M., & Wiersma-Mosley, J. D. (2015). The role of alcohol consumption patterns and pro-social bystander interventions in contexts of gender violence. *Violence Against Women, 21,* 1259–1283.

Gidycz, C. A., Orchowski, L. M., & Berkowitz, A. D. (2011). Preventing sexual aggression among college men: An evaluation of a social norms and bystander intervention program. *Violence Against Women, 17,* 720–742.

Goodwin, R., Graham, J., & Diekmann, K. A. (2020). Good intentions aren't good enough: Moral courage in opposing sexual harassment. *Journal of Experimental Social Psychology, 86.*

Hackman, C. L., Branscum, P., Rush Griffin, S., et al. (2022). Gender differences in bystander intervention intentions to prevent sexual assault: A reasoned action approach. *Journal of School Violence, 21,* 237-251.

Hoxmeier, J. C., Flay, B. R., & Acock, A. C. (2016). Control, norms, and attitudes: Differences between students who do and do not intervene as bystanders to sexual assault. *Journal of Interpersonal Violence, 33,* 2379–2401.

Jouriles, E. N., Krauss, A., Vu, N. L., et al. (2018). Bystander programs addressing sexual violence on college campuses: A systematic review and meta-analysis of program outcomes and delivery methods. *Journal of American College Health, 66,* 457–466.

Jouriles, E. N., McDonald, R., Rosenfield, D., et al. (2016). TakeCARE, a video bystander program to help prevent sexual violence on college campuses: Results of two randomized, controlled trials. *Psychology of Violence, 6,* 410–420.

Kaiser, C. R., Bandt-Law, B., Cheek, N. N., & Schachtman, R. (2022). Gender prototypes shape perceptions of and responses to sexual harassment. *Current Directions in Psychological Science, 31,* 254–261.

Katz, J. (1995). Reconstructing masculinity in the locker room: The Mentors in Violence Prevention project. *Harvard Educational Review, 65,* 163–174.

Katz, J., Heisterkamp, H. A., & Fleming, W. M. (2011). The social justice roots of the Mentors in Violence Prevention model and its application in a high school setting. *Violence Against Women, 17,* 684–702.

Katz, J., & Moore, J. (2013). Bystander education training for campus sexual assault prevention: An initial meta-analysis. *Violence and Victims, 28,* 1054–1067.

Katz, J., Pazienza, R., Olin, R., & Rich, H. (2014). That's what friends are for: Bystander responses to friends or strangers at risk for party rape victimization. *Journal of Interpersonal Violence, 30,* 2775–2792.

Kettrey, H. H., & Marx, R. A. (2019). The effects of bystander programs on the prevention of sexual assault across the college years: A systematic review and meta-analysis. *Journal of Youth and Adolescence, 48,* 212–227.

Kilmartin, C., Smith, S., Green, A., et al. (2008). A real time social norms intervention to reduce male sexism. *Sex Roles, 59,* 264–273.

Koumpilova, M. (2019, January 20). University of Minnesota focuses on enlisting bystanders to fight sexual assault. *Star Tribune.*

Kuntz, J. C., & Searle, F. (2023) Does bystander intervention training work? When employee intentions and organizational barriers collide. *Journal of Interpersonal Violence, 38,* 2934–2956

Lazarus, K., & Signal, T. (2013). Who will help in situations of intimate partner violence: Exploring personal attitudes and bystander behaviours. *International Journal of Criminology and Sociology, 2,* 199–209.

Leading with empathy: Tarana Burke and the making of the Me Too Movement. (2020, November 16). HKS Case Program.

Leone, R. M., & Parrott, D. J. (2019). Misogynistic peers, masculinity, and bystander intervention for sexual aggression: Is it really just "locker room talk?" *Aggressive Behavior, 45,* 42–51.

Levine, M., Philpot, R., & Kovalenko, A. G. (2020). Rethinking the bystander effect in violence reduction training programs. *Social Issues and Policy Review, 14,* 273–296.

Levine, R. M., Prosser, A., Evans, D., & Reicher, S. D. (2005). Identity and emergency intervention: How social group membership and inclusiveness of group boundaries shape helping behavior. *Personality and Social Psychology Bulletin, 31,* 443–453.

Lonsway, K., Banyard, V., Berkowitz, A. D., et al. (2009). *Rape prevention and risk reduction: Review of the research literature for practitioners.* VAWnet, a project of the National Resource Center on Domestic Violence and the Pennsylvania Coalition Against Domestic Violence.

Lukacena, K. M., Reynolds-Tylus, T., & Quick, B. L. (2019). An application of the reasoned action approach to bystander intervention for sexual assault. *Health Communication, 34,* 46–53.

Mainwaring, C., Gabbert, F., & Scott, A. J. (2023). A systematic review exploring variables related to bystander intervention in sexual violence contexts. *Trauma, Violence, & Abuse, 24,* 1727–1742.

McMahon, S., & Banyard, V. L. (2012). When can I help? A conceptual framework for the prevention of sexual violence through bystander intervention. *Trauma, Violence, & Abuse, 13,* 3–14.

McMahon, S., Postmus, J., & Koenick, R. (2011). Conceptualizing the engaging bystander approach to sexual violence prevention on college campuses. *Journal of College Student Development, 52,* 115–130.

Moynihan, M. M., Banyard, V. L., Arnold, J. S., et al. (2011). Sisterhood may be powerful for reducing sexual and intimate partner violence: An evaluation of the bringing in the bystander in-person program with sorority members. *Violence Against Women, 17,* 703–719.

Mujal, G. N., Taylor, M. E., Fry, J. L., et al. (2019). A systematic review of bystander interventions for the prevention of sexual violence. *Trauma, Violence, & Abuse, 22,* 381–396.

Nickerson, A. B., Aloe, A. M., Livingston, J. A., & Feeley, T. H. (2014). Measurement of the bystander intervention model for bullying and sexual harassment. *Journal of Adolescence, 37,* 391–400.

O'Brien, J. (2001). The MVP program: Focus on student-athletes. *Sexual Violence on Campus,* 141–161.

Oesterle, D. W., Orchowski, L. M., Moreno, O., & Berkowitz, A. (2018). A qualitative analysis of bystander intervention among heavy-drinking college men. *Violence Against Women, 24,* 1207–1231.

Piliavin, J. A., & Piliavin, I. M. (1972). Effect of blood on reactions to a victim. *Journal of Personality and Social Psychology, 23,* 353–361.

Planty, M. (2002). *Third-party involvement in violent crime, 1993–1999* (Report No. NCJ 189100). U.S. Department of Justice.

"Police: As many as 20 present at gang rape outside school dance." (2009, October 28). CNN.

Porat, R., Gantman, A., Green, S. A., et al. (2024). Preventing sexual violence: A behavioral problem without a behaviorally informed solution. *Psychological Science in the Public Interest, 25,* 4–29.

Potter, S. J. (2012). Using a multimedia social marketing campaign to increase active bystanders on the college campus. *Journal of American College Health, 60,* 282–295.

Potter, S. J., Moynihan, M. M., & Stapleton, J. G. (2011). Using social self-identification in social marketing materials aimed at reducing violence against women on campus. *Journal of Interpersonal Violence, 26,* 971–990.

"Powerful men confronted as 'Weinstein effect' goes global." (2017, November 14). CBS News. Associated Press.

Rawski, S. L., Foster, J. R., & Bailenson, J. (2022). Sexual harassment bystander training effectiveness: Experimentally comparing 2D video to virtual reality practice. *Technology, Mind, and Behavior, 3,* 1-20.

Robinson, S. R., Casiano, A., & Elias-Lambert, N. (2022) "Is it my responsibility?": A qualitative review of university students' perspectives on bystander behavior. *Trauma, Violence, & Abuse, 23,* 117–131.

Sand, N. (2017, October 17). The full list of Harvey Weinstein accusers includes fledgling actresses and Hollywood royalty. *Los Angeles Times.*

Sundstrom, B., Ferrara, M., DeMaria, A. L., et al. (2018). It's your place: Development and evaluation of an evidence-based bystander intervention campaign. *Health Communication, 33,* 1141–1150.

Tabachnick, J. (2009). *Engaging bystanders in sexual violence prevention.* National Sexual Violence Resource Center.

van Bavel, J. J., Packer, D. J., & Cunningham, W. A. (2011). Modulation of the fusiform face area following minimal exposure to motivationally relevant faces: Evidence of in-group enhancement (not out-group disregard). *Journal of Cognitive Neuroscience, 23,* 3343–3354.

Vega, C. (2009, November 12). *Richmond rape witness describes the assault.* ABC News.

Weidman, A. C., Sowden, W. J., Berg, M., & Kross, E. (2020). Punish or protect? How close relationships shape responses to moral violations. *Personality and Social Psychology Bulletin, 46,* 693–708.

Weisz, A. N., & Black, B. M. (2008). Peer intervention in dating violence: Beliefs of African-American middle school adolescents. *Journal of Ethnic and Cultural Diversity in Social Work, 17,* 177–196.

Wooley, L., & Stubbs, H. (n.d.). *Engaging the healthy majority: An examination of bystander intervention approaches for alcohol and sexual assault prevention.* https://everfi.com/wp-content/uploads/2017/04/Engaging-the-Healthy-Majority.pdf

Workman, J. E., & Freeburn, E. W. (1999). An examination of date rape, victim dress, and perceiver variables within the context of attribution theory. *Sex Roles, 41,* 261–278.

Wrightson-Hester, A. R., Allan, A., & Allan, M. M. (2022). "I'm not batman" and other factors impacting bystander intervention against sexual violence in Australian nightlife settings. *Analyses of Social Issues and Public Policy, 22,* 669–693.

Yule, K., Hoxmeier, J. C., Petranu, K., & Grych, J. (2020). The chivalrous bystander: The role of gender-based beliefs and empathy on bystander behavior and perceived barriers to intervention. *Journal of Interpersonal Violence, 37,* 863–888.

Confronting Bias

7

Key Terms in This Chapter 153

Problems When Encountering Bias 155

Confronting Bias 162
  Applying SMB 162
  Applying TPB 167

Summary 174

Key Terms in This Chapter

aversive racism: both an unconscious avoidance of marginalized groups and a very active denial of such avoidance
code-switching: adjusting style of speech, appearance, and behavior to increase one's chances of being hired, accepted, or promoted
color-blind racial ideology: position that the best way to minimize group differences is by ignoring them (e.g., "I don't see color.")

cultural openness: extent to which an individual is open to, and interested in, the similarities and differences between their own and other groups

discrimination: unfair treatment of others based on their group membership (e.g., race, gender, religion, sexual orientation)

diversity (anti-bias) training: training designed to improve peoples' cultural understanding, knowledge, and interaction with marginalized groups

false consensus: overestimating the number of others who agree with your beliefs

interpersonal racism: biased interactions between people

mindfulness: receptive attention to present-moment experiences

moral licensing: when people do something good, they may feel more permitted to do something bad afterward

pluralistic ignorance: incorrectly assuming that others are thinking and feeling the same as us

precarious manhood: idea that manhood is a fleeting state that must be constantly earned because it can be lost or taken away

prejudice: prejudging people based on their group membership

recategorization: create an inclusive category of "we" by redefining boundaries of "us" vs. "them"

rubber hand illusion: watching a rubber hand being stroked synchronously with one's own unseen hand causes the rubber hand to be attributed to one's own body

situational model of bystander intervention (SMB): proposes that bystanders typically go through a series of five decision-making steps before help will be given

social referencing: seeking out someone from one's in-group to understand an event

sympathetic empathy: caring about another person's distress and wanting to help in some way

systemic racism: unfair practices within a system such as school, law, housing, etc.

theory of planned behavior (TPB): proposes that the intent to do a behavior depends on three antecedent factors: one's *personal attitude* toward the behavior, the perceived *subjective norms* that relevant others hold about the behavior, and the degree of *perceived behavioral control* (i.e., self-efficacy) one has to do the behavior

zero-tolerance policies: severe disciplinary actions in response to specific types of misbehavior, regardless of the context of the improper behavior

Problems When Encountering Bias

Defining the Problem

I've been called the n-word more than 100 times. All the time. From little kids, and grownups sitting right next to them didn't say anything.
—Baseball player Torii Hunter on fan abuse and the fact nobody challenged the racist chants. (Mazza, 2020)

Prejudice involves prejudging people based on their group membership, while **discrimination** refers to unfair treatment of others based on their group membership (e.g., race, gender, religion, sexual orientation). These types of bias range from subtle (often unintentional) comments to offensive jokes/slurs and more blatant forms of mistreatment like the vivid example described in the quote above. Although many people believe that discrimination is a thing of the past, contemporary research shows a high level of bias still exists today. For example, trends in hiring discrimination have remained stagnant. One US study found that compared to a White applicant, a non-White applicant must submit 30 percent more applications to get a call-back (Quillian & Lee, 2023). Likewise, a field study in the United States investigating racial discrimination in high-end retail stores found that salespersons showed higher levels of suspicion (e.g., staring, following) when dealing with Black customers, especially Black males shopping in groups (Schreer, Smith, & Thomas, 2009).

Discrimination is also prevalent in the justice system. When using actual felony criminal photos of Black and White offenders, researchers found that the more Afrocentric features the offender had (e.g., dark skin, wide nose, full lips), the harsher the sentence (on average, 7–8 months longer for same crime) (Blair, Judd, & Chapleau, 2004). Relatedly, Black college students attending predominantly White institutions in the United States report encountering high levels of racially offensive posts on social media attempting to justify excessive use of force and violence by law enforcement against unarmed Black people (Hurd, Trawalter, Jakubow, et al., 2022).

Racial discrimination has even been found in hospital settings. In one study, White doctors from American hospitals showed similar verbal communication patterns when discussing end-of-life care with Black and White patients; however, the doctors tended to show fewer rapport-building nonverbal cues (such as open posture, touch, closeness) with Black patients, which not coincidentally, led Black patients to choose less effective treatment options (Elliott, Alexander, Mescher, et al., 2016). Likewise, a substantial number White doctors and interns show a racial bias in pain assessment (specifically, Black people have a higher pain tolerance). This racial bias has been associated with biased treatment toward Black patients by dismissing complaints of pain and underprescribing pain medication (Hoffman, Trawalter, Axt, & Oliver, 2016).

These repeated slights and unfair treatment can take a heavy toll. Those experiencing repeated incidents of bias often report an increase in mental and physical health problems, social withdrawal, mistrust, fear, an undermining of their sense of belonging, lower job satisfaction, and drops in academic and work performance (Benner, Wang, Chen, & Boyle, 2022; Dessel, Goodman, & Woodford, 2017; Hurd et al., 2022; Kroeper, Sanchez, & Himmelstein, 2014). Even though an inappropriate comment may have been unintentional, these slights can have long-term negative consequences. For example, women from an American university asked to keep diaries reported one to two sexist incidents per week (e.g., gender role stereotypes, demeaning comments, sexual objectification) and these events, in turn, negatively affected their psychological well-being by intensifying their feelings of anger and depression, and decreasing their self-esteem (Swim, Hyers, Cohen, & Ferguson, 2001).

To manage everyday discrimination, People of Color (PoC) ore often forced to use compensatory strategies in order to fit in and be accepted. One common strategy is racial **code-switching**—adjusting one's style of speech, appearance, and behavior to increase one's chances of being hired, accepted, or promoted. Racial code-switching requires marginalized employees to "suppress their cultural identity" (e.g., talk more "White," smile more, or avoid natural hairstyles). This sort of prejudice can become so normalized in organizations that Black employees who engage in racial code-switching are often seen as more professional by both Black and White employers compared to those who elect not to code-switch (McCluney, Durkee, Smith II, et al., 2021; Richeson & Shelton, 2007). Importantly, the extra effort needed to be accepted by mainstream society can be emotionally exhausting. As one Black professional lamented, *"I find myself constantly trying to be aware of my mannerisms to ensure that I don't portray myself or the people I represent in a negative light"* (Melaku, Beeman, Smith, & Johnson, 2020).

Discrimination can also negatively affect physical well-being. For example, studies have found that the cumulative effects of racism-related stress in Black people tends to increase physiological stress, weaken the immune system, and elevate cortisol levels, which are all risk factors for coronary heart disease (Lepore, Revenson, Weinberger, et al., 2006; Pieterse & Carter, 2007). Likewise, Black women from the United States who experienced more race-based discrimination during their pregnancy also reported higher levels of late pregnancy distress, which increased their odds of getting post-partum depression (Weeks, Zapata, Rohan, & Green, 2022) and also led to adverse pregnancy outcomes in the newborn child such as attention deficits and lower ability to regulate emotions (van Daalen, Kaiser, Kebede, et al., 2022).

Fortunately, despite the negative consequences of bias and discrimination, bystanders can play a pivotal role in combating both **interpersonal racism**—biased interactions between people, and **systemic racism**—unfair practices within a system such as school, law, housing, etc. As one large anti-bias review concluded, *"there is a largely untapped potential of bystander anti-racism as part of a holistic approach to anti-racism"* (Nelson, Dunn, & Paradies, 2011, p. 264).

Unfortunately, as we have seen all too often, the default when encountering incidences of bias is typically to remain silent. Research consistently shows that people are far more likely to contemplate confronting bias than to actively engage in confrontation. For example, when White Canadian college students were asked to imagine a scenario where they overhear a White "participant" make a blatantly racist comment *("clumsy 'n-word'")* after a Black "participant" inadvertently bumped their knee, most claimed they would be outraged and directly confront the instigator. In reality, however, the vast majority failed to intervene and often responded with little emotion or concern. This prompted the researchers to conclude that *"One reason why racism remains so prevalent in society may be that people do not respond to overt acts of racism in the way that they anticipate"* (Kawakami, Dunn, Karmali, & Dovidio, 2009, p. 278). Likewise, although most White students from an American university believe people should report racist posts on social media, most admitted that they had witnessed, but not challenged online discrimination (Hurd et al., 2022). This default is also present in work environments where not surprisingly, *"Exit interviews with minority employees often reveal that it is not just inappropriate remarks by individuals that sting, but the silence of a wide array of bystanders"* (Scully & Rowe, 2009, p. 2).

This same pattern has been shown for those experiencing sex discrimination. In one US study, a majority of female participants thought that they would directly confront a male job interviewer who asked them totally inappropriate questions such as *"Do you think it is important for women to wear bras to work?"* but when women were actually placed in such a situation, the vast majority did not confront the perpetrator directly (Woodzicka & LaFrance, 2001). Likewise, female students from an American university working on a group exercise involving being stranded on a desert island often failed to confront a male "partner" who made a blatantly sexist comment *("She's pretty hot. I think we need more women on the island to keep the men satisfied"),* especially when other women were present (Swim & Hyers, 1999). Apparently, the researchers concluded, the fear and discomfort of confronting someone saying an offensive sexist remark replaced the participants' initial anger and disgust.

Research also shows that even though people report witnessing high rates of bias aimed at the LGBTQ+ community, they often fail to intervene (Poteat & Vecho, 2016). For example, heterosexual male students from an American university were less likely to confront a homophobic commenter if they believed masculinity was a fleeting state (known as **precarious manhood**) or others would think they might be gay (Kroeper et al., 2014). Together these studies show that despite being bothered or offended by discrimination, bystanders rarely respond to these acts in the way that they anticipate.

Given these findings, it is somewhat ironic that many people still maintain the unrealistic expectation that they would help during an obvious case of bias. Rather than accurately predicting their behavior, it seems many people have a sense of moral superiority over others facing the same situation such as believing they are more likely than their peers to give up their bus seat to a pregnant woman (Myers & Twenge, 2019). In an extremely vivid display of self-bias, Robert George, a professor at Princeton University (U.S.), posed this question to his students: *"If you were a White Southerner in 1850, would you have been anti-slavery?"* Not surprisingly, given the liberal climate of many higher education institutions, almost everyone claimed that, of course, they would have been abolitionists. Before accepting their answer, however, George challenged them to think of a single instance in which they supported an unpopular cause at great personal cost. When almost no one could come up with an example, it became readily apparent that although most people want to believe they would be morally courageous, they grossly underestimate the level of antipathy they would have faced for supporting such an unpopular cause (Frederick, 2020).

Traditional Strategies

To counteract bias incidents, many schools and businesses have adopted **zero-tolerance policies** requiring bystanders to report any acts of discrimination and severe disciplinary actions for perpetrators of bias. Although well-meaning, as applied to bullying, there is little evidence to suggest zero-tolerance policies reduce discrimination in any measurable way. In order for these policies to work, some form of bias must be detected. Unfortunately, due to the subtle nature of contemporary biases (such as avoidance, small changes in nonverbal behavior), discrimination is often hard to detect, especially for people from non-stigmatized groups (Ashburn-Nardo, Morris,

& Goodwin, 2008). Thus, people in the majority may only see intentional acts of discrimination, while people in the minority often experience more unintentional acts (Nordell, 2017). In addition, zero-tolerance policies, ironically, tend to *inhibit* reporting because most people do not wish to be labeled as a "snitch" or may fear loss of a relationship or retaliation. Still, other bystanders may fail to intervene because they may not trust those in power to conduct a fair investigation or they might believe the people making disparaging comments are closeminded and beyond help (Hodson & Esses, 2005; Rowe, Wilcox, & Gadlin, 2009).

Another common intervention strategy for bias incidents is **diversity (anti-bias) training**—training designed to improve peoples' cultural understanding, knowledge, and interaction with marginalized groups. Typically these trainings educate people about how certain beliefs and actions may have adverse effects, and how they can overcome their biases, reduce intergroup anxiety, and develop more positive interactions with out-group members (Ben, Kelly, & Paradies, 2020). Diversity training remains the go-to solution for companies and colleges dealing with campus intolerance. Nearly all Fortune 500 companies do training, and the majority of colleges and universities have training for faculty and students (Dobbin & Kalev, 2018). Although many institutions are sincere in their renunciation of prejudice of discrimination, ideal anti-bias training outcomes has had mixed success at best (Dobbin & Kalev, 2018).

One reason for the inconsistent findings is that there is little consensus on what constitutes diversity training, what the overarching goals should be, and what best practices should be used to achieve these goals (Devine & Ash, 2022). Another problem with diversity training is that it is often mandatory at many institutions. One large American survey found that most corporations require mandatory diversity training, and about half of colleges and universities require participation (Dobbin & Kalev, 2018). The rationale for mandatory training is simple: people who oppose diversity or think they are non-racist will not attend voluntarily. The problem with making participation mandatory, however, is that people often react negatively to top-down efforts to control them by coercing them to participate (Dobbin & Kalev, 2018; Kachanoff, Kteily, & Gray, 2022). Of course, making these programs voluntary has its own set of problems, such as only people with progressive views or those with concerns about a climate of bias will knowingly attend these trainings. If programs remain strictly voluntary, the message is only "preaching to the choir"—and not getting to the people who need to hear it most (Dobbin & Kalev, 2018).

Another, somewhat surprising, problem with diversity training is that it could lead to an increase, rather than a decrease in discrimination! This may sound counterintuitive, but researchers suggest this may have to do with **moral licensing**—when people do something good (e.g., attend training) they feel more licensed to do something bad afterward (e.g., show bias). For example, studies have found that when employees are told that their employers have pro-diversity measures, they presume that the workplace is free of bias and may become complacent regarding their own biases (Kaiser, Major, Jurcevic, et al., 2013). Thus, diversity training in isolation does not appear to be that helpful, and, in some cases, can actually do more harm than good if not implemented correctly.

On more of an individual level, many people think the best way to handle bias incidents is by adopting a **color-blind racial ideology**—a position that argues that the best way to minimize group differences is by ignoring them. The premise is simple: *"Talking about racial issues causes unnecessary conflict, so if I don't see race, I can't be racist."* Not surprisingly, however, colorblindness is associated with behaviors that run contrary to diversity and social justice, such as greater racial bias, less engagement with PoC, and less empathic concern toward racial minorities (Apfelbaum, Sommers, & Norton, 2008; Mekawi, Bresin, & Hunter, 2017). For example, students from an American university with higher levels of colorblindness scored lower in intergroup empathy and rated themselves as less likely to intervene when encountering prejudice (Yi, Todd, & Mekawi, 2020). Further, when marginalized people work with others who take a color-blind stance they often report feeling alienated, devalued, and invalidated (Plaut, Thomas, & Goren, 2009). Thus, despite its apparent intention, a color-blind racial ideology actually helps to legitimize bias and inhibits people from taking action in bias incidents.

Unique Barriers

Beyond the general obstacles that inhibit helping in emergency situations (see Chapter 2), there are a unique set of barriers preventing bystanders from intervening during situations involving prejudice and discrimination. One unique barrier facing bystanders is that prejudice and discrimination is much more subtle today compared to the overt racist acts during the days of Jim Crow ("separate but equal") laws. Most incidents today do not involve using the N-word in a derogatory way or refusing service to someone based on the color of their skin, but instead are more nuanced and harder to detect (Ashburn-Nardo et al., 2008). Prejudice is often veiled in humor making it difficult to discern its potential harm to targets (Ford, Boxer, Armstrong, & Edel, 2008). For example, if one person in a group of other White people says a joke that could be perceived as racist, it is much easier to awkwardly laugh it off and let the moment pass than to confront the speaker.

During interpersonal encounters, contemporary bias is not only hard to see, it is also relatively easy to hide. In one study, data revealed that employers of American companies were less likely to interview openly gay male candidates for entry-level sales jobs compared to a control group with identical resumes (Tilcsik, 2011). Similarly, compared to "job hunters" applying for jobs in mall stores wearing caps with "Texan & Proud" on the brim, those wearing caps with the words "Gay & Proud" experienced considerably more interpersonal discrimination (e.g., shorter interaction, less eye contact) by the store managers (Hebl, Foster, Mannix, & Dovidio, 2002). Likewise, gay and lesbian callers were less likely to be given help after "dialing the wrong number" than were their same-gender heterosexual counterparts across American (Shaw, Borough, & Fink, 1994), British (Ellis & Fox, 2001), and German (Gabriel & Banse, 2006) samples. Together, these studies show how relatively easy it is to hide unfair treatment, how difficult it can be to detect, and how potential acts of bias can leave targets wondering whether or not certain interactions were biased because of the color of their skin or their sexual orientation.

Another unique barrier facing bystanders today has to deal with the impression that because bias has become far less overt, many people may falsely assume that acts of prejudice is largely a thing of the past. According to recent surveys conducted in the United States, many Whites no longer see racial discrimination as a problem today. In fact, although sociological data still show large racial disparities in quality of life (e.g., Blacks have infant mortality, unemployment, and poverty rates 2 to 3× higher than Whites), a majority of Whites now see anti-White bias as a *bigger* social problem than anti-Black bias (Norton & Sommers, 2011). Similarly, other studies show that men believe they face *more* discrimination than women (Kehn & Ruthig, 2013). This implies that it may be more difficult today for Whites to recognize anti-Black discrimination and for men to recognize gender discrimination against women.

Another unique barrier to helping when encountering bias incidents is that some White individuals may hold ambivalent attitudes toward PoC. According to **aversive racism**, White people may hold egalitarian values toward PoC, while simultaneously holding unconscious negative attitudes (Gaertner & Dovidio, 2005). This type of contemporary racism leads to both an unconscious avoidance of PoC, and a very active denial of such avoidance. Even benign interracial interactions may be perceived as threatening by White individuals and evoke higher physiological arousal, which in turn, may lead to less interracial contact (Mendes, Blascovich, Lickel, & Hunter, 2002).

In support of aversive racism, a meta-analysis of helping behavior found that White participants justified helping Black people less, particularly when a failure to help could be attributed to a reason other than race (such as high risk or a high degree of effort needed) (Saucier, Miller, & Doucet, 2005). For example, in one set of studies, White students from an American university watched over closed-circuit television a staged fall from another "student" in an adjoining room. For some subjects the fall was rather minor, while for others the fall was more severe. To make helping more deliberate and personal in nature, the experimenter collected the subject's cell phones earlier so they could not simply call 911 or campus security. Consistent with aversive racism, Black victims received less help than White victims but only when the severity of the accident was high. On average, White subjects also took twice as long to help Black victims compared to White victims. According to the researchers, *"the prolonged and close contact necessary to help someone who is seriously injured may amplify some White people's aversion and desire to avoid interracial contact"* (Kunstman & Plant, 2008, p. 1500). In addition, to help justify their lack of helping as well as reduce the impression they might be biased, White subjects tended to "see" the emergency as less severe when the victim was Black. This led the researchers to conclude that *"racial bias seems particularly likely to rear its head at the worst possible time, namely, in events where victims need help the most"* (Kunstman & Plant, 2008, p. 1499).

Confronting Bias

In this section, we will look at how both bystanders and diversity educators can develop strategies to overcome the various obstacles bystanders face when witnessing acts of prejudice and discrimination.

Applying SMB

As with each type of emergency situation covered in this book, the obstacles preventing bystanders from helping when witnessing bias incidents can be mapped onto the **situation model of bystander intervention (SMB)**. For example, using the **SMB**, researchers developed a model to help bystanders confront bias in the workplace. To illustrate the model, participants are given a scenario such as a male boss suggesting to the lone female employee in a company meeting that she bake cookies for their next meeting because *"women are good at that sort of thing."* Participants are then asked to reflect upon what questions may be playing out in their minds and them map it to the SMB. Typical responses are *"What did he just say?"* (step 1), *"Was that a sexist remark?"* (step 2), *"Is anyone going to say something?"* (step 3), *"Is there something I should say to make him aware that was inappropriate?"* (step 4), and *"If I say something will it jeopardize my job?"* (step 5) (Ashburn-Nardo et al., 2008). While addressing these questions, the participants are then given practical strategies to overcome each step in order to formulate a clear plan on how to become more active responders. Next we will look at some of these practical strategies.

Recognize Warning Signs

To detect bias, bystanders must remain vigilant in their immediate social environment as many acts of bias are much less overt today. Due to the subtle nature of bias, people often look to others for cues on how to react and behave. To reduce ambiguity, we often use **social referencing**—seeking out others from one's in-group to understand an event. Consistent with this theory, White participants observing a racist comment made in front of a Black person focused more on the Black target if they believed he heard the comment; however, if they believed he did not hear the comment, they showed little interest in the target and tended to focus more on other in-group members (Crosby, Monin, & Richardson, 2008). This implies, that in ambiguous situations (i.e., where it is unclear whether a biased comment was heard by the target), bystanders may incorrectly assume that the in-group does not find it offensive, and thus neither should they (i.e., **pluralistic ignorance**). To overcome this problem, bystanders should consistently take action, regardless of whether they believe the target heard it, or the in-group is in support, or not.

Besides becoming more vigilant to the impact the incident might have on the target, bystanders (especially those from non-stigmatized groups) must become more knowledgeable about the various forms of contemporary bias. Often bystanders fail to notice less obvious forms of racial bias such as avoidance behaviors (e.g., shorter interactions, minimal eye contact, appearing distracted), discomfort (e.g., speech dysfluency, body rigidity) or even the use of "positive" stereotypes to describe a specific group (e.g., *"Black people are natural athletes"*). To illustrate the latter, Black participants from an American university (but not White participants, importantly) watching a White actor interviewing for a position on a diversity task force rated the actor as *more* prejudiced when he made a reference to Black people's superior athletic ability (Czopp, 2008). This implies that while Black people may find an interaction awkward or a comment racially insensitive, White bystanders might assume (incorrectly) that the comment is harmless, thus reducing the chance they would confront the speaker in this case. And as we know, when bystanders remain silent, they fail to communicate the salience of anti-racist norms to other bystanders (Shelton, Richeson, Salvatore, & Hill, 2006).

Bystanders also need to understand that just because the target does not protest or other bystanders do not say anything, that does not automatically mean that no bias took place. Often times the targets of discrimination do not say anything for fear they will be labeled as "whiners" or "playing the race card." For example, one study conducted in the United States found that Black people who attributed being denied an employment opportunity to what was a clearly a blatant act of discrimination, were more likely to be perceived as playing the race card than if the decision was attributed to factors unrelated to discrimination (Kaiser & Miller, 2001). Likewise, a female confederate expressing her dissatisfaction to a male's sexist remark about appropriate roles for women at work was rated less likable by male perceivers compared to when she remained silent (Dodd, Giuliano, Boutell, & Moran, 2001). Together these studies show that targets of bias may not confront the speaker due to the likelihood of being perceived negatively. Fortunately, bystanders have the advantage of advocating for those directly affected by bias without concerns of being viewed negatively for challenging the speaker.

Promote Re-Categorization from "Them" to "Us"

We tend to categorize people into "us" versus "them," and generally speaking, we tend to feel more responsible to help the "us" than the "them" (Tajfel, 1970). So, in order to increase a sense of responsibility, bystanders can learn to recategorize out-group members from the remote "them" to the more inclusive "us." As we saw in Chapter 3, self-identified English football fans were more likely to help a male victim if he presumably was a fan of the same football club they supported (Manchester United) than a football club they despised (Liverpool). However, when the categories were broadened from the exclusive "Manchester fan" to the more inclusive "football fan," bystanders were just as likely to help a victim in a Manchester United shirt as they were to help a victim in a Liverpool shirt (Levine, Prosser, Evans, & Reicher, 2005).

Recategorization can work effectively in mixed race (e.g., Black/White) interactions where the in-group/out-group mentality is more salient. For example, White participants are often less likely to help a Black victim screaming in pain than a White victim, presumably because they felt less responsibility to help out-group members than in-group members (Kunstman

& Plant, 2008). One potential way to extend a sense of responsibility toward out-group members is by expanding common group boundaries. In one study, White students from a prestigious American university showed less prejudice when they used recategorization by shifting boundaries from "White/Black student" to "White/Black student from their proud university" (Scroggins, Mackie, Allen, & Sherman, 2016). Together, these studies show that as shared identity between bystander and target increases, the likelihood of helping can be extended to those who were previously seen as out-group members (Dovidio & Gaertner, 1999).

Increase Cultural Openness via Intergroup Contact

Calls for increasing racial diversity are prominent across business and academia. The presence of diversity may increase intergroup contact and foster more positive intergroup attitudes. In one study, White children from American schools with little intergroup contact were more likely to interpret ambiguous scenarios (e.g., seeing a picture of two children at a swing with one on the ground) in a racially biased way. In this example, when the White child was on the ground, White children from homogeneous schools were more likely to say the Black child pushed the White child off the swing, but when the Black child was on the ground, they were more likely to say he fell off. Importantly, White children from heterogenous schools did not show this bias. Thus diversity in school composition can lead to more positive intergroup attitudes (McGlothlin & Killen, 2010).

Intergroup contact alone, however, is not enough to foster meaningful intergroup interactions. For example, White students from an American college who kept daily diaries of cross-race interactions reported far fewer interactions than would occur at chance given the racial and social class diversity of their student bodies. In addition, these same students experienced less satisfaction (e.g., *"I felt the interaction did not go well"*) in cross-race compared to same-race interactions (Carey, Stephens, Townsend, & Hamedani, 2022). For contact to be effective, diversity educators must try to create intergroup contact that builds empathy and trust and reduces threat and defensiveness (Hodson, Choma, & Costello, 2009).

Increasing diversity will not automatically increase bystander intervention either. Fortunately, there is evidence that people high in **cultural openness**—the extent to which an individual is open to, and interested in, the similarities and differences between their own and other groups—tend to be more assertive bystanders. In one study, adolescent students from more ethnically mixed neighborhoods in the UK tended to report higher levels of cultural openness, and had greater intentions to intervene in instances of offensive name-calling toward minority group members (Abbott & Cameron, 2014). Cultural openness can also be achieved through friendships, intergroup dialogue, and academic pursuits. For example, students from an American university who identified as straight reported greater intention to help an LGBT-identified student encountering harassment when they had LGBT+ friends, were part of a gay-straight-alliance, or took courses with social justice and LGBT+ content (Dessel et al., 2017). For diversity educators, framing diversity programs as an opportunity to learn about someone different ("intercultural exchange") should lead to more productive outcomes than framing programs using a prevention mindset ("avoid being prejudiced") (Dweck, 2012).

Adopt a Growth Mindset

Another way to get people to become better bystanders when encountering bias is to change their mindsets (implicit theories) about, well . . . mindsets. Some people have fixed mindsets about prejudiced people (e.g., *"People have a certain amount of prejudice and they can't really change that"*), while others have more of a growth mindset (e.g., *"No matter who somebody is they can always become a lot less prejudiced"*) (Dweck, 2012). In one study, compared to students of color from an American university who believe people's level of prejudice is fixed, those who believe that a person's level of prejudice is malleable were more likely to challenge another "student" during an online chat who made inappropriate comments about affirmative action policies (Rattan & Dweck, 2010). In a follow-up study, predominantly White students who believed prejudice is malleable reported greater intentions to confront a White male intern who made the offensive comment *"I'm really surprised at the types of people who are working here . . . with all of this "diversity" hiring—women, minorities, foreigners, etc., I wonder how long this company will stay on top?"* Consistent across both studies, those who believed that the prejudiced person could change were more likely to confront him in a non-hostile way (e.g., calmly educating the speaker rather than trying to humiliate them) (Rattan & Dweck, 2010).

Emphasize Costs of Not Intervening

To become a better bystander, we must learn to see that, in many cases, the costs to intervene are often lower than the costs to not to intervene (Poteat & Vecho, 2016). Yes, there are many social costs when confronting acts of bias such as awkwardness, damaging one's relationship with a friend, colleague, or supervisor, or even being labeled the "thought police." For example, one study showed that perceived social pressure to intervene predicted whether people confronted an anti-gay perpetrator (Dickter & Newton, 2013). Likewise, although adolescents typically evoke moral objections to race-based humor, they are also keenly aware of the social exclusion that may result from calling out the instigator (Mulvey, Palmer, & Abrams, 2016). Confrontation is also challenging in organizations with a hierarchical structure where people may not confront biased acts committed by their superior due to perceived risks of "career suicide" such as fear of losing their job, hurting their chance of promotion, or being blackballed (Ashburn-Nardo, Blanchar, Petersson, et al., 2014). Not surprisingly, these studies show that when inappropriate (sexist/racist) comments are made by people in high-power positions (e.g., supervisors), people felt less responsible, reported less competence, and rated the costs to intervene higher.

To overcome concerns of retaliation, companies should provide an option where people may feel safe (anonymously) reporting their supervisor's offensive behavior to other supervisors (Ashburn-Nardo et al., 2014). Diversity educators should also emphasize the many advantages of confronting prejudice immediately after it happens. For example, research shows that confronting a person who makes a prejudiced comment makes them more likely to reflect on their statements and avoid using them again. In one study, White students from an American university who were confronted for using a negative stereotype about Black people subsequently used significantly fewer stereotypes about Black people than those not confronted. Further, challenging someone's use of bias toward one group might reduce the use of stereotypes toward other stigmatized groups. In a follow-up study, confronting people for their use of negative Black stereotypes not only led to fewer Black stereotypes one week later but also resulted in fewer Latino and gender stereotypes (Chaney, Sanchez, Alt, & Shih, 2021). Together these studies imply that bystanders need to become more concerned with the consequences of ignoring harmful behavior and focus more on the potential benefits of confronting acts of bias.

Applying TPB

Let's take a look at how the **Theory of Planned Behavior (TPB)** can be used to increase bystander intentions to help when encountering prejudice and discrimination. The TPB holds that strengthening attitudes about stigmatized groups, emphasizing subjective norms that support confronting discrimination, and increasing behavioral control by developing practical

Theory of Planned Behavior

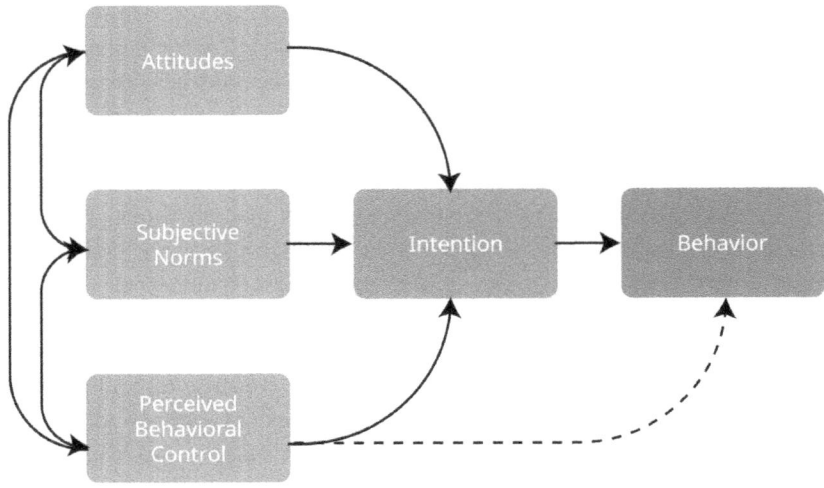

Figure 7.1 Theory of Planned Behavior

strategies on what to say and what actions to take can increase bystanders' intentions to help when faced with bias incidents.

Strengthen Attitudes by Building Empathy

To become active responders in situations involving bias, bystanders must develop strong positive attitudes toward helping out-group members. One way to strengthen attitudes is through teaching people how to develop empathy toward those who are stigmatized and mistreated. Empathy can take several forms: *cognitive empathy* (understanding what another person is feeling), *affective empathy* (sharing another person's feelings such as hurt or anger), and **sympathetic empathy**—caring about another person's distress and wanting to help them in some way. Although all forms of empathy are necessary, sympathetic empathy has been shown to be the best predictor of helping intentions (Brazil, Volk, & Dane, 2022).

To develop sympathetic empathy, diversity educators can expose people to the negative impact of those experiencing the daily hassle of discrimination (Ashburn-Nardo et al., 2008). For example, White students from an American university who read posts from Black peers documenting how personally harmed they felt by online discrimination showed a higher degree of concern and willingness to help (Hurd et al., 2022). Sympathetic empathy training can also be used effectively to help those facing anti-gay prejudice. In one study, Canadian university students asked to imagine what their life would be like after crash-landing on an alien planet where same-sex relationships are the norm and public displays of affection are strictly prohibited (see Hillman & Martin, 2002 for details) showed elevated empathy and favorable attitudes toward people who identify as gay compared to a control group that was not asked to reflect on this experience (Hodson et al., 2009).

Another, more transformative way to experience empathy for different racial groups involves using the **rubber hand illusion**—watching a rubber hand being stroked synchronously with one's own unseen hand creates the illusion the rubber hand is part of one's own body. White participants under the illusion that they have a dark skinned hand displayed more positive racial attitudes, presumably because the illusion creates a physical similarity between the self and the out-group member, resulting in White people feeling more empathy between themselves and those with darker skin (Maister, Slater, Sanchez-Vives, & Tsakiris, 2015). Although somewhat impractical, the researchers believe *"This methodology could be transformed into engaging educational tools that can allow people to experience the world from the perspective of someone different from themselves"* (M. Tsakiris, personal communication, June 3, 2022).

These engaging educational tools can allow adults to experience the world from the perspective of someone different from themselves, but early childhood may be the most critical time to begin providing educational tools to help White children empathize with children of color dealing with bias (Spinrad, Eisenberg, Xiao, et al., 2023). To begin, parents can promote racial empathy and the willingness to confront prejudice by asking their children *"how would you feel if you were treated differently because of the color of your skin or the style of your hair?"* White parents often avoid talking about the impact of race on PoC, yet it is important for children to learn early in life that not everyone is treated the same.

As for diversity educators, a classic experiment documented in the film (*"Eye of the Storm,"* 1970, *ABC*) can be used to develop empathy. While covering the recent assassination of Martin Luther King in her third-grade class, teacher Jane Elliott asked her all-White students *"Do you think you understand how it feels to be judged by the color of your skin? Would you like to find out?"* When the class enthusiastically responded "yes" to both questions, Elliott then declared that blue-eyed children are superior (e.g., smarter, more respectful), and they will be given special privileges (e.g., extra time at recess) over their inferior brown-eyed classmates. The next day, she reversed the status of the two groups. The film vividly documents the students' reactions as they move from being privileged to powerless or vice-versa. As one precocious child exclaimed while discussing the impact of the exercise, *"On top- I felt like a king, like I ruled them brown-eyes. On the bottom- I felt down, unhappy, like I was tied up and couldn't get loose."* (*"Eye of the Storm"*). This documentary was followed up with a second documentary (*"A Class Divided,"* 1985, *Frontline*) in which *Eye of the Storm* was shown to the original students—now fifteen years older—and Elliott is given a chance to hear what long-term impact the lesson had on her students. Many students commented on how that memorable classroom exercise helped to shape their attitudes about Black people and other stigmatized groups. After the students left, a proud Elliott remarked, *"I hope the exercise has produced a group of young people who, when they encounter racism, will feel at least a twinge of opposition, along with a strong sense that what they are seeing is wrong"* (*"A Class Divided"*).

Ideally, adopting lessons from the "brown-eyed vs. blue-eyed" experiment or creating realistic videos of social rejection against PoC (such as insults about hair or clothing) can help children develop empathy toward their peers and motivate them to challenge racism and provide comfort to those encountering discrimination (Spinrad et al., 2023).

Correct Misperceptions of Norms of Silence[1]

It may well be that we will have to repent in this generation not merely for the vitriolic words and actions of the bad people, but for the appalling silence of the good people.—Dr. Martin Luther King Jr during his address to Cornell College, Mount Vernon, Iowa. (October 15, 1962)

According to the TPB, while strengthening attitudes through empathy is essential, shifting social norms is also important for bystanders to increase their willingness to help (Hurd et al., 2022). Social norms have a strong influence on behavior, but like many interpersonal encounters in this book, these crucial norms are often misperceived, leading people to follow an incorrect norm (**pluralistic ignorance**). And as MLK's quote above powerfully illustrates, when it comes to acts of oppression, the norm of silence is not "golden" because the inaction of bystanders who privately condemn the bias sends a message of implicit approval to other bystanders.

---

1 A recent study suggests diversity educators avoid "equating silence with violence" because White people may feel threatened and defensive, and thus tune out messages that equate silence with blatant racism. In contrast, when White people see silence as a building block toward violence (and not a synonym), they feel less of a backlash and may be more likely to support anti-racism programs (Kachanoff et al., 2022).

In order to address contemporary forms of prejudice, new norms of action and intolerance must be established. Public condemnation through bystander anti-racism can reduce **false consensus**—overestimating the number of others who agree with your beliefs—which persists when people overestimate the number of people who remain silent (Nelson et al., 2011). For example, Hungarian adolescent students tended to underestimate how often their peers reject racial bias in their classes, and over time they adjusted their own intentions to this falsely perceived class norm. The researchers concluded that teachers can help students take action by *"creating an environment in which the voices of those who do not agree with prejudiced remarks are heard, ensuring that this becomes a 'visible' norm for students in the class"* (Váradi, Barna, & Németh, 2021, p. 15).

Many studies show that shifting social norms toward intolerance and public disapproval can be effective. For example, White students attending an American university who heard a condemnation of racism increased their public support of anti-racism policies (Blanchard, Crandall, Brigham, & Vaughn, 1994). Likewise, conveying social norms in favor of confronting online discrimination (e.g., *"Most of the people who are important to me challenge racially offensive posts or comments"*) increased White students' sense of personal responsibility to challenge online discrimination posted by their White peers (Hurd et al., 2022). Furthermore, the researchers conclude that encouraging White bystanders to be more vocal in opposition to online discrimination may not only help the target in that situation, but also help to bolster minority students' sense of belonging at the institution and potentially create a domino effect leading to an actual change in existing social norms (Hurd et al., 2022). Together, this research implies that even a few outspoken bystanders can dramatically influence the current normative climate.

Increase Perceived Behavioral Control

Confronting someone who said something offensive or hurtful takes a level of competence and assertiveness that many of us lack. Often when faced with these challenges, the default is to remain silent and rationalize not getting involved (e.g., *"What's the point? I'm sure nothing I say will make a difference"*). By remaining silent, bystanders alleviate any concerns that their comments will be met with anger and defensiveness, and thus avoid any feelings of awkwardness and discomfort. For the few who do confront the speaker, the typical, knee-jerk responses do little to alleviate the problem. These include: insulting the speaker's character *("You're morally bankrupt")*, expressing self-righteous anger *("That's so racist")*, or challenging the accuracy of a statement without explaining why *("You can't say that")* (Lawson & Veraldo, 2022; Martinez, Hebl, Smith, & Sabat, 2017; Plous, 2000).

To increase competence, bystanders must learn to replace these gut-level responses with more mindful ones that will not make the speaker defensive or dismissive. One highly effective way to promote self-efficacy without coming across as hostile or self-righteous is by developing a toolkit designed to reduce defensiveness.[2] These training exercises include: framing the comment in the form of a question (e.g., *"Do you feel that way about every person in that group?"*) rather than a statement (e.g., *"That's racist"*), pointing out the discrepancy between the speaker's prejudiced comments and their equality-minded self-image (e.g., *"I'm surprised to hear you say that, because I've always thought of you as someone who is very open-minded"*), or focusing on how the hurtful comments made you feel (e.g., *"It makes me uncomfortable when you say things like that"*) (Lawson & Veraldo, 2022; Martinez et al., 2017; Plous, 2000). Respectively, these exercises are effective because statements generate resistance, whereas questions generate answers; inducing dissonance increases guilt and motivates action; and although the biased speaker can dispute who they are or how they should behave, they cannot dispute how you feel or what they said (see video on "How to tell someone they sound racist" by Jay Smooth at https://youtu.be/b0Ti-gkJiXc).

Several studies have found these role-playing exercises to be highly effective in helping bystanders confront prejudice. An Australian team of researchers found exercises such as these promoted proactive bystander replies in response to racism in both students and teachers (Priest, Alam, Truong, et al., 2021). Likewise, student athletes from an American college who participated in the training demonstrated a significant improvement in their ability to effectively respond to prejudiced comments, compared to athletes who did not receive the training (Lawson & Veraldo, 2022).

These self-efficacy exercises can also be adapted for younger bystanders. To encourage children to intervene when observing racist name-calling, Canadian researchers had children watch videos of peer models confronting a person making a racist remark with assertive replies such as (*"Why would you want to call him that?"* or *"No one deserves to be called that"*). Later, when the children were shown a bias incident (without the model present)

---

2 In a popular TED talk, social activist, Loretta J. Ross suggests that instead of "calling people out," we should "call them in." Ross argues that calling out people through public "shaming and blaming" (e.g., *"you're racist/toxic/despicable"*) only leads to defensiveness. Instead, Ross provides a toolkit for calling wrongdoers "in" by starting productive conversations (e.g., *"How can I reconcile the good person I know you are with the words that just came out of your mouth?"*). Ideally, this allows people to grow by giving them the opportunity to choose a better self (see https://www.youtube.com/watch?v=xw_720iQDss).

and asked what they would do, they were more assertive, and not by simply repeating the phrases verbatim, but by paraphrasing and adding their own words (Aboud & Joong, 2008).

Although scripted role-playing exercises can be highly effective in increasing self-efficacy in bias incidents, it does come with some challenges. Because the training is done in a public setting, some learners may feel uncomfortable practicing these new behaviors in front of others. Recently, researchers found using an avatar-based simulation (see https://youtu.be/_BofiRjUq3E?si=Ncqb9xGEab36lQYz), that offers a more private learning environment, to be quite successful at increasing intervention to bias incidents (Chen, Carboni, & Tutwiler, 2023).

"What Can Bystanders Do?"

Based on research incorporating the **SMB** and **TPB**, there are several practical strategies you can do to become an active responder the next time you witness an act of bias including:

- becoming more aware of the subtle nature of contemporary bias such as avoidance behaviors (e.g., shorter interactions, minimal eye contact, appearing distracted), and discomfort (e.g., speech dysfluency, body rigidity)
- understanding that just because the target does not protest or other bystanders do not say anything, that does not automatically mean that no bias took place
- realizing that bias is often veiled in humor making it difficult to discern its potential harm to targets
- adopting a growth mindset implying that people are capable of becoming less prejudiced
- realizing that remaining silent fails to communicate anti-racist norms to other bystanders
- learning to recategorize out-group members from the remote "them" to the more inclusive "us"
- developing a sense of cultural openness by being open and curious to learn about other cultures and social groups
- rather than staring in stunned silence to biased comments, practice responding in a non-defensive/nonjudgmental way such as: *"Do you feel that way about every person in that group?" "I'm surprised to hear you say that, because I've always thought of you as someone who is very open-minded,"* or *"It makes me uncomfortable when you say things like that"* (remember, a speaker can dispute who they are, but not how you feel)

> ### "What Can Diversity Educators Do?"
>
> Based on research incorporating the **SMB** and **TPB**, there are several additional practical strategies (beyond those above) that diversity educators can do when designing programs to get bystanders to confront bias incidents including:
>
> - framing diversity programs as educational opportunities to learn about someone different ("intercultural exchange") rather than using a prevention mindset ("avoid being prejudiced")
> - helping White people see silence as a building block toward violence (and not a synonym), can help them feel less of a backlash and increase their support of anti-racism programs
> - providing intergroup contact opportunities that build empathy and trust rather than threat and defensiveness
> - promoting sympathetic empathy by exposing people to the negative impact of the daily hassles of bias and discrimination
> - emphasizing the many immediate advantages of confronting prejudice such as causing the speaker to reflect on what they said, bolstering members of stigmatized group's sense of belonging, and even possibly changing existing passive social norms to norms of action and intervention

Summary

Bystanders are in the unique position to help people during interpersonal encounters of bias and discrimination. To become an active responder, bystanders can learn to recognize the signs of subtle bias, develop a sense of cultural openness, and practice responding to acts of bias in a non-defensive manner. For positive change to occur, diversity educators should frame diversity programs as educational opportunities for intercultural exchange, and create inclusive environments in which the voices of those affected by biased remarks are heard. When bystanders proactively intervene on behalf of the target of bias, they can cause the speaker to reflect on what they said, bolster members of targeted group's sense of belonging, and ultimately help to change norms of silence into norms that call out and challenge bias incidents.

In addition to being better bystanders when immediate emergencies arise, we also need to become better allies by advocating for those facing systemic acts of social injustice and inequality. In the final chapter, we will discuss the importance of allyship and various ways to become a proactive ally.

References

Abbott, N., & Cameron, L. (2014). What makes a young assertive bystander? The effect of intergroup contact, empathy, cultural openness, and in-group bias on assertive bystander intervention intentions. *Journal of Social Issues, 70,* 167–182.

Aboud, F. E., & Joong, A. (2008). Intergroup name-calling and conditions for creating assertive bystanders. In S. R. Levy & M. Killen (Eds.), *Intergroup attitudes and relations in childhood through adulthood* (pp. 249–260). Oxford University Press.

Apfelbaum, E. P., Sommers, S. R., & Norton, M. I. (2008). Seeing race and seeming racist? Evaluating strategic colorblindness in social interaction. *Journal of Personality and Social Psychology, 95,* 918–932.

Ashburn-Nardo, L., Blanchar, J. C., Petersson, J., et al. (2014). Do you say something when it's your boss? The role of perpetrator power in prejudice confrontation. *Journal of Social Issues, 70,* 615–636.

Ashburn-Nardo, L., Morris, K. A., & Goodwin, S. A. (2008). The confronting prejudiced responses (CPR) model: Applying CPR in organizations. *Academy of Management Learning & Education, 7,* 333–342.

Ben, J., Kelly, D., & Paradies Y. (2020). Contemporary anti-racism: A review of effective practice. In J. Solomos (Ed.), *Routledge international handbook of contemporary racisms* (pp. 205–215). Routledge.

Benner, A. D., Wang, Y., Chen, S., & Boyle, A. E. (2022). Measurement considerations in the link between racial/ethnic discrimination and adolescent well-being: A meta-analysis. *Developmental Review, 64,* 101025.

Blair, I. V., Judd, C. M., & Chapleau, K. M. (2004). The influence of Afrocentric features in criminal sentencing. *Psychological Science 16,* 674–679.

Blanchard, F. A., Crandall, C. S., Brigham, J. C., & Vaughn, L. A. (1994). Condemning and condoning racism: A social context approach to interracial settings. *Journal of Applied Psychology, 79,* 993–997.

Brazil, K. J., Volk, A. A., & Dane, A. V. (2022). Is empathy linked to prosocial and antisocial traits and behavior? It depends on the form of empathy. *Canadian Journal of Behavioral Science, 55,* 75.

Carey, R. M., Stephens, N. M., Townsend, S. S. M., & Hamedani, M. G. (2022). Is diversity enough? Cross-race and cross-class interactions in college occur less often than expected, but benefit members of lower status groups when they occur. *Journal of Personality and Social Psychology, 123,* 889–908.

Chaney, K. E. Sanchez, D. T., Alt, N. P., & Shih, M. J. (2021). The breadth of confrontations as a prejudice reduction strategy. *Social Psychological and Personality Science, 12,* 314–322.

Chen, J. A., Carboni, I., & Tutwiler, M. S. (2023). EDI skill-building tools: Preparing learners to effectively intervene in bias incidents. *Scholarship of Teaching and Learning in Psychology, 9,* 419–434.

Crosby, J. R., Monin, B., & Richardson, D. (2008). Where do we look during potentially offensive behavior? *Psychological Science, 19,* 226–228.

Czopp, A. M. (2008). When is a compliment not a compliment? Evaluating expressions of positive stereotypes. *Journal of Experimental Social Psychology, 44,* 413–420.

Dessel, A. B., Goodman, K. D., & Woodford, M. R. (2017). LGBT discrimination on campus and heterosexual bystanders: Understanding intentions to intervene. *Journal of Diversity in Higher Education, 10,* 101–116.

Devine, P. G., & Ash, T. L. (2022). Diversity training goals, limitations, and promise: A review of the multidisciplinary literature. *Annual Review of Psychology, 73,* 403–429.

Dicker, C. L., & Newton, V. A. (2013). To confront or not to confront: Non-targets' evaluations of and responses to racist comments. *Journal of Applied Psychology, 43,* 262–275.

Dobbin, F., & Kalev, A. (2018). Why doesn't diversity training work? The challenge for industry and academia. *Anthropology Now, 10,* 48–55.

Dodd, E. H., Giuliano, T. A., Boutell, J. M., & Moran, B. E. (2001). Respected or rejected: Perceptions of women who confront sexist remarks. *Sex Roles, 45,* 567–577.

Dovidio, J. F., & Gaertner, S. L. (1999). Reducing prejudice: Combating intergroup biases. *Current Directions in Psychological Science, 8,* 101–105.

Dweck, C. S. (2012). Mindsets and human nature: Promoting change in the Middle East, the schoolyard, the racial divide, and willpower. *American Psychologist, 67,* 614–622.

Elliott, A. M., Alexander, S. C., Mescher, C. A., et al. (2016). Differences in physicians' verbal and nonverbal communication with black and white patients at the end of life. *Journal of Pain and Symptom Management, 51,* 1–8.

Ellis, J., & Fox, P. (2001). The effect of self-identified sexual orientation on helping behavior in British sample: Are lesbians and gay men treated differently? *Journal of Applied Social Psychology, 31,* 1238–1247.

Ford, T. E., Boxer, C. F., Armstrong, J., & Edel, J. R. (2008). More than "just a joke": The prejudice-releasing function of sexist humor. *Personality and Social Psychology Bulletin, 34,* 159–170.

Frederick, S. (2020). Suppose you were a white southerner before abolition. *Psychology Today.* https://www.psychologytoday.com/us/blog/cognitive-reflections/202007/suppose-you-were-white-southerner-abolition

Gabriel, U., & Banse, R. (2006). Helping behavior as a subtle measure of discrimination against lesbians and gay men: German data and a comparison across countries. *Journal of Applied Social Psychology, 36,* 690–707.

Gaertner, S. L., & Dovidio, J. F. (2005). Understanding and addressing contemporary racism: From aversive racism to the common ingroup identity model. *Journal of Social Issues, 61,* 615–639.

Hebl, M. R., Foster, J. B., Mannix, L. M., & Dovidio, J. F. (2002). Formal and interpersonal discrimination: A field study of bias toward homosexual applicants. *Personality and Social Psychology Bulletin, 28,* 815–825.

Hillman, J., & Martin, R. A. (2002). Lessons about gay and lesbian lives: A spaceship exercise. *Teaching of Psychology, 29,* 308–311.

Hodson, G., Choma, B., & Costello, K. (2009). Experiencing alien-nation: Effects of a simulation intervention on attitudes toward homosexuals. *Journal of Experimental Social Psychology, 45,* 974–978.

Hodson, G., & Esses, V. M. (2005). Lay perceptions of ethnic prejudice: Causes, solutions, and individual differences. *European Journal of Social Psychology, 35,* 329–344.

Hoffman, K. M., Trawalter, S., Axt, J. R., & Oliver, M. N. (2016). Racial bias in pain assessment and treatment recommendations, and false beliefs about biological differences between blacks and whites. *Proceedings of the National Academy of Sciences, 113,* 4296–4301.

Hurd, N. M., Trawalter, S., Jakubow, A., et al. (2022). Online racial discrimination and the role of white bystanders. *American Psychologist, 77,* 39–55.

Kachanoff, F. J., Kteily, N., & Gray, K. (2022). Equating silence with violence: When white Americans feel threatened by anti-racist messages. *Journal of Experimental Social Psychology, 102,* 104348.

Kaiser, C. R., Major, B., Juncevic, I., et al. (2013). Presumed fair: Ironic effects of organizational diversity structures. *Journal of Personality and Social Psychology, 104,* 504–519.

Kaiser, C. R., & Miller, C. T. (2001). Stop complaining! The social costs of making attributions to discrimination. *Personality and Social Psychology Bulletin, 27,* 254–263.

Kawakami, K., Dunn, E., Karmali, F., & Dovidio, J. F. (2009). Mispredicting affective and behavioral responses to racism. *Science, 323,* 276–278.

Kehn, A., & Ruthig, J. C. (2013). Perceptions of gender discrimination across six decades: The moderating roles of gender and age. *Sex Roles, 69,* 289–296.

Kroeper, K. M., Sanchez, D. T., & Himmelstein, M. S. (2014). Heterosexual men's confrontation of sexual prejudice: The role of precarious manhood. *Sex Roles, 70,* 1–13.

Kunstman, J. W., & Plant, E. A. (2008). Racing to help: Racial bias in high emergency helping situations. *Journal of Personality and Social Psychology, 95,* 1499–1510.

Lawson, T. J., & Veraldo, C. M. (2022). A psychology role-playing exercise improves student-athletes' ability to confront prejudiced comments. *Scholarship of Teaching and Learning in Psychology, 10,* 488-495

Lepore, S. J., Revenson, T. A., Weinberger, et al. (2006). Effects of social stressors on cardiovascular reactivity in Black and White women. *Annals of Behavioral Medicine, 31,* 120–127.

Levine, R. M., Prosser, A., Evans, D., & Reicher, S. D. (2005). Identity and emergency intervention: How social group membership and inclusiveness of group boundaries shape helping behavior. *Personality and Social Psychology Bulletin, 31,* 443–453.

Maister, L., Slater, M., Sanchez-Vives, M. V., & Tsakiris, M. (2015). Changing bodies changes minds: Owning another body affects social cognition. *Trends in Cognitive Sciences, 19,* 5–12.

Martinez, L. R., Hebl, M. R., Smith, N. A., & Sabat, I. E. (2017). Standing up and speaking out against prejudice toward gay men in the workplace. *Journal of Vocational Behavior, 103,* 71–85.

Mazza, E. (2020, June 8). *Ex-MLB all-star Torii Hunter names city he'd never play for due to racist abuse.* Huff Post. https://www.yahoo.com/huffpost/torii-hunter-boston-no-trade-clause-040952102.html

McCluney, C. L., Durkee, M. I., Smith II, R. E., et al. (2021). To be, or not to be ... Black: The effects of racial codeswitching on perceived professionalism in the workplace. *Journal of Experimental Social Psychology, 97,* 104199.

McGlothlin, H., & Killen, M. (2010). How social experience is related to children's intergroup attitudes. *European Journal of Social Psychology, 40,* 625–634.

Mekawi, Y., Bresin, K., & Hunter, C. D. (2017). Who is more likely to "not see race"? Individual differences in racial colorblindness. *Race and Social Problems, 9,* 207–217.

Melaku, T. M., Beeman, A., Smith, D. G., & Johnson, W. B. (2020). Be a better ally. *Harvard Business Review.* Retrieved from https://hbr.org/2020/11/be-a-better-ally

Mendes, W. B., Blascovich, J., Lickel, B., & Hunter, S. (2002). Challenge and threat during social interactions with White and Black men. *Personality and Social Psychology Bulletin, 28,* 939–952.

Mulvey, K. L., Palmer, S. B., & Abrams, D. (2016). Race-based humor and peer group dynamics in adolescence: Bystander intervention and social exclusion. *Child Development, 87,* 1379–1391.

Myers, D. G., & Twenge, J. M. (2019). *Social psychology* (13th ed.). McGraw Hill.

Nelson, J. K., Dunn, K. M., & Paradies, Y. (2011). Bystander anti-racism: A review of the literature. *Analyses of Social Issues and Public Policy, 11,* 263–284.

Nordell, J. (2017, May 2). Is this how discrimination ends? *The Atlantic, 7.*

Norton, M. I., & Sommers, S. R. (2011). Whites see racism as a zero-sum game that they are now losing. *Perspectives on Psychological Science, 6,* 215–218.

Pieterse, A. L., & Carter, R. T. (2007). An examination of the relationship between general life stress, racism-related stress, and psychological health among Black men. *Journal of Counseling Psychology, 54,* 101–109.

Plaut, V. C., Thomas, K. M., & Goren, M. J. (2009). Is multiculturalism or color blindness better for minorities? *Psychological Science, 20,* 444–446.

Plous, S. (2000). Responding to overt displays of prejudice: A role-playing exercise. *Teaching of Psychology, 27,* 198–200.

Poteat, P., & Vecho, O. (2016). Who intervenes against homophobic behavior? Attributes that distinguish active bystanders. *Journal of School Psychology, 54,* 17–28.

Priest, N., Alam, O., Truong, M., et al. (2021). Promoting proactive bystander responses to racism and racial discrimination in primary schools: A mixed methods evaluation of the 'Speak Out Against Racism' program pilot. *BMC Public Health, 21,* 1–17.

Quillian, L., & Lee, J. J. (2023). Trends in racial and ethnic discrimination in hiring in six Western countries. *Proceedings of the National Academy of Sciences, 120,* e2212875120.

Rattan, A., & Dweck, C. S. (2010). Who confronts prejudice?: The role of implicit theories in the motivation to confront prejudice. *Psychological Science, 21,* 952–959.

Richeson, J. A., & Shelton, J. N. (2007). Negotiating interracial interactions: Costs, consequences, and possibilities. *Current Directions in Psychological Science, 16,* 316–320.

Rowe, M., Wilcox, L., & Gadlin, H. (2009). Dealing with—or reporting— "unacceptable" behavior. *Journal of the International Ombudsman Association, 2,* 52–64.

Saucier, D. A., Miller, C. T., & Doucet, N. (2005). Differences in helping whites and blacks: A meta-analysis. *Personality and Social Psychology Review, 9,* 2–16.

Schreer, G., Smith, S., & Thomas, K. (2009). Shopping while Black: Examining racial discrimination in a retail setting. *Journal of Applied Social Psychology, 39,* 1432–1444.

Scroggins, W. A., Mackie, D. M., Allen, T. J., & Sherman, J. W. (2016). Reducing prejudice with labels: Shared group memberships attenuate implicit bias and expand implicit group boundaries. *Personality and Social Psychology Bulletin, 42,* 219–229.

Scully, M., & Rowe, M. (2009). Bystander training within organizations. *Journal of the International Ombudsman Association, 2,* 1–9.

Shaw, J. I., Borough, H. W., & Fink, M. I. (1994). Perceived sexual orientation and helping behavior by males and females: The wrong number technique. *Journal of Psychology and Human Sexuality, 6,* 73–81.

Shelton, J. N., Richeson, J. A., Salvatore, J., & Hill, D. M. (2006). Silence is not golden: The intrapersonal consequences of not confronting prejudice. In S. Levin & C. van Laar (Eds.), *Stigma and intergroup inequality* (pp. 65–81). Erlbaum.

Spinrad, T. L., Eisenberg, N., Xiao, S. X., et al. (2023). White children's empathy-related responding and prosocial behavior toward White and Black children. *Child Development, 94,* 93–109.

Swim, J. K., & Hyers, L. L. (1999). Excuse me—what did you just say?!: Women's public and private responses to sexist remarks. *Journal of Experimental Social Psychology, 35,* 68–88.

Swim, J., Hyers, L., Cohen, L., & Ferguson, M. (2001). Everyday sexism: Evidence for its incidence, nature, and psychological impact from three daily diary studies. *Journal of Social Issues, 57,* 31–54.

Tajfel, H. (1970). Experiments in intergroup discrimination. *Scientific American, 223,* 96–103.

Tilcsik, A. (2011). Pride and prejudice: Employment discrimination against openly gay men in the United States. *American Journal of Sociology, 117,* 586–626.

van Daalen, K. R., Kaiser, J., Kebede, S., et al. (2022). Racial discrimination and adverse pregnancy outcomes: A systematic review and meta-analysis. *BMJ Global Health, 7,* e009227.

Váradi, L., Barna, I., & Németh, R. (2021). Whose norms, whose prejudice? The dynamics of perceived group norms and prejudice in new secondary school classes. *Frontiers in Psychology, 11,* 3621.

Weeks, F., Zapata, J., Rohan, A., & Green, T. (2022). Are experiences of racial discrimination associated with postpartum depressive symptoms? A multistate analysis of pregnancy risk assessment monitoring system data. *Journal of Women's Health, 31,* 158–166.

Woodzicka, J. A., & LaFrance, M. (2001). Real versus imagined gender harassment. *Journal of Social Issues, 57,* 15–30.

Yi, J., Todd, N. R., & Mekawi, Y. (2020). Racial colorblindness and confidence in and likelihood of action to address prejudice. *American Journal of Community Psychology, 65,* 407–422.

Promoting Allyship

8

Key Terms in This Chapter 181

Importance of Allyship 183
How to Become an Anti-Racist Ally 185

Summary 204

Final Thoughts 204

Key Terms in This Chapter

allyship: the practice of supporting and advocating for marginalized groups, even if you are not a member of those groups

anti-racism: any policy that creates equitable outcomes between people of different races

anti-racist ally: someone who supports anti-racist policies through their actions

civil courage: acting on one's moral values to help others even in the face of likely opposition and potential harm to oneself

code-switching: adjusting their style of speech, appearance, and behavior to fit into a particular culture and increase their chances of being hired, accepted, or promoted.

color-blind racial ideology: position that the best way to minimize group differences is by ignoring them (e.g., "I don't see color.")

gaslighting: form of psychological manipulation that creates doubt in victims perceptions of an event by invalidating their experience

heroic imagination: seeing oneself as capable of handling risky situations, the hypothetical problems these situations generate, and the actions needed to resolve the situation

implicit association test (IAT): a useful tool for detecting implicit (unconscious) bias by assessing how quickly subconscious associations come to mind

implicit bias: any bias that has formed unintentionally

microaggressions: small, covert acts of bias often unnoticed by those who perpetrate them

post-racial society: theoretical society free from racial preference, prejudice, and discrimination

privilege: automatic unearned benefits bestowed upon dominant groups based on social identity

redlining: a banned discriminatory practice that consisted of the systematic denial of services such as mortgages, insurance loans, and other financial services to residents in predominantly Black neighborhoods

situational model of bystander intervention (SMB): proposes that bystanders typically go through a series of five decision-making steps before help will be given

systemic racism: unfair practices within a system such as school, law, housing, etc.

weapon bias: tendency to see an imaginary gun more frequently when primed with a Black person than White person

zero-sum game: belief that one group's gain is another group's loss

Every single person actually has the power to protest racist and antiracist policies, to advance them, or, in some small way, to stall them.

—Ibram Kendi, author of *How to Be an Antiracist*

In Chapter 2, we learned that when it comes to helping others in emergency situations, the default is often to remain neutral or invoke ways to justify not helping. We also learned that for most people, lack of helping is not due to apathy and indifference, but rather competing forces that create obstacles preventing us from helping; forces that are often exacerbated in the presence of other passive bystanders. Fortunately, the succeeding chapters provided us with many evidence-based ways to overcome these obstacles.

In addition to becoming better bystanders, however, we also need to become better allies to those facing systemic bias and oppression. Like the inspirational quote above implies, we all have the power to become active responders to symbols of oppression. Not only should we be prepared to act when we witness bias and oppression, we should also advocate for positive change to help uproot the injustice and inequality that perpetuate the conditions for bias to exist. In this chapter, we will discuss the importance of allyship and how to become a proactive ally.

Importance of Allyship

An **ally** is someone who uses their position of power to advocate for positive change within marginalized communities targeted by oppression (e.g., PoC, LGBTQ+, immigrants, disabled) by taking tangible, ongoing actions to dismantle systems of oppression (Williams, Sharif, Strauss, et al., 2021). Allies are socially conscious people who recognize patterns of injustice and feel a sense of responsibility for changing these patterns (Collins, Zhang, & Sisco, 2021). Even though care and concern for others is necessary for becoming an ally, compassion alone is not enough. As one study showed, American school personnel typically showed openness toward transgender youth and concern for their well-being, however, audio transcriptions of focus groups revealed that many perceived trans students as outside of normal (i.e., conflated diversity with strangeness) and used transphobic tropes such as trans people are seeking attention and overly dramatic (Marx, 2017). Thus, to move beyond passive egalitarianism and the accepted status quo, allies must operate in solidarity with those facing oppression, and encourage others in positions of power to do so as well (Salter & Migliaccio, 2019).

It is important to understand that allies are motivated by an intrinsic desire to advocate for equity rather than by guilt or to seek glorification as a savior (Sue, Alsaidi, Awad, et al., 2019). To differentiate these motives for helping, let's use anti-racist activism as an example: White allyship is helping to amplify the voices of PoC in order to achieve social justice and equality. White saviorship, on the other hand, is helping PoC for one's own benefit, self-image, or recognition (Williams et al., 2021). A great way to envision allyship can be seen using a conveyor belt metaphor (Tatum, 1997). According to this allegory, the conveyor belt quickly moves people in positions of power toward biased institutional practices. Most people are oblivious to the power and privilege that propels them forward. Allies, however, are not only aware, but they deliberately move in the opposite direction to disrupt the movement of the belt.

Allies actively listen to and are sympathetic to those encountering systemic injustice. Allies avoid **gaslighting**—a form of psychological manipulation that creates doubt in people's perceptions of an event by invalidating their experience (e.g., *"I'm sure he didn't mean any harm by that. That's just his way."* or *"You need to learn to be less sensitive."*) (Ashburn-Nardo, 2018).

Allies are not only supportive to those facing injustice, they also display **civil courage**—acting on one's moral values and caring for others even in the face of likely opposition and social harm to oneself (Staub, 2019; Williams, Faber, Nepton, & Ching, 2022). Allies must learn to disregard the cliché that *"nothing I say or do will make a difference"* and be confident enough to take action despite the potential social costs of being shunned or rejected.

Although becoming an ally takes practice, courage, and dedication, allies can be an invaluable source for helping disadvantaged groups fight injustice. Because an ally often has a relatively higher degree of status and privilege, and more importantly, recognizes said privilege, they can be powerful voices beside those whose voices are often unheard, diminished, or disregarded. As we saw in Chapter 7, targets of racial injustice, may avoid speaking up for fear they will labeled as "whiners" or "playing the race card" (Kaiser & Miller, 2001). Because allies are often advocating for causes that do not affect them directly, they are less likely to be viewed negatively for speaking up. For example, one study found that White students from an American university watching a White person confront another White person who made an explicitly racist comment rated the confrontation more favorably compared to when a Black person confronted the speaker (Rasinski & Czopp, 2010). Likewise, students from an American university rated confrontations from White people as more effective in inducing feelings of guilt and self-criticism in White perpetrators than confrontations from Black people (Czopp & Monteith, 2003).

Allies also have the advantage of promoting social change without the perception they are doing it for personal gain, so their message may be perceived by others as more authentic and selfless (Salter & Migliaccio, 2019).

In one study, female students from a German university who read a fictitious scenario of a person confronting a shop owner about the need to remove a sexist advertisement showed more gratitude when a man was the confronter (Kutlaca, Becker, & Radke, 2020).[1] Furthermore, women faculty from the United States and Canada who perceived their male colleagues as allies in fighting sexism felt more energized and inclusive at work (Warren, Bordoloi, & Warren, 2021). Together, these studies show that because advantaged allies are viewed as more genuine and not motivated by self-interests, they can be highly persuasive in standing up to injustices facing disadvantaged groups.

How to Become an Anti-Racist Ally

> *Allyship is not self-defined—our work and our efforts must be recognized by the people we seek to ally ourselves with.*
> —Layla Saad, author of Me and White Supremacy.

As the quote above implies, one cannot proclaim themselves an ally simply because they refrain from discriminating against others or openly declare their positive attitudes about diversity. Instead, allyship entails taking action such as promoting the rights of disempowered groups or working to eliminate social inequalities, even those that might benefit allies (Williams et al., 2021). Specific examples of allyship include: White people walking in solidarity with PoC during a Black Lives Matter protest, men participating in a Women's March, or a White supervisor asking a PoC to lead a meeting in order to gain visibility by the company's all-White executives (Melaku, Beeman, Smith, & Johnson, 2020). Allies are vital for fighting social injustice. Since much of the research deals with becoming a White advocate (i.e., an **anti-racist ally**), that is what we will focus on here.

Detect Hidden Biases and Blind Spots

We tend to have a blind spot when it comes to seeing bias in ourselves. In general, we are remarkably adept at seeing bias in others, yet fail to see the same biases in ourselves. The reality is that even highly egalitarian people tend to have bias blind spots (Ashburn-Nardo, 2018). One reason for this blind spot is that people tend to look inwardly to determine if they are biased (e.g., *"Was my decision not to help that person biased in some way? Hmm . . . No, I don't believe so."*), but look outwardly to see if others are biased (e.g., *"I can't believe that person didn't help. How selfish."*) (Pronin & Hazel,

---

[1] This could partially explain why although Weinstein's wrongdoings were exposed by the work of several female journalists, Jodi Kantor and Megan Twohey, of *The New York Times*, it was mainly credited to one male journalist Ronan Farrow, of *The New Yorker* (Kutlaca, 2021).

2023). To overcome these bias blind spots, we must learn to recognize our own biases and preconceptions by using the same standard of assessment we would use to evaluate someone else.

Another way to see your blind spots is to recall a previous experience in which you engaged in a bias-related behavior that you regretted, and then think about how you would respond differently if the situation presented itself again. For example, an American participant in one study described her regret of having been fearful of a group of African American men on a subway train because they were dressed in baggy clothes and listening to loud music. After reflecting on her stereotypical thoughts and realizing that there was no reason to fear a group simply because of cultural and generational differences, she felt better prepared to behave more impartially if presented with that scenario again (Ashburn-Nardo, 2018).

A popular way to diagnose blind spots is to examine your hidden or **implicit biases**—any bias that has formed unintentionally, by taking the **Implicit Association Test (IAT**; https://implicit.harvard.edu/implicit/takeatest.html). The IAT is a useful tool for detecting implicit (unconscious) bias by assessing how quickly subconscious associations come to mind (Greenwald & Banaji, 1995). Let's use the Gender-Career IAT as an example. One group of participants is told to press the E key if the word relates to "female or family" (e.g., "children" or "home"), and press the I key if the word relates to "male or career" (e.g., "salary" or "office"). The associations are then reversed (i.e., "male or family" and "female or career"). To counterbalance the responses, another group of participants are given the same two conditions in the reverse order. Based on millions of participants from countries across the world, the Gender-Career IAT reveals a quicker association between female and family (than male and family) and between male and career (than female and career). Similarly, those taking the Race-IAT tend to show a quicker association for "White and good" (than "Black and good") and "Black and bad" (than "White and bad") (Nosek, Greenwald, & Banaji, 2005). Taking various IAT's on the website (there are more than twenty to choose from) can help reveal unconscious biases you may not be aware you have. Feeling a slight "response competition" when trying to pair certain groups together (e.g., "Black and good" or "White and bad") may result in a feeling of uneasiness and apprehension, however this discomfort is a necessary step toward weakening those implicit negative associations.

After taking the IAT, an important question to ask yourself is *"Do these implicit biases subconsciously influence how I treat and interact with others?"* Research shows that scores on the IAT can, in fact, predict intergroup interactions. For example, White students from an American university scoring high on the race-based IAT (i.e., higher implicit bias) displayed more negative social interactions (e.g., acted less friendly) toward a Black (vs. a White) experimenter (McConnell & Leibold, 2001). Another critical question to ask is *"Where do these implicit biases originate?"* As a budding ally, it is important to understand that even the situational roles one regularly takes part in can increase implicit bias. For example, people in positions of power may unknowingly and automatically show implicit bias. In one study, White female students from an American university assigned to a high-power role as a superior of a Black female employee revealed more implicit bias than those assigned to a subordinate role. Importantly, this power differential had no influence on automatic bias during same-race interactions (Richeson & Ambady, 2003).

Implicit bias not only stems from the roles we play, but also the media we watch. In one clever study done on students from an American university, clips from TV shows of two actors having a dialogue were edited to remove both the audio track and one of the characters in the scene. This made it possible to see whether the *unseen* "target" (Black or White) character was treated differently while interacting with a White character. Typically, the unseen Black characters (vs. unseen White character) elicited *less* favorable nonverbal responses while interacting with the observed White character. Further, the more TV shows that participants reported watching with this nonverbal bias pattern, the higher they scored on the Race-IAT (Weisbuch, Pauker, & Ambady, 2009).

Weaken Negative Associations

Humans see age and gender and skin color: That's vision. Humans have associations about these categories: That's culture. And humans use these associations to make judgments. That, is habit . . . Prejudice is a habit that can be broken.

—Patricia Devine, (cited in Nordell, 2017)

To become an ally, we must make a habit of replacing negative associations with positive associations. As the quote above implies, to break the habit of prejudice, we must learn to align unwanted implicit biases with non-biased explicit attitudes. Classic research on implicit bias has found that White participants who learn to actively replace automatic stereotypes with unbiased personal beliefs showed less implicit prejudice (Devine, 1989). Likewise, linking racial categories to specific counterstereotypic thoughts can also be effective at reducing real-world problems such as the **weapon bias**—being more likely to see an imaginary gun when primed with a Black person than a White person. To counter the weapon bias, White students from an American university who learned to make new associations *("When I see a*

Black person I will think "safe" instead of fear") were less likely to associate Blacks with guns compared to those who simply tried to avoid thinking about the bias (Payne, 2005).

There are many potential ways to weaken negative associations, but some have been found to work better than others. A meta-analysis looking at seventeen possible interventions to reduce implicit bias revealed that exposure to admired Black people (e.g., Oprah Winfrey), pairing Black people with positive traits (e.g., strong, proud, family-oriented), and setting goals to override implicit biases once they have been activated (e.g., *"If I see a Black person, then I will think good"*) were superior to broader strategies such as watching a video designed to induce moral virtue, reading about historic racial injustices, or reflecting on one's own egalitarian values (Lai, Marini, Lehr, et al., 2014). Likewise, White students from an American university who reflected on positive qualities and strengths of Black Americans (e.g., hard-working, family-oriented) showed less implicit bias toward Black people (Legault, Coleman, Jurchak, & Scaltsas, 2022). Moreover, White students from an American university trained to use positive nonverbal behavior (e.g., smiling, leaning in) toward a Black partner formed more positive impressions toward that person and showed less implicit racial bias toward Black people in general (Willard, Isaac, & Carney, 2015).

Although implicit attitudes can be gradually changed at the individual level, to reduce implicit bias, change must also occur at the societal level (Charlesworth & Banaji, 2019). For example, prominent displays of structural inequality and historic racism often found on American university campuses (e.g., presence of confederate monuments, a lack of racial diversity among full-time faculty, and lower social mobility for low-income students after graduation) were associated with higher average levels of implicit bias. These findings prompted the researchers to state: *"more energies should be directed toward identifying and dismantling the structures that are the source of injustice and promote individual bias in the first place"* (Salter, Adams, & Perez, 2018, p. 153). In support of this, anti-racism allies protesting together with Native American and Civil Rights groups were instrumental in restructuring social environments designed to reclaim Columbus Day for indigenous peoples and dismantling prominent confederate monuments, respectively (Salter et al., 2018).

Approach Interracial Interactions with a Promotion Mindset

It is important to realize that a reduction in negative attitudes toward the out-group does *not* necessarily translate into an *increase* in positive attitudes toward out-group members, in general. To move beyond a simple "tolerance" of marginalized group members, we must also learn to feel comfortable around out-group members, deliberately seek interactions with persons from these groups, and develop a sense of curiosity and respect toward outside group members (Pittinsky, 2009).

For many people, unfortunately, initiating interracial contact can be an awkward and emotionally draining experience, often due to the fear of saying something inappropriate or perceived disinterest from out-group members. Despite these concerns, research shows that most Black and White people would like to have more contact with each other (outside the work environment), but each group attributes their own avoidance to fear of being rejected while attributing the other group's avoidance to lack of interest (Shelton & Richeson, 2005). Ironically, both groups fail to recognize that out-group members' avoidance of intergroup contact reflects the same interpersonal concerns as their own. This mutual misunderstanding may lead to an unnecessary outcome of self-segregation outside of work settings.

To better visualize the extent of segregation in your life, you can map your friendships into a network diagram. By seeing who is in your friendship network, you can easily see whether you have few or many cross-racial friendships. To foster close connections with out-group members, researchers have found that the best predictors include displaying a combination of *enthusiasm* (feeling inspired about spending time with the out-group) and *engagement* (a desire to know and learn more about out-group experiences) (Collins et al., 2021; Williams & Gran-Ruaz, 2021). As a start, fostering connections can be accomplished by immersing oneself in another culture either directly (e.g., by attending events in which you are in the distinct minority) or indirectly (e.g., reading books written from the perspective of a person from another social group). Developing these interpersonal connections via cultural immersion could also have the added benefit of helping you to critically examine your our own (in some cases, privileged) identity (see *Examine White Identity* below).

Interracial contact cannot only be awkward, but it can also create feelings of mistrust. Research has consistently shown that White Americans/Canadians often exhibit subtle, negative nonverbal behaviors toward Black people (e.g., less eye contact, fewer smiles, greater physical distance), which lead to feelings of wariness and distrust (Goff, Steele, & Davies, 2008; Word, Zanna, & Cooper, 1974). Furthermore, during interracial interactions, White people often report that the interaction went well, while Black people often report seeing the White person as somewhat disengaged and avoidant (Dovidio, Gaertner, Kawakami, & Hodson, 2002). Ironically, White peoples' insistence that they are non-biased may ultimately perpetuate mistrust in Black people (Rosenblum, Jacoby-Senghor, & Brown, 2022). One explanation for this difference in perceptions is White people tend to focus on their verbal behaviors, while Black people tend to focus on White peoples' nonverbal behavior. To help build interpersonal trust and allyship, researchers have established optimal conditions for intergroup contact. These include contact that is cooperative, equal status, and institutionally supported (Tropp, 2008). Together these conditions can help build a promotion mindset ("intercultural exchange") rather than the usual prevention mindset ("avoid being prejudiced").

Recognize the Malleability of Prejudice

Sadly, research shows that children typically start to show a decline in interracial friendships in late elementary grades (Pauker, Apfelbaum, Dweck, & Eberhardt, 2022). One explanation for the decline in cross-race interaction, especially for White children, is the concern over being labeled prejudiced. To counter this expectation, researchers had children from American schools watch an illustrated digital storybook that diverged in how prejudice was described. The *fixed* version indicated that prejudice cannot change (e.g., *"Prejudice is permanent because after it develops, it usually does not change"* or *"Changes in laws to give equal rights to all people are important, even if prejudice deep down cannot be erased"*), while the *malleable* version emphasized that prejudice can change (e.g., *"Prejudice is not permanent, because even after it develops, it can be changed"* or *"Changing prejudice is important because with enough effort, even prejudice deep down can be erased"*). White children led to believe that prejudice is malleable expressed greater interest in engaging in interracial interactions, had more diversity in their friendship, and showed less interracial anxiety (Pauker et al., 2022). Thus, adopting a view that prejudice is malleable may free you to explore people different from yourself and exhibit greater interest in fostering interracial interactions.

Stand Up to Acts of Everyday Bias

Do you value social justice? Are you bothered when you see acts of bias and discrimination? Do you actively fight against injustice and unfairness? For most of us, despite valuing fairness and being disturbed by inequality (typical answers to the first two questions), fighting injustice can be a daunting task because we often lack the assertiveness needed to intervene, and we are typically unprepared to deal with "cultural pushback" (Sue, 2017). As we saw in Chapter 7, people who actually overheard a racist slur tended to respond with indifference and rarely intervened, whereas those asked to imagine the same event emphatically stated they would be outraged (Kawakami, Dunn, Karmali, & Dovidio, 2009). This shows that although people report having strong feelings against racial slurs, they often underestimate how likely they will actually stand up to it.

Consistent with the **Situational Model of Bystander Intervention (SMB)**, researchers have identified a number of reasons for people's failure to stand up to racial bias, including the invisibility of modern forms of bias (step 1), trivializing an incident as harmless (step 2), assuming others will intervene (step 3), paralysis of not knowing what to do (step 4), and the fear of negative consequences (step 5) (Shelton, Richeson, Salvatore, & Hill, 2006). On the bright side, however, research on White allyship shows allies tend to be more be aware of implicit biases, interpret implicit bias incidents as real problems, and feel a sense of responsibility to do something (Sue et al., 2019). The primary obstacle, however, seems to be a lack of competence on how to handle the situation. Fortunately, despite the challenges of becoming an ally, there are several concrete strategies we can use to build the efficacy needed to become anti-racist allies.

Let's start with building efficacy when encountering one form of bias receiving a lot of attention: **microaggressions**—small, covert acts of bias often unnoticed by those who perpetrate them. Often racially biased in nature, microaggressions are different from trivial slights or rudeness in that they are constant and continual in the lives of PoC, cumulative in nature, and serve as a constant reminder of a group's subjugation and persecution (Sue et al., 2019).[2]

If confronted by either a target or ally for using a microaggression, there are both proper and improper ways to respond. Futile responses include reacting with defensiveness, righteous indignity, accusing the person of being overly sensitive, or arguing that you were misunderstood. A better, more culturally sensitive approach is to show empathy with the target's perspective, apologize sincerely, convey a sense of accountability, and attempt to avoid using that comment or doing that behavior in the future (Clark & Spanierman, 2018).

As for confronting a person who uses a microaggression against someone else, there are several tactics allies can use. One strategy is to "make the invisible, visible." This can help in situations where the perpetrator is unaware that they have engaged in demeaning behavior or offensive comments. As an

---

[2] Some scholars have questioned the validity of the term microaggression (see Lilienfeld, 2017; Tulshyan, 2022). Others (e.g., Kendi, 2019) believe it is a valid construct in theory, but prefer to use the term "everyday abuse" because the persistent daily occurrences of racial bias is not minor (micro), and the intent of the behavior (something typically present in aggression) is often unclear. Regardless of the terminology used, a growing body of work shows there is validity that microaggressions are linked to negative outcomes such as well-being and job turnover (Haynes-Baratz et al., 2021; Kanter, Williams, & Kuczynski, 2017; Sue et al., 2019).

example, let's say while standing in an elevator, you witness your friend, a White woman, clutch her purse tighter when a Black man enters. Rather than passively stand by, you can make your friend more mindful of their behavior *("Are you aware what you did when that man entered the elevator?")* (Haynes-Baratz, Metinyurt, Li, Y., et al., 2021; Sue et al., 2019).

Another tactic is to focus on the *impact* of the statement, rather than the intent. Focusing on intent typically leads to defensiveness and the perception that you are being oversensitive, whereas focusing on the impact gets the perpetrator to consider the pain they might have unintentionally caused the target. To practice refocusing the discussion on the impact instead of intent, the next time somebody tells an offensive joke, try stating *"I'm sure you meant it as a joke, but it kind of came off offensive"* or *"I know you didn't realize this but that comment you made about [individual] was demeaning because it portrays [disadvantaged group] in a negative light."* You could also try to disarm the microaggression directly by steering the conversation away from the offensive remark. So, for example, if you overhear a manager say. *"I'm putting you on the finance committee, because 'you people' are good at that kind of stuff,"* you can proclaim *"Ouch!"* or *"Whoa, let's not go there."* (Rogers, 2020).

When confronting microaggressions said in front of PoC (e.g., *"Racism may have been a problem in the past, but it is not an important problem today"* or *"I understand that you are multiracial, but it's more important for you focus on your identity as a human being"*), it is important not to speak for and over the PoC. Black people are very used to the microaggressions and might have chosen not to speak out because of exhaustion, unwanted attention, or fear of negative consequences. In a recent study, Black people preferred White allies who did not disparage the commenter, but rather called out the bias in question and connected the individual act of racial bias to a higher, systemic level (Bak, Jurcevic, & Trawalter, 2024).

Practicing these tactics can be quite helpful in increasing efficacy. In one bystander training workshop, faculty provided with a list of strategies they could use when dealing with microaggressions reported higher levels of bystander efficacy (e.g., *"I would express my discomfort if I saw a [disadvantaged] colleague being repeatedly interrupted and/or ignored when speaking"*) 3-months later compared to their baseline levels (Haynes-Baratz et al., 2021).

Cultivate Civil Courage

Civil courage is acting on one's moral values to help others even in the face of likely opposition and potential danger to oneself. While physical courage requires bravery in the face of danger (e.g., jumping into a freezing lake to save a drowning dog), civil courage requires bravery in the face of social pressure (e.g., confronting your boss who made a clearly offensive remark) (Sanderson, 2020; Williams et al., 2022). Situations requiring civil courage can also be differentiated from typical helping situations. Applying the **SMB**, German researchers found that civil courage situations tend to be associated with: quicker awareness that help is needed (Stages 1 and 2), more perceived responsibility (Stage 3), less perceived intervention skills (Stage 4), and a higher degree of expected risks and negative social consequences (Stage 5) (Greitemeyer, Fischer, Kastenmüller, & Frey, 2006).

Despite the challenges of perceived higher risks and feelings of incompetence, there are concrete ways to cultivate civil courage in order to overcome these challenges. Whether confronting bullying, sexual assault, or discrimination, we all have the ability to become allies and morally courageous people. A good place to start is to stop seeing courageous and heroic behavior as something only a few "superheroes" can do, but rather something we all have the ability to do. As one team of social activist states, *"By conceiving of heroism as a universal attribute of human nature, not as a rare feature of the few, heroism becomes something that seems in the range of possibilities for every person, perhaps inspiring more of us to answer that call"* (Franco & Zimbardo, 2006, p. 31).

To become an everyday hero, social activists believe we must nurture our **heroic imagination**—seeing oneself as capable of handling risky situations, the hypothetical problems these situations generate, and the actions needed to resolve the situation (see *Heroic Imagination Project: www.heroicimagination.com*). According to these prosocial advocates, the steps we must take to foster the heroic imagination include: resisting the urge to rationalize inaction, remaining mindful of each situation we encounter, developing the personal hardiness necessary to stand up to injustice, and accepting any negative consequences associated with heroism. Through inspiration (reading stories and watching others showing acts of moral courage), education (uncovering the invisible barriers preventing heroism), and preparation (practicing confronting bias and standing up to others), we all have the potential to be everyday heroes (Franco, 2006; Sanderson, 2020).

Examine White Identity

Most White people have little experience thinking about their White identity. Like the classic tale where two young fish are asked by an elderly fish, "Hey, how's the water?" upon which one young fish turns to the other and says, "What the hell is water?" White people are often oblivious to their own race because their race often fades into the background. As the parable implies, sometimes the most obvious realities are often the hardest to see.

For White people to begin examining their identity, they must understand the difference between "ethnicity" and "race." Ethnicity encompasses heritage and genetic background (e.g., Irish, German, Italian) and is fluid, while race is socially constructed and often redefined (Williams et al., 2022). For example, who is considered "White," as defined by the US Census has changed to fit political ideologies. In one remarkable historic case, Mexican immigrants to the United States were considered White in the 1920s (to increase the labor force), non-White in the 1930s (to limit immigration), and White again in the 1940s (to increase the labor force again) (Whitley & Kite, 2009). The message to many immigrants to the United States is clear: only immigrants given the label of "White" can become part of American society (DiAngelo, 2018).

White people living in an increasingly diverse America can no longer ignore their racial identity (Knowles, Lowery, Chow, & Unzueta, 2014). Despite the "melting pot" (read as assimilation) opportunity, most White people and PoC live in racial segregation. Racial groups tend to have separate neighborhoods, schools, shopping areas, places of worship, and social gatherings. Although for many White people the segregation is described as unintentional *("We are just seeking 'good schools' and 'good neighborhoods' to raise our kids")*, the result is that many White people are woefully unprepared to think critically about race, thus allowing them to remain in a cocoon of "racial innocence" (DiAngelo, 2011).

"Whiteness" is still the standard in many societies today. In the United States, for example, White images are represented in historical textbooks, people in power, standards of beauty, money (currency), the media, and religious icons. Exposure to primarily White imagery makes Whiteness the standard which allows Whites to ignore their race and maintain the privilege of seeing themselves as non-racialized. While PoC are seen as "having a race" and described in racial terms ("the Black teacher"), White people are seen as the non-racialized default ("the teacher") (DiAngelo, 2011).

Although White people need to become more aware of their White identity, getting White people to critically look at their identity can be a daunting process. White people need to understand that it is not wrong to think about race (i.e., being White); however, for many White people, thinking about their race is highly unsettling and often leads to discomfort, stress, and feelings of fragility (DiAngelo, 2011). Whiteness is also part of a system that includes the unspoken expectation that White people will not cause racial discomfort to other White people (Williams et al., 2021). As long as White people feel non-racialized they can maintain a sense of comfort and neutrality in regards to race-related issues.

For many White people, talking about their White identity can lead to feelings of awkwardness. Because White people are often seen as the default category to which other racial groups are compared, the absence of a meaningful cultural identity can foster feelings of invisibility, lack of uniqueness (homogeneity), and that their contribution to diversity issues is minimal at best (Rios & Mackey, 2022). In one study, White people made to feel "nondiverse" (i.e., their White identity made salient) believed they had less to contribute to diversity and endorsed multiculturalism less (possibly due to eschewing the celebration of other groups' diversity) compared to Whites whose sense of uniqueness was not threatened (Rios & Mackey, 2022). To overcome this perception that White identity is inherently ordinary and pedestrian, diversity training could highlight the complexity and nuance of White identity. Because the category of "White" can threaten people's sense of uniqueness,[3] White people might benefit if they are reminded of other social identities they currently hold (e.g., Italian, LGBTQ+, Jewish). In theory, these culturally rich identities may help White people *"feel that they personally contribute more to diversity and hence exhibit a heightened affinity toward racial and ethnic minorities"* (Rios, 2024, p. 8). Furthermore, "White identity" is not something people can (or should) take pride in (unlike taking pride in Irish, Italian, or Polish identities), so shifting the conversation away from a strict "White" identity allows (i.e., gives permission) for White people to see their "Whiteness" in a more positive light as it pertains to contributing to diversity and ultimately a greater appreciation for multiculturalism.

In addition to awkwardness, when White people are asked to think about their Whiteness in diversity trainings (e.g., *"What does being White mean to you?"*), it can also lead to defensiveness or re-direction. Typical responses include: *"Focusing on race only divides us," "I don't see color, I see people,"* or *"I don't care if someone is pink, purple, or polka-dotted, we are all the same inside"* (DiAngelo, 2018). One major problem with these knee-jerk responses is: *If you do not see race, how can you possibly spot racism?* The same holds true when somebody hearing "Black lives matter" argues that "All lives matter." People must understand that a call to help an oppressed racial group does not mean "only Black lives matter," but rather "Black lives matter, *too*." Using a powerful metaphor as an illustration: *"When a house is on fire, the fire truck doesn't come and hose water on all the houses on the street saying, 'All houses matter.' They've come to help the*

---

3 The perception of White identity as insufficiently unique could partially explain the rising popularity of genetic testing services such as 23andme.com and ancestry.com (Rios, 2024).

house that's burning" (Rogers, 2020). It is also important to understand that a **color-blind racial ideology** presumes that a PoC's experience with race is the same as a White person's, and devalues a PoC's social identity, rendering them invisible.

Endorsing colorblindness also implies that we now live in a **post-racial society**—free from racial preference, prejudice, and discrimination. A post-racist society is something we should all strive for; a post-racial society, however, is not. As one Black actress, Kerry Washington, eloquently states, *"I'm interested in living in a 'post-racist world', where being African American doesn't dictate limitations on what I can do—but I don't want to live 'post-race'. Our differences are so fascinating and wonderful. We don't want to all be the same. Who wants that?"* (see https://www.theguardian.com/culture/2013/jun/28/kerry-washington-scandal-interview).

Thinking about race and reflecting on systematic acts of racial bias (e.g., police killings of unarmed Black men) can lead to feelings of discomfort and defensiveness. As one might expect, participants told to avoid facing the negative feelings associated with deep-rooted racism in the United States were less likely to acknowledge **systemic racism**—unfair practices within a system such as school, law, housing, etc.. On the bright side, however, people taught to accept their racial discomfort were more open to recognizing systemic racism (Koopmann-Holm, Beccari, & Oosthuizen, 2024). For anti-bias trainings to be successful, they must avoid promoting racial colorblindness and protecting White people against negative feelings (Banks, Adams, AuBuchon, et al., 2022). To become an anti-racist, people must learn to accept that dealing with race can be a source of discomfort, but refusal to deal with negative emotions only helps in maintaining the racist status quo.[4]

Besides awkwardness and defensiveness, examining one's racial (White) identity can also trigger feelings of guilt, especially in regards to racism. Although guilt can be a motivator for change, it is often motivated by a lack of action. Rather than using the temporary feeling of guilt as a call to action, thinking about one's responsibility for perpetuating these inequities is a far better option. As one ant-iracist advocate states, *"I was socialized as a white in racism-based society, I have a racist worldview, deep racial bias, and investments in the racist system that elevates me. Still, I don't feel guilty about racism. I didn't choose this socialization . . . But I am responsible for my role*

---

[4] One social activist, Verna Myers, contends, *"You are not going to get comfortable before you get uncomfortable."* She suggests we walk toward our discomfort by looking at whose missing in our social circles and strengthening casual relationships with other racial groups. When we begin to see other groups as family *"we cease to become [passive] bystanders, and we become actors, we become advocates, and we become allies"* (see https://www.youtube.com/watch?v=uYyvbgINZkQ).

in it." (DiAngelo, 2018, p. 149). If you typically respond to racial issues with hurt feelings and guilt, you should not be surprised if most people are unwilling to take on the herculean task of moving you in a forward direction. To become a racial ally, a White person must feel comfortable within their (White) skin and redirect any guilt to something less temporary and more substantive (Helms, 1995).

Examine White Privilege

After reflecting upon their White identity, the White anti-racist ally must also think about their identity in relation to other social groups. Being White in many societies means having greater access to wealth, health, education, jobs, and social justice than other groups (Knowles et al., 2014). **Privilege** refers to the "automatic unearned benefits bestowed upon members of dominant groups based on their social identity" (McIntosh, 1989). To examine White identity and privilege in a productive way, White people need to accept that they have *"been bestowed with a power and privilege that was fundamentally created as a way to entrench an entire class of people with generational power"* (M. Williams & S. Faber, personal communication, June 10, 2023).

Most White people see bias and discrimination as something that puts certain groups at a disadvantage, rather than something that puts those in power at an advantage. For example, it is not uncommon for fair-skinned immigrants who enter the United States to recall the exact moment when they realized that they would be treated better than people around them with darker skin (Williams et al., 2021). These immigrants soon realize that White neighborhoods are often described as "safe and clean," while minority neighborhoods are described as "dangerous and sketchy." They also understand that upward mobility moves you to Whiter spaces, where not coincidentally, White people can enjoy access to relatively unpolluted neighborhoods in part because non-Whites are relegated to more polluted areas (Knowles et al., 2014).

White people are often oblivious to the invisible privilege that surrounds them. To become a White ally, one must visualize how unearned advantages can play a role in one's success. If a White person honestly reflects on privilege across various contexts, they are more likely to come to the stark realization: *"if a cop pulls me over, I know I haven't been singled out because of my race"; "if people of my race engage in riots they are not usually referred to as 'animals' or 'thugs'";* and *"if I am mistreated, I can call people out without worrying that they will accuse me of playing the 'race card'"* (McIntosh, 1989). White people are also far less likely to have to use **code-switching**—adjusting their style of speech, appearance, and behavior to increase their chances of being hired, accepted, or promoted. This extra work and effort can also take an emotional toll; As one Black professional acknowledged, *"I find myself constantly trying to be aware of my mannerisms to ensure that I don't portray myself or the people I represent in a negative light"* (Melaku et al., 2020).

Despite these racial preferences in numerous social institutions, White people will often argue that any privilege they may have once had no longer applies today. Maintaining this view helps explain the wide racial gap in the United States (between Whites and PoC) in regards to racial progress. For example, one study found that White respondents tend to believe there has been significant racial progress because they tend to compare the present day with the Jim Crow ("separate but equal") past, while Black respondents see much less racial progress because they tend to compare the present day with an ideal, yet unrealized society (DeBell, 2017). Ironically, many White people continue to romanticize the past as the ""good old days"" when "we" were better off." *But was the past really better for everybody?* If we use the 1950s (an often chosen time period of said "glory days"), Blacks and other minorities faced mandatory segregation, inferior schools, lower home values, redlining, and large-scale incarceration for minor drug offenses (Knowles et al., 2014).

To become a White ally, people must grapple with how institutions maintain inequities. Racism is often seen as a heinous act committed by an individual, rather than something that is systemic in almost every known social institution. White people must learn to let go of the individual narrative and look at how systemic advantages help perpetuate racism (DiAngelo, 2018). Accepting White privilege is difficult. Accepting White privilege implies that any success is due to their race and not to individual merit and determination. When reminded of White privilege, White people will often emphasize personal hardships (e.g., divorce, family history of alcoholism) or other forms of discrimination they have faced (e.g., classism, sexism, homophobia) (Rios & Mackey, 2022). When someone argues that *"I'm Polish/Armenian/Italian and my family came to this country with nothing,"* they must understand that although that might be true, as European immigrants they could assimilate relatively easy into the dominant White culture and thus reap the benefits of a preferential system.

To become an anti-racist ally, we must: recognize our unearned privilege, make the connection that privilege leads to the oppression of disadvantaged groups, and feel a sense of responsibility for changing these patterns (Radke, Kutlaca, Siem, et al., 2020). Rather than becoming defensive and protective of White privilege, White people must develop a positive sense of self-identity by acknowledging unearned privileges inherent in social systems, and then working to dismantle these advantages (Williams et al., 2021). As current research shows, White participants' anti-racist practices increased the more they rejected color-blind ideology, the more they were aware of their White privilege, and the more they acknowledge negating those systems of inequality (Collins & Walsh, 2024).

Talk to Children about Race

Although most White American parents believe it is beneficial to talk to children about race, many parents are reluctant to discuss racism with their children or downplay the importance of race when they have these conversations (Perry, Wu, Abaied, et al., 2024). In one vivid example, half of White Minneapolis mothers contacted one month after the George Floyd murder made no mention of the murder or discussed the highly publicized event only superficially. On a positive note, the mothers aware of their White racial identity were much more likely to talk to children about BLM, systemic racism, and White privilege (Ferguson, Eales, Gillespie, & Leneman, 2022).

If White parents do talk about race with their children, they often delay talking about race until their children are older, but child development experts say they should start much earlier, preferably before out-group racial biases develop. Before age six, White children tend to show an in-group White bias; basically, *"what is familiar to me is good,"* while not displaying out-group negativity due to their limited capacity for abstract thinking. By age seven, however, children begin to pick up on social meanings attached to skin color and start showing signs of out-group hostility (Aboud, 2003; Cameron, Alvarez, Ruble, & Fuligni, 2001). For older children, feelings about out-group members often shift from concrete (*"she's* mean") to the more abstract (*"they* are mean"). Because children by age seven begin to pick up on negative social connotations attached to skin color, it is best to talk about race before any out-group bias develops (Cameron et al., 2001; Kite, Whitley, & Wagner, 2022).

When talking to children about race, experts recommend avoiding color-blind strategies (e.g., "race doesn't matter" or "we don't see race"), which may inadvertently communicate the message that racial inequalities stem from racial minorities' individual failings, as opposed to racial discrimination. Instead, parents of young White children should stress similarity with children from other racial groups. For example, if a White child says "her skin looks dirty," an effective response would be *"She is not dirty. Her skin is as clean as yours. It's just a different color. Even though she has darker skin, she likes dolls too."* For older children, however, parents should also stress the importance of diversity. For example, if a White child asks, "Why do they all look and talk ghetto," an effective response could be *"We don't all dress or talk the same, so if we are all different we can assume there is much diversity in other groups too, right?)* (see Corridan, 2024). In one study, White American parents encouraged to have color conscious conversations with their children found that both parent's and children's racial biases were reduced after the discussion, especially when talking about how they would feel if they were the recipients of real-world examples of subtle bias (Perry et al., 2024).[5]

Support Dismantling Systems of Inequality

The opposite of racist isn't "not racist." It is "antiracist."
—Ibram Kendi, author of *How to Be an Antiracist*

In his seminal book, *How to Be an Antiracist*, Kendi (2019/2023) differentiates "not racist" from "anti-racist." He points out that although many people throughout history have disavowed racism (i.e., claimed to be "not racist"), a remarkably few have supported policies that might remedy the effects of racial inequality. Kendi defines **anti-racism** as any policy that creates equitable outcomes between people of different skin colors, and an **anti-racist ally** as someone who supports anti-racist policies through their actions. According to Kendi, current policies on climate change are racist because they disproportionately affect communities of color who are more likely to live near industrial areas with polluted air and water, whereas affirmative action in college admissions is anti-racist because it is designed to remedy or dismantle past systems of inequality.

Racist ideas in social policies have a widespread impact by threatening the equity of systems and the fairness of our institutions. **Systemic racism**—unfair practices within a system such as school, criminal justice, housing, etc. can help maintain and perpetuate racial group disparities. To reflect on group disparities more vividly the Antiracist Research and Policy Center at American University (https://www.american.edu/centers/antiracism/) suggests trying the following activity: first think about which racial groups in the United States get the best service/experience/outcomes in Education, Healthcare, Employment, Housing, and Criminal Justice systems. Then, think about which groups get the worst service/experience/outcomes. For

---

5 Here is one example: "Stephanie (White) doesn't have any Black friends. She usually picks White kids, like Sarah (White), to be on her team instead of Black kids, like Maiah (Black). Do you think that there was something wrong with Stephanie's behavior? How do you think that Stephanie's behavior made Maiah feel? How would you feel if you were Maiah?" (Perry et al., 2024).

Photo 8.1 © iStock/Vladimir Vladimirov.

most the pattern becomes obvious, PoC often experience the highest levels of systemic bias.

Let's examine one form of systemic racism that historically transfuses several major social systems: **redlining**—a discriminatory practice that consists of the systematic denial of services such as mortgages, insurance loans, and other financial services to residents in predominantly Black neighborhoods. Beginning in the 1930s, government-sponsored agencies (e.g., Home Owners' Loan Corporation) drew different color lines on maps around certain neighborhoods where green indicated "best," yellow indicated "declining, and red indicated 'hazardous.'" The "redlines" were typically drawn around poor neighborhoods consisting of Black people and other minorities based on the rationale that the presence of these people would undermine property values. Private lenders and government agencies (e.g., Veterans Administration, Federal Housing Authority) used these map lines to effectively bar Black home buyers from qualifying for home loans to secure mortgages. Although redlining has been officially banned since the late 1960s its negative impact can still be felt today in the form of racialized poverty, health inequities, educational barriers, and limited intergenerational wealth (see Badger, 2017; Zenou & Boccard, 2000).

Concurrent with the advent of redlining, after the Second World War the US government implemented national programs to help lift White people out of poverty by creating access to home ownership (e.g., GI Bill), but specifically excluded PoC. This resulted in minority communities having limited access to home ownership, the primary driver of wealth accumulation in the United States, and less property taxes to fund local public schools (Osta, 2020; Osta & Vasquez, 2018). To this day, public school systems still use property taxes that ensure inequities and limit access to academic excellence for minority students. For example, schools with a predominantly minority population are for more likely to have crowded classrooms, less resources, and less access to quality teachers (Nowicki, 2018). Systematic racism is also prevalent in how teachers discipline students from different racial groups. In one study, researchers produced videos of White, Black, and Latino teenage male actors performing three identical disruptive behaviors (slamming a door, texting during a test, and crumpling a test booklet in frustration) and had teachers rate what they believed their punishment should be. Compared to the White boys, teachers assigned more blame to the Black and Latino boys for the classroom disruptions and were more likely to refer them to the principal's office (Owens, 2022).

Anti-racist allies must face the realization that "bad" neighborhoods and "low-quality" schools are often created through restrictive housing policies, systematic disinvestment, and resource hoarding (Osta, 2020). To reverse the long-term, harmful consequences of redlining, anti-racist allies should advocate for more equitable policies such as: investing in historically disenfranchised areas via neighborhood revitalization programs, utilizing inclusionary zoning ordinances to improve the amount of high quality housing, and distributing hazardous waste sites so they are not concentrated in low-income and minority areas (Egede, Walker, Campbell, et al., 2023).

Anti-racist allies must acknowledge that many current social institutions sustain and reinforce inequality. By advocating for dismantling these systems, anti-racist allies can help to replace these harmful, systemic policies with policies that provide equal treatment and opportunity for all. Dismantling the systems of inequality requires a reframing about how people in positions of privilege should perceive inequities. Rather than asking *"How can I use my power and expertise to help marginalized people with their problems?"* the better questions to ask are: *"How is my own role in upholding systems of oppression helping to create this inequality?" and "How can I work together with historically marginalized groups to dismantle systems of inequality?"* (Nixon, 2019). By reframing how best to help, we can reverse who is presumed to be the expert from the people in power to the people battling for equality.

To dismantle systemic racism more broadly, anti-racist allies must reflect on how the social structures (e.g., schools, businesses, governments) continue to reinforce systems of inequality. They must intentionally look for ways to shift resources to the oppressed, develop ways to share space accumulated through unearned advantages, and encourage elected officials to support racial justice policies (Kendi, 2023). White anti-racist allies need to understand that dismantling privilege is not a **zero-sum game** where one group's gain is another group's loss, but rather a way to benefit society as a whole. As Anne Braden, a prominent White anti-racism activist, firmly asserts, *"The fight against racism is our issue. It's not something we're called on to help people of color with. We need to become involved with it as if our lives depended on it because, really, in truth, they do."* (The Anne Braden Institute for Social Justice Research, University of Louisville College of Arts and Sciences; see Mission and Vision—Anne Braden Institute for Social Justice Research.) Anti-racist allies must understand that by removing the barriers that keep talented and creative people from sitting at the table, everyone can benefit. If a dedicated group of activists adopts the norm of allyship and advocates for positive change collectively with marginalized communities, social justice can be promoted and ultimately achieved.

"What Can I Do to Become an Anti-Racist Ally?"

- learn about the social injustice and oppression that minority groups face by researching a particular social group's history
- recall a previous experience in which you engaged in a bias-related behavior that you regretted, and then think about how you would respond differently
- take online IAT's in order to detect what implicit biases you may have
- adopt the view that prejudice is malleable, rather than fixed
- call out microaggressions you encounter in public settings
- deliberately seek out positive intergroup contact (avoid tendency to segregate)
- avoid using a "color-blind" strategy when dealing with race-related issues
- align yourself in solidarity with marginalized groups
- promote physically and emotionally safe spaces for all groups to share their ideas, initiate change, and contribute to social justice
- acknowledge that even though you may feel pain, guilt, and discomfort, avoiding that discomfort ultimately maintains the privilege status quo
- harness the many facets of White identity to reduce feelings of threat while still recognizing the power White people wield in society

- understand that dismantling privilege is not a zero-sum game where one group's gain is another group's loss, but rather a way for everyone to thrive
- let go of the individual narrative ("I wasn't given any handouts") and instead look at how systemic bias helps perpetuate social injustice
- focus on the impact of the statement, rather than the intent when an offensive comment is made
- accept that you will make mistakes when trying to help, but is important to persevere
- become a visible sign of acceptance by validating (rather than invalidating) people's experiences
- offer support to disadvantaged groups without expecting acknowledgment or thanks
- embrace policies and behaviors aimed at dismantling in-group privilege

[see Bishop, 2002; Collins et al., 2021; Lautenberger, 2023; Melaku et al., 2020; Rios, 2024; Salter & Migliaccio, 2019; Spanierman & Smith, 2017]

Summary

In addition to becoming better bystanders when emergencies arise, we must also become better allies when observing the systemic injustices that face many people today. To become a proactive ally, we must consciously commit to disrupting cycles of injustice, and work to dismantle the social institutions that continue to impede the growth of disadvantaged groups. To become an anti-racist ally, White people must understand that it is not wrong to think about being White. Equally important, they must also understand that not talking about Whiteness is complicit with allowing bias to remain deeply embedded in society. Successful White anti-racist allies are those who demonstrate nuanced understanding of institutional racism and White privilege, and who express a sense of responsibility and commitment to using their racial privilege in ways that promote equity and prosperity for all.

Final Thoughts

Hopefully this book has helped you realize that whether we encounter alcohol/medical emergencies, bullying, sexual assault, or discrimination, we all have the ability to become better bystanders, morally courageous people, and antiracist allies. Like the inspiring beach study that began the book reminds us: when we truly feel accountable for each other's well-being, no barrier is too great. We'll leap into action, chase down the thief, and embody the very best of humanity.

References

Aboud, F. E. (2003). The formation of in-group favoritism and out-group prejudice in young children: Are they distinct attitudes? *Developmental Psychology, 39,* 48–60.

Ashburn-Nardo, L. (2018). What can allies do? In A. J. Colella & E. B. King (Eds.), *The Oxford handbook of workplace discrimination* (pp. 373–386). Oxford University Press.

Badger, E. (2017, August 24). How redlining's racist effects lasted for decades. *The New York Times.* Retrieved from https://www.nytimes.com/2017/08/24/upshot/how-redlinings-racist-effects-lasted-for-decades.html

Bak, H., Jurcevic, I., & Trawalter, S. (2024). What black people value when white people confront prejudice. *The Journal of Social Psychology, 164,* 187–198.

Banks, B. M., Adams, D. F., AuBuchon, S., et al. (2022). Factors influencing satisfaction with a microaggression bystander intervention. *Journal of Human Behavior in the Social Environment, 33,* 163–179.

Bishop, A. (2002). *Becoming an ally: Breaking the cycle of oppression* (2nd ed.). Zed Books.

Cameron, J. A., Alvarez, J. M., Ruble, D. N., & Fuligni, A. J. (2001). Children's lay theories about ingroups and outgroups: Reconceptualizing research on prejudice. *Personality and Social Psychology Review, 5,* 118–128.

Charlesworth, T. E. S., & Banaji, M. R. (2019). Patterns of implicit and explicit attitudes: I. Long-term change and stability from 2007 to 2016. *Psychological Science, 30,* 174–192.

Clark, D. A., & Spanierman, L. (2018). "I didn't know that was racist": Costs of racial microaggressions to white people. In G. C. Torino, D. P. Rivera, C. M. Capodilupo, K. L. Nadal, & D. W. Sue (Eds.), Microaggression theory: Influence and implications (pp. 138–155). Wiley.

Collins, C. R., & Walsh, C. (2024). Colorblind racial ideology as an alibi for inaction: Examining the relationship among colorblind racial ideology, awareness of White privilege, and antiracist practices among White people. *Journal of Social Issues, 80,* 651–669.

Collins, J. C., Zhang, P., & Sisco, S. (2021). Everyone is invited: Leveraging bystander intervention and ally development to cultivate social justice in the workplace. *Human Resource Development Review, 20,* 486–511.

Corridan, K. (2024, February 4). *Your age-by-age guide to talking about race and skin color with your child.* Retrieved from https://www.parents.com/parenting/better-parenting/teaching-tolerance/talking-about-race-with-kids/#:~:text=Ages

%204%20to%206,-It's%20common%20for&text=3%20As%20a%20result%2C%20you,all%20different%20skin%20colors%22

Czopp, A. M., & Monteith, M. J. (2003). Confronting prejudice (literally): Reactions to confrontations of racial and gender bias. *Personality and Social Psychology Bulletin, 29,* 532–544.

DeBell, M. (2017). Polarized opinions on racial progress and inequality: Measurement and application to affirmative action preferences. *Political Psychology, 38,* 481–498.

Devine, P. G. (1989). Stereotypes and prejudice: Their automatic and controlled components. *Journal of Personality and Social Psychology, 56,* 5–18.

DiAngelo, R. J. (2011). White fragility. *International Journal of Critical Pedagogy, 3,* 54–70.

DiAngelo, R. J. (2018). *White fragility: Why it's so hard for White people to talk about racism.* Beacon Press.

Dovidio, J. F., Gaertner, S. E., Kawakami, K., & Hodson, G. (2002). Why can't we just get along? Interpersonal biases and interracial distrust. *Cultural Diversity and Ethnic Minority Psychology, 8,* 88–102.

Egede, L. E., Walker, R. J., Campbell, J. A., et al. (2023). Modern day consequences of historic redlining: Finding a path forward. *Journal of General Internal Medicine, 38,* 1534–1537.

Ferguson, G. M., Eales, L., Gillespie, S., & Leneman, K. (2022). The Whiteness pandemic behind the racism pandemic: Familial Whiteness socialization in Minneapolis following #GeorgeFloyd's murder. *American Psychologist, 77,* 344–361.

Franco, Z., & Zimbardo, P. (2006). The banality of heroism. *Greater Good, 3,* 30–35.

Goff, P. A., Steele, C. M., & Davies, P. G. (2008). The space between us: Stereotype threat and distance in interracial contexts. *Journal of Personality and Social Psychology, 94,* 91–107.

Greenwald, A. G., & Banaji, M. R. (1995). Implicit social cognition: Attitudes, self-esteem, and stereotypes. *Psychological Review, 102,* 4–27.

Greitemeyer, T., Fischer, P., Kastenmüller, A., & Frey, D. (2006). Civil courage and helping behavior: Differences and similarities. *European Psychologist, 11,* 90–98.

Haynes-Baratz, M. C., Metinyurt, T., Li, Y. L., et al. (2021). Bystander training for faculty: A promising approach to tackling microaggressions in the academy. *New Ideas in Psychology, 63,* 100882.

Helms, J. E. (1995). An update of Helms' White and People of Color racial identity models. In J. G. Ponterotto, J. M. Casas, L. A. Suzuki, & C. M. Alexander (Eds.), *Handbook of multicultural counseling* (pp. 181–198). Sage.

Kaiser, C. R., & Miller, C. T. (2001). Stop complaining! The social costs of making attributions to discrimination. *Personality and Social Psychology Bulletin, 27,* 254–263.

Kanter, J. W., Williams, M. T., Kuczynski, A. M., et al. (2017). A preliminary report on the relationship between microaggressions against Black people and racism among White college students. *Race and Social Problems, 9,* 291–299.

Kawakami, K., Dunn, E., Karmali, F., & Dovidio, J. F. (2009). Mispredicting affective and behavioral responses to racism. *Science, 323,* 276–278.

Kendi, I. X. (2019). *How to be an antiracist*. One World.
Kendi, I. X. (2023). *How to be an antiracist*. One World. (paperback)
Kite, M. E., Whitley, B. E., Jr., & Wagner, L. S. (2022). *Psychology of prejudice and discrimination* (4th ed.). Routledge.
Knowles, E. D., Lowery, B. S., Chow, R. M., & Unzueta, M. M. (2014). Deny, distance, or dismantle? How White Americans manage a privileged identity. *Perspectives on Psychological Science, 9*, 594–609.
Koopmann-Holm, B., Beccari, A., & Oosthuizen, M. (2024). Individual and cultural differences in compassion, noticing suffering, and well-being: Consequences of wanting to avoid feeling negative. *Social and Personality Psychology Compass*, e70000.
Kutlaca, M. (2021, August 9). *"Do we appreciate or shun those who confront discrimination?"* Retrieved from https://www.spsp.org/news-center/blog/kutlaca-confronting-discrimination
Kutlaca, M., Becker, J., & Radke, H. (2020). A hero for the outgroup, a black sheep for the ingroup: Societal perceptions of those who confront discrimination. *Journal of Experimental Social Psychology, 88*, 103832.
Lai, C. K., Marini, M., Lehr, S. A., et al. (2014). Reducing implicit racial preferences: I. A comparative investigation of 17 interventions. *Journal of Experimental Psychology: General, 143*, 1765–1785.
Lautenberger, D. (2023). Allyship and being an 'active bystander'. *ABC of Equality, Diversity and Inclusion in Healthcare, 93*.
Legault, L., Coleman, D., Jurchak, K., & Scaltsas, N. (2022). Reducing prejudice by enhancing the other rather than the self. *Self and Identity, 21*, 687–709.
Lilienfeld, S. O. (2017). Microaggressions: Strong claims, inadequate evidence. *Perspectives on Psychological Science, 12*, 138–169.
Marx, R., Roberts, L., & Nixon, C. (2017). When care and concern are not enough: School personnel's development as allies for trans and gender non-conforming students. *Social Sciences, 6*, Article 11.
McConnell, A. R., & Leibold, J. M. (2001). Relations among the Implicit Association Test, discriminatory behavior, and explicit measures of racial attitudes. *Journal of Experimental Social Psychology, 37*, 435–442.
McIntosh, P. (1989, July/August). White privilege: Unpacking the invisible knapsack. *Peace and Freedom*, 10–12.
Melaku, T. M., Beeman, A., Smith, D. G., & Johnson, W. B. (2020). Be a better ally. *Harvard Business Review, 98*, 135–139.
Nixon, S. A. (2019). The coin model of privilege and critical allyship: Implications for health. *BMC Public Health, 19*, 1–13.
Nordell, J. (2017). Is this how discrimination ends? *The Atlantic, 7*.
Nosek, B. A., Greenwald, A. G., & Banaji, M. R. (2005). Understanding and using the implicit association test: II. Method variables and construct validity. *Personality and Social Psychology Bulletin, 31*, 166–180.
Nowicki, J. (2018). *Discipline disparities for Black students, boys, and students with disabilities*. Government Accountability Office.
Osta, K. (2020). *White women: Our role in racial (in)justice*. Retrieved from https://medium.com/@nationalequityproject/white-women-racial-justice-is-our-work-3c233b0b6eb0

Osta, K., & Vasquez, H. (2018). *Implicit bias and structural inequity. National Equity Project.* Retrieved from https://www.nationalequityproject.org/frameworks/implicit-bias-structural-racialization

Owens, J. (2022). Double jeopardy: Teacher biases, racialized organizations, and the production of racial/ethnic disparities in school discipline. *American Sociological Review, 87,* 1007–1048.

Pauker, K., Apfelbaum, E. P., Dweck, C. S., & Eberhardt, J. L. (2022). Believing that prejudice can change increases children's interest in interracial interactions. *Developmental Science, 25,* e13233.

Payne, B. K. (2005). Weapon bias: Split-second decisions and unintended stereotyping. *Current Directions in Psychological Science, 15,* 287–291.

Perry, S., Wu, D. J., Abaied, J. L., et al. (2024). White parents' racial socialization during a guided discussion predicts declines in white children's pro-white biases. *Developmental Psychology, 60,* 624–636.

Pittinsky, T. L. (2009). Allophilia: Moving beyond tolerance in the classroom. *Childhood Education, 85,* 212–215.

Pronin, E., & Hazel, L. (2023). Humans' bias blind spot and its societal significance. *Current Directions in Psychological Science, 32,* 402–409.

Radke, H. R., Kutlaca, M., Siem, B., et al. (2020). Beyond allyship: Motivations for advantaged group members to engage in action for disadvantaged groups. *Personality and Social Psychology Review, 24,* 291–315.

Rasinski, H. M., & Czopp, A. M. (2010). The effect of target status on witnesses' reactions to confrontations of bias. *Basic and Applied Social Psychology, 32,* 8–16.

Richeson, J. A., & Ambady, N. (2003). Effects of situational power on automatic racial prejudice. *Journal of Experimental Social Psychology, 39,* 177–183.

Rios, K. (2024). Harnessing the many facets of White identity to reduce feelings of threat and improve intergroup relations. *Group Processes & Intergroup Relations.*

Rios, K., & Mackey, C. D. (2022). "White" self-identification: A source of uniqueness threat. *Social Psychological and Personality Science, 13,* 416–424.

Rogers, K. (2020, June 6). Dear anti-racist allies: Here's how to respond to microaggressions. https://www.cnn.com/2020/06/05/health/racial-microaggressions-examples-responses-wellness/index.html?utm_source=feedburner&utm_medium=feed&utm_campaign=Feed%3A+rss%2Fcnn_topstories+%28RSS%3A+CNN+-+Top+Stories%29

Rosenblum, M., Jacoby-Senghor, D. S., & Brown, N. D. (2022). Detecting prejudice from egalitarianism: Why Black Americans don't trust white egalitarians' claims. *Psychological Science, 33,* 889–895.

Salter, N. P., & Migliaccio, L. (2019). Allyship as a diversity and inclusion tool in the workplace. *Diversity Within Diversity Management, 22,* 131–152.

Salter, P. S., Adams, G., & Perez, M. J. (2018). Racism in the structure of everyday worlds: A cultural-psychological perspective. *Current Directions in Psychological Science, 27,* 150–155.

Sanderson, C. A., (2020). *Why we act: Turning bystanders into moral rebels.* Belknap/Harvard University Press.

Shelton, J. N., & Richeson, J. A. (2005). Intergroup contact and pluralistic ignorance. *Journal of Personality and Social Psychology, 88,* 91–107.

Shelton, J. N., Richeson, J. A., Salvatore, J., & Hill, D. M. (2006). Silence is not golden: The intrapersonal consequences of not confronting prejudice. In S. Levin & C. Van Laar (Eds.), *Stigma and group inequality: Social psychological perspectives*. Psychology Press.

Spanierman, L. B., & Smith, L. (2017). Roles and responsibilities of White allies: Implications for research, teaching, and practice. *The Counseling Psychologist*, *45*, 606–617.

Staub, E. (2019). Witnesses/bystanders: The tragic fruits of passivity, the power of bystanders, and promoting active bystandership in children, adults, and groups. *Journal of Social Issues*, *75*, 1262–1293.

Sue, D. W. (2017). The challenges of becoming a White ally. *The Counseling Psychologist*, *45*, 706–716.

Sue, D. W., Alsaidi, S., Awad, M. N., et al. (2019). Disarming racial microaggressions: Microintervention strategies for targets, White allies, and bystanders. *American Psychologist*, *74*, 128–142.

Tatum, B. D. (1997). *Why are all the black kids sitting together in the cafeteria?* Basic Books.

Tropp, L. R. (2008). The role of trust in intergroup contact: Its significance and implications for improving relations between groups In *Improving intergroup relations: Building on the legacy of thomas F. Pettigrew* (pp. 91–106). Wiley.

Tulshyan, R. (2022, March 28). We need to retire the term "microaggressions." *Harvard Business Review*.

Warren, M. A., Bordoloi, S. D., & Warren, M. T. (2021). Good for the goose and good for the gander: Examining positive psychological benefits of male allyship for men and women. *Psychology of Men & Masculinities*, *22*, 723–731.

Weisbuch, M., Pauker, K., & Ambady, N. (2009). The subtle transmission of race bias via televised nonverbal behavior. *Science*, *326*, 1711–1714.

Whitley, B. E., Jr., & Kite, M. E. (2009). *The psychology of prejudice and discrimination* (2nd ed.). Thomson/Wadsworth.

Willard, G., Isaac, K. J., & Carney, D. R. (2015). Some evidence for the nonverbal contagion of racial bias. *Organizational Behavior and Human Decision Processes*, *128*, 96–107.

Williams, M. T., Faber, S., Nepton, A., & Ching, T. H. W. (2022). Racial justice allyship requires civil courage: A behavioral prescription for moral growth and change. *American Psychologist*, *78*, 1–19.

Williams, M. T., & Gran-Ruaz, S. M. (2021). Can anti-racism training improve outgroup liking and allyship behaviours? *Whiteness and Education*, *8*, 20–38.

Williams, M. T., Sharif, N., Strauss, D., et al. (2021). Unicorns, leprechauns, and White allies: Exploring the space between intent and action. *The Behavior Therapist*, *44*, 272–281.

Word, C. O., Zanna, M. P., & Cooper, J. (1974). The nonverbal mediation of self-fulfilling prophecies in interracial interaction. *Journal of Experimental Social Psychology*, *10*, 109–120.

Zenou, Y., & Boccard, N. (2000). Racial discrimination and redlining in cities. *Journal of Urban Economics*, *48*, 260–285.

Index

#MeToo movement 127, 143

alcohol myopia 67, 129
alcohol-related emergencies 65–75
 binge-drinking 66–9
 intoxication 52, 65, 67, 72, 74
 poisoning 65–71
altruistic helping 6–7
anti-bullying programs 115–18
anti-racist ally 181–204
anti-sexual assault programs 139–44

belief in the just world 25–7
benevolent sexism 130
bias 153–74
 racism (*see* racism)
bullying 57–8, 99–119
 cyberbullying 101–9
bystander effect 9–10, 29 52

cell phones 18–19, 44
 smart phone apps 86
code-switching 156, 197
colorblind racial ideology 160, 196, 199
compassion fatigue 21–2
competence (*see* self-efficacy)
cost-reward model 53, 69, 134
COVID-19 pandemic 77–8, 90
critical mass 113

cultural openness 165–6
 intergroup contact 165, 189–90

diffusion of responsibility 25–6, 48, 108
discrimination (*see* bias)
diversity (anti-bias) training 159–60, 195

egoistic helping 6–7
embarrassment/social inhibition 33–4, 54
 reducing inhibition 54
empathy
 active listening skills 107
 affective empathy 111–12, 168
 cognitive empathy 111, 168
 sympathetic empathy 87–8, 168

false consensus 171
fixed *vs.* growth mindset 166, 190

gaslighting 184
Good Samaritan laws 30, 52, 70

health-related emergencies 75–95
 cardiac arrest/CPR 78–80, 84–7
 mental health 89–90
 seizures 82–4
 stroke 80–2

hegemonic masculinity   136
heroic imagination   193

implicit bias   186–8, 191
  implicit association test (IAT)   186

kin-selection theory   49
Kitty Genovese   4–5, 8

medical amnesty policies   70
microaggressions   191–2
mindfulness   44–5
morality
  moral agency   87–8, 109–10
  moral (civic) courage   135, 184, 192–3
  moral disengagement   109–10
  moral distress   110
  moral licensing   160

norms
  descriptive and injunctive norms   58, 72–3, 112–13
  inhibiting attention   8, 14–15
  of silence   174
  social responsibility norms   6, 48–9
  trending norms   88

pluralistic ignorance   23–4, 47, 68, 163, 170
post-racial society   196
precarious manhood   158
prevention mindset   166, 188–90

racism
  aversive racism   161–2

interpersonal racism   157
systemic racism   157, 196, 199–203
talking to children   197–200
recategorization   50–1, 133, 164–5
redlining   201–2
rubber hand illusion   169

self-efficacy   27–9, 51–2, 74–6, 80–9, 114–20, 137–43
sensory overload   19–20
sexual assault/misconduct   126–46
  sexual assault training   43–7, 53
situational ambiguity   23
  reducing   132–3, 163
situational model of bystander intervention (SMB)   8–10, 14–34, 42–55, 67–71, 78–86, 131–4, 137–8, 162–7, 191–3
social exchange theory   30–1
social identity theory   50, 196–7
social modeling   47–8
social referencing   163

theory of planned behavior (TPB)   55–9, 71–4, 86–90, 108–15, 134–8, 167–73
  reasoned action approach   138–9
time pressures   16–17, 44

weapon bias   187–8
White identity   193–7
White privilege   197–9

zero-sum game   203
zero-tolerance policies   45, 66, 103, 158–9

About the Author

George Schreer has been a member of the Department of Psychology at Manhattanville University for more than twenty-five years. He currently teaches courses in Social Psychology, Social Influence & Persuasion, Stereotyping & Prejudice, and courses emphasizing critical and quantitative reasoning, including Psychological Mythbusting, Statistics, and Research Methods. He chaired the Institutional Review Board for ten years and was a founding member of the Bias Education Response team on campus. He has published studies in a wide array of areas, including institutionalized and interpersonal racism, the link between narcissism and aggression, and pet ownership and well-being. (see https://www.mville.edu/faculty/george-schreer.php).